Family Reunion

A Novel

Family Reunion

Carole Gift Page

CROSSWAY BOOKS • WESTCHESTER, ILLINOIS
A DIVISION OF GOOD NEWS PUBLISHERS

Cover photography: Robert M. Lightfoot III
                       Mark Schramm

First printing, 1989

Printed in the United States of America

Library of Congress Catalog Card Number 89-50332

ISBN 0-89107-474-0

To my own
dear family,
with love that
goes beyond words

1

GOING HOME.

Two days on the road now.

Justin Cahill was traveling east on Interstate 90 with his wife Robyn and their son Eric, heading for America's heartland in their silver-blue Toyota Corolla. It was mid-December. Nearly Christmas.

Heat, dry and oppressive, belched from the dashboard heater, parching Justin's throat. Too much heat, giving off a hot electric smell, repugnant, a stark, ironic contrast to the icy sworls on the windshield, belying the bitter, bone-numbing cold outside, the endless stretches of barren, ice-swept landscape.

Going home.

The phrase summoned images of familiar, aging faces, comfortable old rooms, crackling fires, child voices singing, *Over the river and through the woods* . . . Long dormant feelings blended with faint, moldering sensations—tricks of the mind. Memories sprang from shadowed crevices, from nowhere, sharp and surreal, with a stinging, swift reality, and then rebounded with the sudden snap of a slingshot.

Going home.

The radio blared, static-scratchy, not quite tuned in. Willie Nelson was singing, his voice low and gravelly, throbbing with a husky passion, a familiar song, something Justin had heard before—maybe from one of Eric's albums. Eric liked Willie Nelson and Billy Joel and Lionel Richie—better them than Prince or Van Halen or Led Zeppelin, Justin figured—better his son liked the mellow sounds than punk rock or

7

heavy metal. Eric was seventeen, too young to appreciate the old-timers—Bob Dylan, Neil Diamond, Simon and Garfunkel. But then Justin hadn't appreciated them either, hadn't been caught up in the music of his day like Eric was now. Eric would rather strum his guitar or play his keyboard than play sports or eat. Music had never touched Justin the way it captivated Eric, the way it nearly obsessed Eric, often driving a painful wedge between father and son.

"Dad, tune in the radio," Eric said from the backseat. "It sounds terrible."

Justin reached for the dial. He was fighting the first nauseating waves of a migraine. He arched his upper back, futilely trying to relieve the vise-like throbbing between his shoulder blades. "How about me turning the radio off, son? I'd like to drive a few hours in peace and quiet before we get to Southfield."

"Then just turn up the back speakers, Dad."

Pain radiated down Justin's torso into his thigh, cramping his right calf. He let up lightly on the gas pedal, savoring a moment's relief. "Why don't you just listen to your Walkman, Eric? You've got earphones."

Eric pushed his knees against the back of the seat. "Come on, Dad. I'll wear out my batteries."

Before Justin could utter another protest, Robyn's voice came light and coaxing as she touched his arm. "Justin, please . . ."

He looked over at his wife, glimpsing her delicately sculpted face and finely drawn features. Her skin glistened like porcelain. He felt momentarily warmed. She caught his gaze and flashed her cryptic Mona Lisa smile; then she turned to the frosted window. She was taking Eric's side as usual, always their son's defender, cushioning Justin's abrasiveness with a gentle word, a tender smile, a maternal touch.

Sometimes Justin accused her of pampering the boy— "What do you want?—you want him to be soft, spineless? Look at him—look! He's growing up, Robyn. Let him be a man!"

And always Robyn's quiet reply: "A man can have feelings, Justin, can be sensitive, gentle. He's not you, Justin, not a carbon copy of you—"

"Dad, did you hear me? The back speakers—"

"Yes, son, I heard!" Grudgingly Justin relented and adjusted the radio.

Going home. Home to Southfield.

It had been three long years . . .

"Dad—" Eric's voice seemed to come now from a distance. "Keep your eyes peeled for a gas station, okay? I could use a john."

Three long years since Justin had been home . . .

"Dad, are you listening to me?"

No.

He wasn't listening.

He was thinking of the monumental task that faced him: To comfort his grieving mother . . . and confront his estranged father. In spite of their age-old differences. In spite of the festering bitterness neither father nor son acknowledged anymore. Justin would give anything in the world to avoid this ordeal, to turn around and go back to his own meticulously ordered life as associate pastor of Redeemer Christian Church. He would turn the car around this instant if he could, if he dared. He would turn tail and run.

"Justin, did you hear Eric?" Robyn prodded. "He needs to stop."

Stop?

No, Justin couldn't stop, although he wanted to stop, wanted to turn back. But where would he go? There was no escape. He had a mission to carry out. His own father's soul was at stake. The prideful, beloved, stubborn old man was dying.

Justin and his family had been on the road two days now—Great Scott!—two days of monotonous driving, the highway stretching ahead, endless—how much longer? Forever? For hours on end he stared hypnotized at the long, blank, anonymous ribbon of road punctuated only by garish billboards, weather-worn signs, and rolling hills dotted with ramshackle farmhouses and zigzag patterns of rickety fences. He stopped for gas at snow-crusted service stations and made dismal bathroom trips (some johns clean, but most foul-smelling closets of dirt and grime); they wolfed down

C

burgers—tasteless, dry, hard to swallow—at rinky-dink fast food places or homely, crowded cafes. And always there was the blaring noise—the hard rock, the insane, pounding beat—Justin blocking out the noise, closing his ears, his mind, thinking instead of home—of what lay ahead at home for him—his father, his mother, his brother, all of them waiting for him, ready to blame him for his father's condition. If only Justin had been there . . .

The silent accusations played in his mind: *You listening, Justin? If you had been there, your father would not be dying!*

Would his family say the words aloud, to his face, eye to eye? No, but in a hundred different ways they would let him know how they felt; somehow he was to blame. If he hadn't headed for seminary sixteen years ago, if he had taken over his father's furniture business right after college, if he had fulfilled all their dreams, if he had been the perfect son . . .

Remembering—heaven help me!—can't stop remembering see his face my father's face hear his voice hear the anger read it in his eyes: Justin, you call yourself my son? I've slaved all my life to build a future for you and you throw it back in my face! How can you do this to me—betray me like this?

Betray you, Father?

Every day of my life I turn the question back to you how could you do this to me Dad you talk about betrayal you talk about hurt and disappointment did you ever stop to think what you did to me? Can't think of this now can't dwell on the past must forget but it's there always there, Justin, in the fiber of your being eating at you eating at your joy your peace. Justin man of God how can you live at peace with your Heavenly Father when you can't live at peace with your earthly father?

God, You're bigger than my father; why do You let him torment me this way?

"Dad? Hey, Dad, listen. Did you hear me?" Eric, cramped in the backseat, his legs too long for the narrow space, croaked in exasperation, "Dad, I said I gotta stop—when's the next gas station? All that Coke I drank—"

"Eric, really, come on," Justin shot back irritably. "We just stopped an hour or so ago." He glanced over and met Robyn's mildly scolding gaze. The winter sun caught the burnished gold in her long auburn hair, and her velvety green eyes shone with a conciliatory plea.

"Justin, if he says he's got to stop—"

"Okay, we'll stop, but if we stop every hour we'll never get to Southfield by dark. What about it, Eric? Can't you wait?"

"No, Dad. Give me a break. If Mom didn't say something, you wouldn't stop until we got to Grandpa's."

"All right, Eric, cut the sarcasm; we'll stop. Watch for a place, will you?" Slowly Justin forced his irritation back down, quelled it—the racing pulse, the sudden hotness in his chest. It was crazy, the way his son could stir such sudden, fierce, blood-red emotion from depths Justin couldn't even fathom. Where did the anger come from? Why?—when Eric's remarks were usually so innocuous—just simple, innocent throw-away remarks? Did Eric have any sense of his power, any idea of the effect of his words?

Usually Justin could handle it—the minor clashes with his son. But not now, not today. Surely Eric knew that. Surely Eric sensed that he should tread carefully around his father now. Justin's nerves were riding the edge, had been since the telephone call from his younger brother—was it really only three days ago?—Chris's voice thin and incredulous—"It's Dad—his heart—the doctor says it won't be long . . ."

"Come on, Dad," Eric wheedled. "Hurry up. Find a john."

Justin didn't want to provoke a confrontation with his son now, not when the world was caving in on him, so he swallowed his angry retort and said levelly, "I'm looking for a place, Eric."

But silently Justin fumed that no one cooperated with him; no one appreciated the enormity of his situation. For his wife and son this was simply another trip back to the old hometown; another trip, hardly more than an unexpected vacation, a handful of days off from school for Eric—nothing life or death like it was for Justin, like it was for Justin's father.

When Justin finally spotted a Shell station ahead, he swerved off the highway, braking skittishly on the icy concrete near the side of the rustic brick building.

He was the first one out of the car, striding toward the pumps, breathing in the heavy odors of gasoline and oil as the malodorous fumes mingled with the chill wind. He gulped in several short breaths. His chest felt heavy; he needed more air to expand his lungs and remove some of the mounting pressure, but the icy December air only ached in his chest.

He stared at the barren, snow-shrouded fields skirting the highway—fields that in the summer had likely been lush and green and productive, but were dead now, their rash of weeds broken and stiff, everything dead, decaying under a rippling, mud-speckled blanket of snow. Justin wanted to bolt from this spot, bolt from his family and take off running across those frosty fields, run until the air filled his lungs, burst his lungs, until his pulse raced with life, and his muscles and sinews tingled with energy—like an athlete, a runner, someone in a race, winning a race; but he'd been in a race all his life and had never won, hadn't won yet—would he ever win? Would anyone let him win?

"Dad, we're ready to go!" Eric called as he climbed back into the car. "Come on, hurry! It's freezing!"

Justin strode back to the Toyota, climbed in and fastened his seat belt.

"I miss California already," said Robyn, hugging her arms.

"Me too," said Justin.

"I couldn't take this weather again," she told him. "I don't know how we stood it so many years—"

"We didn't know any better," said Justin as he merged again with the traffic. "It's how we grew up."

"I like the snow," said Eric. "I could live with it."

"Who knows? Maybe someday you'll have to," said Justin.

"What kind of remark is that?" asked Robyn.

"Nothing. Just thinking—what it would be like—"

"What, Justin?"

"If we went home to Southfield . . . for good."

"You're not actually thinking—?"

"What about the church, Dad?—your job? Would you quit just because they didn't make you senior pastor? Would you really move back to Southfield?"

"No, of course not, Eric," Justin said testily. He didn't want to be reminded of the fiasco at Redeemer Christian, the new man Bradford, his own disappointment, that gnawing sense of humiliation . . . "I'm just talking, son. It's nothing. I've got the old homestead on my mind, that's all . . ."

Going home.

Long forgotten images flashed in Justin's mind—vivid, nearly tactile in their intensity. Decades-old wallpaper, yellowed and crinkling near the cornices, its faded pattern more familiar than the planes and angles of Justin's own face. The dark polished solidity of the bannister rail; the pine fragrance in the dresser drawers, the faint smell of mothballs in the closets, the damp musty smell of the cellar, the stuffy mildewed odor of the attic. Every inch of the house summoned fragile moth wings of memory. His boyhood. A mixture of darks and lights. Happy. Not so happy. The sunshine laughter was marbled all too often with smoldering tensions, unspoken resentments, suppressed jealousies, buried too deep to remember, but too painful to forget.

Going home.

It ought to be a pleasant time, Justin reflected somberly—a time of love and warmth and renewal. How he needed renewal now, some glimmer of affirmation in his life. A whispered promise, a thread of hope.

Hope?

Was there hope?

Death summoned him home. Death, waiting in the wings, hovered like a gleeful fiend ready to pounce. Even the wintry world mocked—the snow-shrouded ground, the drizzling sky decked out for mourning, the trees stripped of all life. Hope was as elusive as the filigrees of frost on their dusky, drooping limbs.

2

ROBYN CAHILL studied her husband from the corner of her eye. He drove in glum silence, refusing to let anyone else drive, his hands heavy on the wheel, his expression blank, impossible to read. But then Justin was never an open book, Robyn reflected darkly. No. Resoundingly no. *The strong, silent type.* That was how Robyn described him to family and friends during the early days of their marriage. Those had been glorious days filled with wonder and romance. She and Justin shared a special camaraderie even when they were silent. But these days she wondered what strength, what joy there was in silence.

Justin was a sturdy, imposing man, not lean but not overly muscular, with broad shoulders and a narrow waist, well-earned by compulsive jogging every morning. His immaculately combed raven-black hair was etched with gray at the temples, giving him an air of distinction that set him apart from other men who were merely handsome, yet unremarkable.

Justin's darkly brooding, no-nonsense eyes possessed a disarming directness; his riveting gaze bore into others with an intimidating frankness. It was Justin's eyes that had drawn and captivated Robyn the first time he asked her out over eighteen years ago. He was home from college for the summer. His junior year. Of course, she had known him before. At sixteen, he had begun attending her church, Southfield Community, but he was a boy then, rather ordinary, almost forgettable. And she was in love with charming, affable Alex Lanigan, practically engaged to him—Alex, the very boy who

15

had first invited Justin to church. In retrospect, what irony! Who would have guessed that she would ever love anyone but Alex?

But that one summer when Justin came home from college, everything changed. Robyn changed. From the moment Justin looked into her eyes, she knew he was the one for her. Her impulsive schoolgirl reaction struck her now as mawkishly sentimental, but at the time she was mesmerized by those eyes. She refused even to listen when some of her friends warned her that Justin was cold, remote, unapproachable, or when they argued that his conservative, logic-bound nature would clash with her freewheeling artistic spirit. They said a man like Justin would never tolerate a wife who was an artist, a painter, a dreamer. But Robyn knew better; she sensed the fiery, volatile, passionate man beneath Justin's cool, calm exterior.

Of course, her friends weren't entirely wrong. Justin had his moments. Like now. Robyn could tell by the steely set of his jaw that Justin was irritated with her. She hadn't intended to take Eric's side against him earlier (over, of all ridiculous things, playing the radio and stopping at a bathroom!). But someone had to act as a mediator between father and son.

Why was it that Justin was so abrasive with Eric lately, so quick to confront his son, riling the boy over such silly matters? Then Justin wondered why he and Eric had rarely been close, especially these past few years!

Robyn always felt like a reluctant referee, anxiously biting her tongue during Justin and Eric's heated exchanges, hearing what each said, knowing what each meant, and despairing over the fact that neither father nor son ever managed to grasp the other's intent.

If only Justin could be more easygoing, laid back, as Eric put it, taking their father-son differences in his stride.

But that wasn't Justin. He never took anything in stride. So it was left to Robyn to smooth the rough places and fill the awkward spaces in their daily family life.

At last, as Justin craned his neck with obvious discomfort, Robyn broke the silence with, "You must be stiff from so much driving, honey. Do you want me to drive?"

He flexed his shoulders, grimacing. "No, I'm okay."

"Want a snack then? Apple? Candy bar? There's a Hershey's—"

He kept his eyes on the road. "No, thanks. I'm fine."

"Are you?"

He eyed her skeptically. "Yes. Why?"

"Nothing. I just thought—"

"What? That I'm mad?"

"You are, aren't you?"

"No. Perturbed a little."

"Perturbed? With me?" She wondered, Why would he never admit to plain, ordinary anger?

He shrugged, his face still inscrutable.

"Tell me," she urged.

"What? There's nothing to tell."

She kept her tone casual. "Tell me what you're feeling."

"Nothing."

"Nothing? How can you say that?"

"Nothing I can put into words."

"Try, Justin, please. I know it's going to be hard seeing your folks again. You must be going through so much right now, so many mixed emotions—"

"I'm fine, Robyn."

Her voice cracked slightly. "Honey, I can't help you if I don't know how you feel."

He gave her that look. It always silenced her. "Let it be, Robyn. You always analyze everything to death."

She turned her face to the window and shrank down in her seat, wounded. She closed her eyes and let her thoughts tumble about in her mind pell-mell, random, disconnected. Venting her anger in soundless cries inside her own head. Washing her wounds in a rushing stream of unspoken words:

Sitting next to my husband not touching hardly ever touching anymore riding over endless roads seeing nothing but snow everywhere white and gray shades of bleached, barren landscape, and nothing to think about nothing to do except snack on stale chips listen to the radio and talk but who can talk about anything now in the car with Eric here with Justin's mind too filled with himself and his father and home—why won't he talk?—why won't he tell me

17

how he feels? Locks me out lately—what have I done wrong? How have I failed him?

Precious Lord, help!

What's wrong with my husband? With me? Why don't we touch anymore—our bodies, our minds, our souls?

It'll be worse in Southfield always worse when Justin's back in his hometown. Strange. I think of Southfield as his hometown, but it's mine too, mine as much as Justin's—didn't my parents live there till their deaths?—didn't I grow up in Southfield too? Why does it seem like only his hometown now, just because I have no one left, no relatives waiting to greet me, only in-laws—and heaven knows I've tried to love them as my own but somehow it's not the same; how can it be the same when I'm sucked into this thing between Justin and his father, between Justin and his mother and brother, and all the age-old unspoken anguish erupts, but doesn't quite erupt—no one speaks of it, acknowledges it, but it's always there, and no wonder we never go home anymore; how many times can I stand to see our lives thrown into chaos, our emotions shredded?

How long can I be the understanding wife the eternally passive compassionate wife—not that I don't love Justin—oh, if I loved him less it might be easier, but I do love him, even now with the distance between us, the miles of emotional distance that keep us living in separate cubicles of silence; but the silence might be bearable if there was still the touching, still some connection; and now, now we're going back, allowing ourselves to be absorbed back into the explosive dynamics of the Cahill clan.

Will we survive? Will Justin and I survive intact? Will we make a difference? Oh, God, we should be going to them in Your power and strength! Are we? Am I? I feel so frail, a tender leaf caught in the winter wind. How can I handle these shattering days?

And then there's—don't think it, don't say it—but it's there. Ever since we started our journey to Southfield. How can I deny it? There's Alex. So warm-hearted, affectionate, fun-loving. Face it. He's always been there in a secret pocket of my mind—the bittersweet memories, the poignant feelings. And why not? I would have married Alex if God had given me an ounce of peace. But no, I was convinced God wanted me to marry a minister, a man dedicated to God. Why did I think marrying Justin would erase Alex Lanigan from my heart, render him invisible, as if he'd never existed, as if he hadn't been the most important person in my life for so many years?

Alex will be there in Southfield—Alex, who wrote last year to tell us his wife had died—Alex, alone and grieving. But maybe I won't see Alex—haven't seen him in a dozen years or more; but what if I do see him, what if by chance we meet and speak and it all comes back—the feelings, the desires, the ties that once bound us? It scares me, terrifies me. He's so alone now, and vulnerable. And I feel so alone too.

3

ERIC CAHILL slunk down in his seat, helped himself to a bag of Cheetos and shut out his parents' small talk (did all couples have so little to say to each other after eighteen years of marriage? Man, they were bor-ING!). He concentrated instead on the inner rumblings of his own mind. He was miserable, but if he complained, his dad would just shoot him down. Better to sulk in silence.

Help, I'm a prisoner in the backseat of a silver-blue Toyota-Corolla! Riding hour after hour like some second-rate little kid stuck behind his parents—man, when did they start making backseats so small?—isn't this mental cruelty or cruel and unusual punishment?—my legs so cramped, body doubled over like a pretzel, sitting here stuffed in like a sardine in a can.

Man, I should be behind my own wheels, should be back home in sunny California, the land of surf and fun, back on the beach somewhere with my shades over my eyes and a girl by my side (okay, so there's no girl right now; I can dream, can't I?) and my music blasting and me feeling so smooth and mellow. Man, why can't I be back home? I'd be in English now—no, history; yeah, second seat, middle row, listening to Mrs. Simmons drone on. So, all right, maybe I'm glad I'm not there, but think of all the tests I'll miss and the tons of homework to make up. Don't know why Dad couldn't have waited another week for this trip; then I'd be on Christmas vacation. Gramps has lived this long; no way he's gonna kick off this week.

Awright, so I sound like a selfish jerk. But this is my senior year, and, man, I can't mess up now, not with SATs and GPAs and college entrance exams and a future to worry about.

But how can I think about the future when I'm taking a nosedive into the past? Back to good old Southfield, right out of the Stone Age, retro-fifties stuff.

God, I'm sorry. I shouldn't think that—they're family—my relatives, man! What's wrong with you, Cahill? You got no sympathy for your dying grandfather?

"Hey, Eric, get your knees out of the seat back. You're pushing my seat forward."

"Sorry, Dad, but, man, like I'm fighting off an advanced case of claustrophobia."

"Yeah, well, why don't you move over behind your mother?"

"Same difference, Dad. Both sides of the car are the same."

"But at least you won't be bugging me, always bumping my seat."

"I like this side, Dad. It's my best side."

"Okay. Then turn sideways or something."

Eric sat up and leaned forward. "Hey, Dad, when are we stopping for lunch?"

"After a while, Eric."

"But, Dad, I'm starved."

"Eric, please—!"

Eric reached across the backrest and squeezed his mother's shoulder. "Come on, Mom, aren't you hungry too?"

"Well, yes, I suppose I am. It is past noon, Justin."

"Eric has a ton of snacks back there, Robyn."

"No, I don't, Dad. These Cheetos are stale and I'm sick of candy—"

"We need to get to Southfield by dark, Eric."

"Look, Justin," said Mom brightly, "we're coming to a little town. Maybe there's a restaurant." Then, after a moment: "Yes, see, Justin? Look, sweetheart, there ahead. A restaurant."

Eric saw it too—a hole in the wall, a dump. "Aw, Mom, it's weird. The Dew Drop Inn. What kind of name is that? Let's find a McDonald's."

"This is fine, Eric. It looks nice and homey. If you're hungry you won't complain. Right, Justin? Justin, are you going to stop?"

His father pumped the brake and swerved into the snow-muddy parking lot beside the plain, boxy structure with its plaid cafe curtains and a faded Coca-Cola sign over the door. "Is this it, Robyn? You want to eat in this beanery?"

"Yes. It might be miles before we find something else."

"It looks like a dive to me," said Eric dubiously. "Man, I could sure go for a Big Mac, or even a taco or burrito right now."

"It's this or nothing, son."

They climbed out of the automobile. Eric stretched stiffly. "My legs sure are numb, they were so cramped back there." Gingerly he followed his parents toward the cafe. A blanket of snow carpeted the parking area around the cafe, except where the bric-a-brac of tire tracks had penetrated, revealing slick concrete. A red-cheeked boy in a blue parka stood by the door peddling newspapers. He was maybe ten, Eric noted, and he was gross. His nose was running unchecked as he held out a mittened hand and chattered, "P-paper, mister?"

"No, thanks," said Eric's dad, reaching for the door knob.

"Please, mister," the boy sniffed noisily. "Just two bits."

Eric watched as his dad fished in his overcoat pocket for a quarter, and then accepted the paper with a perfunctory nod. Eric held back as his parents entered the restaurant. Leaning over confidentially to the boy, Eric said, "Hey, kid, why don't you peddle your papers inside? You'll freeze your buns out here."

The boy glared at him, and then suddenly lunged for Eric's arm. Eric had a sudden horrific vision of what the youngster was about to do—wipe his dirty nose all over Eric's new leather jacket! Eric did a quick sidestep and darted into the restaurant, raising his hands placatingly. "Just trying to help, buddy."

Inside, a wave of warm air assailed him, carrying the tantalizing aroma of freshly brewed coffee. Eric hated the bitter burnt-toast taste (give him a Coke any day!), but he loved the warm, nutty, fireside smell coffee always had.

He breathed deeply, then glanced around. The place looked old and dilapidated, like something out of a fifties movie. Man, what happened when he left California? Did the whole world immediately switch from Technicolor to black and white? At least the joint was strung with a few Christmas lights and some cheap garlands. Maybe someone around here even had some Christmas spirit—which was more than anyone could say for Eric.

Across the room, a waitress was already seating his parents—a plump, round-faced lady, probably fifty, with the complexion of day-old oatmeal. Why couldn't their waitress be the cute chick behind the counter? She looked about Eric's age, maybe a little older—that was okay, he liked older girls. He considered sitting down at the counter and striking up a conversation, but his folks would probably think he was out of his tree, and besides, they were into togetherness and eating meals as a family and all that rot.

And what would he talk to the girl about anyway? Face it. Eric Cahill wasn't known for his glibness with the girls; in fact, sometimes he had nightmares of himself coming across as a tongue-tied geek. Did the girls see him that way?

He realized with a start that the girl at the counter was meeting his gaze—and smiling! He smiled back, his slow, cool smile, not too overdone, just a slight upward turn of the lips, his gaze lazy and unruffled. Yeah, she liked him. She was busying herself with something at the counter, clearing away some dishes, but she was still smiling, her gaze lowered, her cheeks flushing red.

Eric took two purposeful strides toward the counter, and then heard his dad's voice boom from the booth across the room. "Eric, son, we're over here."

Eric stopped in mid-step, met the girl's gaze again, and saw the fleeting disappointment. He shrugged; she flashed an "oh well, another time" smile, and he dutifully joined his parents.

"Thought we lost you for a moment," said his dad, casting a knowing glance toward the girl at the counter.

"No, Dad," said Eric, perturbed at being found out. "I was just gonna buy some, uh, gum, that's all. But I can wait."

The dowdy waitress gave him a menu and a chilly fish-eye stare, and said blandly, "Beef stew's real good. Or the chili, except it's real hot, and I do mean hot!" She waited, shifting impatiently from one stubby leg to the other, while they read their menus. Then she turned her glassy gaze on Eric's dad. "So what'll it be, mister? You ready to order or you need more time?"

"Uh—I'll have the ground round and fries. And coffee. Hot."

His mother handed back the menu. "Same here. With a little cottage cheese on the side, please."

"It only comes with peaches. Canned."

"What?"

"The cottage cheese. We only serve it with canned peaches."

"But I only want—oh, never mind, that's fine."

"I'll have the chili," said Eric lightly. "And a fire extinguisher, if the chili's as hot as you say."

"That all?" The stone-faced woman didn't crack a smile.

Eric's bravado collapsed like a punctured balloon. "And a Coke," he said, glowering.

Across the table, his father settled back with his newspaper. "It says here we'll have snow right through Christmas. Sure beats California, huh, Eric? How about that—snow, the real thing, and plenty of it."

"That's not news," Eric groused. "All you gotta do is look outside. Man, it's like all you see. White on white on white."

"I thought a California boy like you would like snow for a change. Maybe try a little sledding, ice skating—"

"Sure, it's okay, if it doesn't freeze your butt."

"Eric, watch your language."

"Come on, Mom. Everyone talks that way."

"I don't care, it sounds crude."

"Okay, how about, it'll freeze your derriere. Same difference."

She smiled. "It sounds better in French."

The waitress came at last with two coffees and a Coke. Eric tore the end off his straw wrapper and blew through the straw, shooting the sheath of paper into the air.

"Aren't you a little old for that?" said his dad mildly.

Eric grinned and quipped, "You're never too old, Dad."

His father managed a wry smile. "Glad to hear it, son. Sometimes you act like I'm a few years short of Methuselah."

"No way, Dad. He's got you beat by a hundred years, at least."

"I'm not so sure. The way my back feels right now, I could be Rip Van Winkle."

"Thank goodness, you don't look like Rip Van Winkle," said Mom, entering into the spirit of things.

Eric smiled, reflecting that moments like this were nice. And unexpected. And all too rare lately.

His dad rustled his paper and scanned the front page.

"Why'd you buy the newspaper from that nerdy punk anyway?" Eric asked.

His dad looked up. "The kid's runny nose got to me."

Eric chuckled. "Yeah? Funny thing. It almost got to me, too."

Mom looked around. "You know, our food should be coming..."

Eric leaned forward, crossing his arms on the table. "So what do you think, Dad? Are we going to stay over in Southfield for Christmas? Or do we get to spend Christmas at home?"

His father's face darkened. "I don't know, son. It depends."

"You mean, on whether Grandpa Cahill gets better?"

There was a heavy pause. Then: "He won't get better, son."

Eric lapsed into silence. He didn't want to hear about Gramps not getting better. It was okay if he was sick—everybody got sick. But dying—being dead—that was another matter. Eric had never had anyone close to him die, not someone where you could say, "Man, I was just talking to him the other day, and now he's gone." Eric couldn't imagine someone that he knew well dying. His other grandparents had died when he was a baby. They meant nothing more to him than an old album of black and white photos and a bunch of stories Mom told when she was in a wistful mood.

But Grandma and Grandpa Cahill, that was different.

Not that he knew them all that well. He had maybe a handful of random memories of Southfield—winter memories, summer memories. Grandpa Cahill always gave him money for his piggy bank rather than candy; Grandma Cahill gave him suits of new clothes instead of cookies. He couldn't recall that they ever gave him a toy or encouraged him to do something frivolous. He always knew he had to be on his best behavior when he went to Southfield. His mother used to say, "Show Grandma and Grandpa what a proper little man you are."

He felt like puking when his mother said that.

Once, many years ago, Grandpa Cahill took him to see the factory where they made furniture—Grandpa's factory. In Eric's mind he could still smell the pungent, heady aroma of new wood and hear the shrill, ear-shattering noise of the machines. And Eric still remembered how proud he felt walking around holding Grandpa's hand—man, he must have been small to be holding the old man's hand—and Gramps kept telling everyone, "This is my grandson. He might look like small potatoes now, but someday he could be your boss."

Eric had no idea what Gramps was talking about, but he sure basked in his grandfather's approval. It was one of the few times he ever felt close to him.

Aloud, Eric said solemnly, "Dad, do you really think Grandpa's going to die?"

His father's voice was husky. "Yes, Eric. I—I'm sorry, son."

"I hardly even knew him," Eric mumbled.

"Time gets away from all of us, Eric. I admit, we—we should have seen Grandpa more often over the years."

Eric's voice caught on a sudden knot of emotion. "Why didn't we?"

Silence.

After a moment, his mother said briskly, "Your grandparents live far away, Eric. And your father's so busy at the church, it's not easy for him to find the time—"

"Don't I know it," Eric said under his breath.

"What's that supposed to mean?" challenged his father.

Eric's shoulders sagged. "Nothing, Dad. It's just that now—now I won't get a chance to really know him, my only grandfather."

His mother cleared her throat and looked around again. "We should have our food by now—"

Eric stared hard at his father. "How come, Dad? How come you hardly ever went home? Is it because Grandma and Grandpa Cahill aren't Christians?"

His father set his coffee cup down jarringly. "No, Eric. That's not it at all. It's just that—it's—"

"You know how demanding your father's work is, Eric. Sometimes he has to forfeit his vacation time."

Eric rubbed at a stain on the dingy red-checkered oilcloth. "That's stupid."

"That's enough, Eric," his mother scolded. "Your father is a very dedicated man."

"I know." Eric peered through one end of his straw as if it were a tiny telescope. "But it seems to me"—he drew out his words deliberately—"with Grandma and Grandpa and Uncle Chris and Aunt Laura not Christians, it seems like they'd be the first ones Dad would want to preach to."

His father grimaced. "It's not that easy, son. No one wants to be preached at, especially your own family—"

"Yeah, yeah, I know. Like you always say, they're the hardest mission field there is." Eric dipped his straw back in his Coke. "You know, it's weird, Dad. How'd you ever get to be a Christian in the first place?"

"I've told you."

"Yeah, you were sixteen, right?—a year younger than me."

"Right. A school friend invited me to church. Alex Lanigan. In fact, he was a good friend of your mother's. Very good, right, Robyn? Anyway, the last thing I ever thought I'd do was walk down that aisle. But I did." His expression grew thoughtful. "I stood at the altar and cried my eyes out."

"You're kidding, Dad. You cried?"

His father blinked several times. His voice came out low and gravelly. "Yes, I cried."

"Come on, Dad. I can't picture you crying."

Mom touched his hand. "Eric's right, Justin. Do you know, I've never seen you cry in all the years of our marriage."

"I guess I haven't," Dad murmured, lowering his gaze. "Not since that night when I was sixteen."

Eric couldn't think of anything to say.

Evidently Mom couldn't either.

Dad shifted uncomfortably and glanced around. "Where's our waitress?" he bellowed. "Our food should have been here by now. If we don't get going, we'll never make it to Southfield by nightfall."

4

IT BOTHERED Justin that his son couldn't believe he had ever cried. It bothered him that Robyn considered his crying, or not crying, a suitable topic of dinner conversation. To ward off any further speculation, Justin buried himself in his newspaper.

"Anything interesting?" Robyn asked at last.

"No." He tossed the paper aside with an impatient sigh. "Small-town papers are all alike. The world's on the verge of collapse, but all they report is how many people attended the last PTA meeting or who was voted president of the local women's club."

"Careful, Justin. You're sounding cynical in your old age."

"Forty's not old," he countered.

But he felt old.

Deflated.

Empty.

When had he first glimpsed the stunning reality that life wouldn't last forever? Incredibly, he was already on the downward side. How many miles, or years, before he was in the home stretch like his father?

Oh, God help him!—his father . . .

"Did you hear me, Justin?" Robyn squeezed his hand. "They say life begins at forty, don't you know? They say—"

"They who?" he complained, his voice edged with acid. "They must have been sixty, or eighty, when they said it. They don't know beans about it. Getting old is for the birds!"

Robyn stared at him.

Eric stared at him.

Justin grabbed up the paper again and cleared his throat. "I'm just not in the mood to think about old age right now. Is that a crime?"

Eric flashed one of his mischievous smiles. "We all gotta go sometime, Dad. Isn't that what you always tell Mom when she complains that you're preaching too many funerals?"

"It's not the same, son," said Justin levelly. He hated that self-righteous, singsong tone in the boy's voice.

"Sure, it's the same, Dad. We're supposed to accept death just like we accept life. I've heard you say so in your sermons."

Justin felt the heat rising in his temples. "We learn to cope with death, son, but death is always the enemy."

"I know that's what the Bible says. But, Dad, maybe if we don't think about it as an enemy—maybe if we pretend Gramps is just another sick old man in the congregation, and he's lived a good long life and now it's his turn to kick off—"

"That's enough, Eric!" For an instant, Justin wanted to hit the boy, slap him across the mouth. "How dare you dismiss your grandfather as just another sick old man? When you speak of him, you speak with respect."

"Don't get all bent out of shape, Dad. I wasn't being disrespectful to Gramps." Eric methodically flattened his straw. "Creepers, a guy gets shot down around here just for trying to help."

Justin rustled his paper irritably. "Let's drop it, okay?"

At last the waitress brought their hamburgers and chili. "Took a while," she muttered, shoving the plates at them. "New cook."

"Well, we hope it's worth waiting for," said Justin in his mock-polite voice. He wasn't in the mood for rude waitresses any more than smart-aleck sons.

"If it's lousy, tell the cook, not me," she shrugged, and lumbered away before Justin could think of a proper retort.

"I told you we should have gone to McDonald's," said Eric.

"Eric, if I hear that one more time . . ."

"Cool it, Dad, or you won't be able to pray over this slop, and I know you're gonna wanna pray long and loud—"

"Drop it, boy, or you're walking to Southfield!"

"Forget that hick town! I'll hitchhike back to California."

"Then start walking!"

"Justin, Eric! Stop it, both of you!"

Eric jumped to his feet, stood a moment looking from Justin to his mother; then, with a scowl, he sat back down, slouching in his seat. He twisted his straw in brisk, snapping gestures. "It's not fair, Dad," he said under his breath. "You can shoot me down any time you please, but I'm not even allowed to defend myself."

Justin shook his head. The pain was back, throbbing, a crushing sensation at the top of his skull. At moments like this his mind short-circuited. He couldn't think straight, couldn't think how to respond to his son. Buying time, he gazed up at the artificial wreath over the lunch counter. Plastic. Not even a very good imitation. He sensed it already—his Christmas was going to be a cheap imitation this year. Maybe that was his whole life—a cheap plastic imitation. "I don't know, Eric," he said finally. "I don't know what to say to you anymore. I hear this garbage come out of your mouth, and I just—"

"Bull!"

"That's just what I mean!"

"I said stop it, you two," cried Robyn. "You're at each other's throat, and neither of you has the slightest idea what you're talking about!"

Eric chewed on his lower lip. "Don't worry, Mom. It's cool."

"Yes," said Justin unevenly. "It's cool. You ask the blessing, Robyn."

"No," she said firmly, biting into her hamburger with rare defiance. "Why should I subject God to our bickering?"

As they ate in ill-humored silence, Justin studied the boy—his son, his only child—the dark, brooding face, the intensely expressive cobalt blue eyes, the swatches of brown-black hair fanning his forehead, and yes, the incredible energy and brash, exasperating youthfulness.

Justin saw himself in Eric, envisioned himself as a boy—callow, gullible, with eyes too open, too easy to read.

Eric hadn't learned yet to curb his expectations, to exercise caution in revealing his emotions. He was too sensitive, idealistic, a dreamer who spent long hours alone strumming his guitar and writing mercurial poetry and sentimental ballads.

It was an obscure part of himself Justin sensed in Eric, the person he had been before the protective barriers went up. *Maybe that's why I sometimes get so irritated with the boy,* he mused silently.

But Justin didn't want to remember his own hapless, awkward, uncertain youth, his own grappling after God in spite of his family's disapproval and his father's scorn. He preferred to concentrate on the man he had become after years of intensive study and discipline—a man of God who felt his greatest satisfaction behind the pulpit. Of course, he wasn't a Jonathan Edwards or Billy Sunday or even a Billy Graham, but he thrived on delivering a solid, meaty, well-researched sermon. And he took pleasure in seeing a sudden glint of understanding flash in someone's eyes. Making the truth known to a needy, unenlightened world—that was his calling. At least, that's how he had felt until the shattering events of the past month.

Justin sipped his coffee—it was hot and black, the sort of good strong brew he liked—and allowed his mind to wander back over the past few weeks. Was it really just three weeks ago that the new man had officially accepted the position of senior pastor at Redeemer Christian? That recent? It seemed like years now.

Justin recalled that fateful afternoon with wincing clarity. Until that day he had nursed his own private hopes that the pulpit committee would relent and promote him to senior pastor. He knew he was bucking tradition; churches rarely promoted from within their own ranks. Still, there had been enough conversation among pulpit committee members to fuel Justin's hopes. Small embers of expectancy remained alive even after the committee extended an invitation to William Bradford. After all, perhaps Bradford would refuse the position. But then came the formal acceptance letter, snuffing out Justin's final, flickering expectations.

After reading Bradford's acceptance letter, Justin said to

Hollister, the minister of music, "So what now? Do we walk the plank? Bury our heads in the sand?" He had tried to sound good-humored about it all but had come across rather flippant, judging by Hollister's retort.

"Good grief, Justin, don't you know what we're up against? The new man—" (they all called him that, not William, or Rev. Bradford) "—he's got a reputation for contrariness. We'll all be out on our ears if he has his way."

The new man Bradford would assume his duties as senior pastor of Redeemer Christian on the third Sunday of January. Next month. A red-letter day. Dreaded. By then all that Justin was facing at home in Southfield would likely be behind him. But in his own mind Justin's problems would just be beginning. His resignation would be expected. Would he hand it in willingly . . . or under protest? Would he go down kicking and screaming? (A repugnant image for a man of Justin's natural restraint!)

Justin considered it a shame that he should be returning home now with a sense of defeat rather than of triumph. He was not one to question God's ways, but it seemed to him that the Lord could have arranged things more advantageously, so that two crises would not be heaped upon him at once.

"God, what are You trying to tell me?" he asked often lately, aloud, when he was alone. "Am I dense, missing a message just under my nose?"

Surely not. He was, if nothing else, a careful, conscientious man who paid great attention to detail. But at the moment, for all his credentials, Justin felt baffled as to God's purposes. Perhaps most lamentable was the growing realization that if there was to be a minister of any real consequence in the family, it appeared that Eric was Justin's last great hope. . . .

Some hope! he reflected sardonically, when he and Eric seemed destined to forever lock horns!

An hour later, after they had eaten and were on the road again and Eric was dozing soundly in the backseat, Robyn reached over and squeezed Justin's hand. "Feeling better?"

He met her gaze and smiled. "How'd you know?"

"That you had a migraine? I can always tell."

"No. That I'm feeling better."

"Easy. The frown lines in your forehead. They're gone. And you're actually smiling."

"You know me too well."

"Never too well," she murmured.

He reached instinctively for her knee. "You're right."

They both laughed.

He glanced over, fixing her laughter in his mind. Even at thirty-eight Robyn had skin as smooth and unblemished as egg shell. Her hair was the color of nutmeg, with sunset-gold highlights, and framed her oval face perfectly. Her thickly lashed green-velvet eyes always stirred something deep within him, as if she were opening her very soul for him alone to read.

And now: She was as lovely as ever. Lovelier.

He didn't tell her that often enough.

And sometimes, lately, he couldn't tell her, couldn't risk inviting her pleasure . . .

But that was something else . . .

Something he refused to think about now . . .

Something he could barely admit to himself.

"You look good," he acknowledged offhandedly. It was safe here, now, in the cozy warmth of the automobile, with Eric in the backseat. He could utter the words that pleased her. Yes. He could tell she was pleased. Her face glowed.

"Goodness! What prompts a compliment in the middle of the day?"

"Uh—remembering how long it's been since I've given one."

"I save them all," she said softly. "Each one is tagged and dated and tucked away in a special place."

"Really? Funny I've never stumbled upon it."

"Oh, but you have." She patted her heart.

He chuckled lightly. "My darling romantic."

She barely breathed the words: "One of us has to be, Justin."

He shifted uneasily. "Then I'm glad it's you, Robyn."

She knows. A wave of panic washed over him. *She feels my rejection, thinks I no longer care, no longer love her. Dear God—!* He gripped the wheel. *If she only knew the truth!*

They were silent for several miles. When Robyn spoke again, her voice was tinged with anxiety. "Are you going to tell your family?"

"Tell them—?" Did she already know? Had she guessed?

"Yes. You know. Tell them about the new senior pastor."

Justin's reply came out harsher than he intended. He was shaken, thinking she had meant their relationship. "You mean, I should admit that the pulpit committee passed me over for new blood, for some golden-tongued orator with more pomp and polish?"

"I'm sorry, Justin. I shouldn't have brought it up. I just wondered what I should say—"

"What you should say?"

"Yes. If your folks ask about the promotion you were expecting. We wrote them, remember?"

"They won't ask," he said curtly, his throat souring with unexpected bitterness.

"How can you say that?"

"Because I know them. Why should they suddenly take an interest in my work now when they never have before?"

Robyn made a half-hearted motion to fluff her hair from under her collar. "Oh, Justin, I've prayed and prayed—"

"I know what you're going to say—"

"—that this time we'll be able to reach your family."

"That's been my prayer since I was sixteen."

"I can't imagine—nearly a quarter of a century—the same prayer—"

"And we're no closer—"

"You can't say that, Justin."

He breathed in sharply. "This will be my father's last chance, Robyn. You know it. I know it."

She cupped her hand over his. "We can't give up, darling."

"No, we can't. Dad's life is on the line now."

The moment had turned somber. They lapsed into silence.

In a way that Justin could not verbalize, and perhaps would not consciously concede, he considered Christianity itself to be on the line as well. Not his own personal faith, but the power of God to enliven and transform cold, dead hearts and lives. Rationally he knew it happened; by faith it had

37

happened to him. But he could not honestly imagine it happening to the people to whom he was intimately and irrevocably bonded by blood and birth. "Oh, ye of little faith," he mumbled cynically, to himself.

"What, Justin?"

"Nothing, Robyn."

5

NIGHTFALL.

Not quite 5:00 P.M. Justin had nearly forgotten the deep, dusky shades of early winter nights back home.

SOUTHFIELD - 25 MILES

His heart started hammering.

Absurd.

He felt like a kid again.

How could it be? The hunger to see and embrace his parents and brother was suddenly a physical ache in his chest.

Why hadn't he realized how much he missed them?

SOUTHFIELD - 15 MILES

Yes, closer. He was getting closer. He recognized familiar landmarks: the old lumberyard, the Howard Johnson's Motor Lodge where the Interstate forked south, the stretch of lush forest . . . and then the friendly, winking farmhouses just before Southfield's city limits. Everything was blanketed in white—everything hushed, spangling like the stars—and oh, on every bright, bucolic house a string of Christmas lights!

He turned to point them out to Robyn and Eric, but they were both dozing now, lulled to sleep by the tedious hours of travel.

Never mind. It didn't matter. This was his moment now.

He was almost home.

He imagined it already—the house, the smells, the sounds. His brother Chris would be there, would probably open the door—yes, of course, Mom would be bustling about in the kitchen, so Chris would greet him—his younger brother, his only brother.

Chris.

Memories flooded back.

Memories of a rare and long-lost comradeship. Two brothers, once the best of friends. When had the friendship faded? He recalled the tender days of new, green summers when he and Chris rose at dawn and walked down the dirt road to the creek and fished for hours, baking in the sun, the creek water as hazy and brown as a storm-smudged sky; days when there were no fish to catch, only polliwogs, which they confined in an old glass milk bottle and carried home. Often they walked home kicking at stones, picking cattails on their way, looking for bits of glass or colored rocks, pretending they were gold or precious stones from some pirate's treasure trove.

He remembered sitting at the old oak breakfast table gulping down Cheerios, arguing with Chris over who would get the cheap plastic toy at the bottom of the box. The winner— usually Justin—would clasp his prize and run to his room and add it to his box of treasures—not an expensive box, just an old round oatmeal box or a cookie tin or a cigar box that still reeked with the thick, odious smell of cigars.

Sometimes he and Chris sat and watched the black and white TV, rooting for the Lone Ranger or Cochise, for Matt Dillon or Palladin. They pretended they were riding the sleek, powerful horses or guarding the stagecoach or shooting it out with desperadoes on the main street of some western town that was probably nothing more than a cardboard backdrop on some movie studio lot—but back then Justin had believed everything in life was real; everything was exactly what it claimed to be.

Now that Justin had let it begin, had unwittingly inched open that long-closed door, memories from the past assailed him with stunning clarity.

He remembered his boyhood in shimmering shades of burnt orange twilights—he and Chris playing kickball out in the weed-torn field down the road, running breathless and shouting into the thin cold night air, all the boys from the neighborhood gathering around shouting back and forth, exchanging catcalls and dirty words and slapping one another around, showing off, pretending to be bold and brave and invincible.

But Chris remained too often on the sidelines. When did Justin first realize that Chris was more frail than the others, his frame not solid like Justin's, his face more open and vulnerable?—even a frightened doe-like look in his eyes, like a startled deer Justin and his dad had seen once while hunting in the woods up north—Chris's expression was like that, and it was a look that irritated Justin; sometimes he wanted to slap his brother, startle him out of that look, take away the odd, half-terrified glint that made other boys take advantage of him, made them chase him and tease him, even when he was just a string-bean eight-year-old.

Why was it? The older Chris got, the less he fought back. He rarely stood up to anyone—not to Justin, not to their father, not to the other boys at school. Sometimes Justin wanted to shake Chris or punch him, bully him into showing some fire, some resistance, but Chris would just draw into himself and close up like a pod, more silent and inscrutable than ever.

During moments like that, their father, the unbending Victor Cahill, had no patience with Chris. He would shout orders and spew out profanity when Chris was too slow or awkward or sniveling. At those times Justin pitied his younger brother. It was a wonder Chris never ran away from home; a wonder he was still here, tied to the old homestead, running the family business, or at least making an attempt to run it. Why hadn't he gotten out during his own youth, gone somewhere where someone would appreciate him and see his talents? He had them—he was keen-minded and sensitive and gentle, never wounding anyone, always the conciliatory agent in any disagreement, and his sense of humor was marvelous when he let it show; he was forever mellow and soft-spoken in a house that rang with Victor Cahill's testy retorts.

But perhaps there was no reason for Justin to pity Chris after all. Chris had ultimately won their father's approval, had slipped right into the mold Victor Cahill had created for his sons. Justin had refused to fit the mold, had refused to be twisted into his father's image; but Chris had been as compliant as wet clay, had slipped without protest into the role their father had created at first for Justin, and then given to Chris by default.

At least now Chris and their father were friends, comrades of sorts; they shared a life, moved in the same circle; perhaps at times they even shared their feelings. Surely Victor Cahill loved his younger son; surely he did. Surely he even loved Justin, the son he could not mold in his own image.

It was something Justin brooded over often: Fathers loved their sons even when they never spoke the words or made a tender gesture. Love was understood. Love was there somewhere in all the silences. Justin loved his father; he loved his brother. Did the words have to be spoken? It was enough, surely, that love was what bound them as a family, as people tied to one another by years and by experiences, by common days and long nights and by pain and need and occasional joys. What else bound them to one another if not love? What else drove Justin even now toward home, back into the unpredictable, disturbing heart of his family? What, if not love?

More than love. Less than love. Need. Instinct. Buried, gut-level drives he could not begin to comprehend. Not just love. Then what? Oh, God, if he was ever to make peace with his family, he had to know, understand, begin to fathom what drove them!

Justin's introspection faded as he spotted another road sign. The headlights of his vehicle illuminated the words: SOUTHFIELD CITY LIMITS.

Yes, this was it. Main Street. It looked just the same—drab, timeworn buildings strung with glittering Christmas lights. And more familiar landmarks: The Rexall Drug Store, Woolworth's Five and Dime, the Frontier Theatre, Ginger's Cafe. Only a handful of hardy shoppers. Years ago, most of the people had deserted downtown for the modern shopping mall just outside the city. Now, Main Street was a virtual wasteland, an anachronism, a relic of the fifties. The fact saddened Justin.

He craned his neck to the right. Just off First Street stood Southfield Community Church where it all began for him—his walk with the Lord, his call to the ministry.

And four blocks south of Main stood the most unforgettable landmark of them all—Cahill Manufacturing—the company that had put the Cahill clan on the map for three generations. But it had also drained his father's and brother's lifeblood, and would have claimed his as well—if the church hadn't claimed him first.

Justin turned right on Arbor Road and drove another mile. "Robyn, Eric, wake up," he said. His voice rumbled in the silent car. "Wake up, sleepyheads. We're almost there. Come on, look—the end of the street—there's the house."

Robyn stirred. "Oh, Justin, why didn't you wake me sooner? My makeup's all smudged. I'm a mess."

He squeezed her shoulder. "You look fine."

Eric sat forward and stretched, his long arms filling the narrow backseat space. "We're here already? Man, my muscles are killing me."

Justin swung his automobile into the familiar circling driveway. In the crystalline starlight the Cahill homestead effused the same tarnished eloquence Justin remembered from his youth. More than four decades ago, his father Victor Cahill had built the home for his new bride Ellen. Justin and Chris were born in the master bedroom upstairs.

It was a large, rambling house punctuated by wide shuttered windows, pointed Gothic arches, and ornamental Victorian gables. It boasted a sprawling front porch with narrow, finely grooved pillars. During Justin's childhood, the porch had attracted restless, chatty, fan-waving neighbors on humid summer nights. But he had loved the porch best when he had it all to himself, when as a youth he had sat limpid and lazy, pondering the immensity of the universe or the weighty meaning of his own existence.

But now it was winter and his youth was far behind him. Too far behind. As Justin parked beside the house, he noted that the porch was bare, stripped of its lounge chairs and redwood swings. Only fragile streamers of lamplight escaped from the bolted shutters, giving an impression that the house was closing in upon itself, resisting all outsiders.

Justin was an outsider.

His parents considered him the eccentric, aberrant son who had deviated from the predictable route they had mapped for him at Cahill Manufacturing. It irritated him that he should feel like the prodigal returning when *he* was the Christian.

Or was it just his imagination that this house was a bastion whose occupants would not grant him access, at least not on the level he deemed crucial?

"Justin?"

He looked over at Robyn. She was running a brush through her silky, shoulder-length hair. "What's wrong?" he asked.

"Nothing. It's you. Just sitting there. Are we going in?"

"Of course. I'm just waiting for you."

"Waiting for me? I'm ready."

"Me too. Let's go."

But where was that sense of anticipation he'd felt moments before? Now there was only a knot in his stomach, a sense of dread.

As they stepped out of the car, Eric stared transfixed at the house. "Dad, it's fantastic! I forgot the old place was so big."

"I've always considered it like something out of *Wuthering Heights*," said Robyn.

Justin smiled. "I don't think it's quite that atmospheric." He took her arm as they climbed the steep porch steps. He half expected everyone inside to pile out upon them before he touched the bell (surely they had heard the engine or the car doors slam), but the house remained silent, imperious. So it was left to Justin to knock and summon someone, to initiate contact.

"Ring again, Dad. It's freezing," said Eric, shivering.

Justin quickly punched the bell a second time. He felt mildly chastened. He wanted to say, *Not so fast, son. A lot's going on here you know nothing about. A trial. We're all on trial. Can't you see that? It would be easier to walk away.*

The porch light went on; then the door opened a crack. Chris looked out, his smoky gray eyes crinkling in recognition.

"Chris—," said Justin.

"It's them, Ma!" Chris shouted, opening the door wide. His gaunt face was more lined than Justin remembered, but his grin was as wide and infectious as ever. He reached out and pulled Justin inside with a near bear hug of a handshake. "Hey, brother, it's been ages!"

"Sure has," said Justin. He put a playful, impulsive arm-lock on his brother's neck, their way of greeting each other as youngsters. He felt suddenly sixteen again.

He gazed around. The house looked the same, nothing out of place, everything comfortably familiar. The furniture and lamps and rugs and paintings were swathed in memories, bits of nostalgia, pieces of himself assailing his senses on a level that went beyond words and thoughts. His nostrils filled with the heady scent of home—a unique blend of roast beef and onions, lemon oil polish, lilac perfume—

"Where's all that California sunshine you promised to bring?" Chris teased. "We've had enough winter around here!" He drew Robyn and Eric inside.

"Oh, it's wonderful in here," said Robyn. "So warm and cozy."

"And you look as beautiful as ever," said Chris, taking Robyn in his arms. "Must be all that sun and surf—"

"And smog!" Robyn laughed.

"Well, guess you can't have it all," said Chris.

Justin studied his brother—the same lean, angular face, sharply drawn chin, and distinctively crooked nose he remembered. But his sandy-brown hair was flecked with gray at the temples, and his shaggy brows nestled a little lower over his eyes, adding a scowl to his usual dubious squint.

But he was laughing now, his eyes merry as he turned to Eric. "Hey, who's this big guy? Come on, not Eric, the little runty kid who used to come teasing for a quarter for the ice cream man!"

Eric smiled. "Don't worry, Uncle Chris. I brought my own quarters this time."

Chris gave Eric's shoulder an affectionate squeeze. "Listen, kiddo, I've always got quarters for my favorite nephew."

"Your *only* nephew."

"Don't get technical, bud." They both laughed.

"Where's Mom, and Laura and the kids?" asked Justin as he removed his overcoat.

"Mom's in the kitchen making homemade noodles, and Laura's changing little Rudy."

"Rudy—the baby—!"

"That's right, you haven't even seen our youngest. He's going on two already, and I'll tell you, he keeps us hopping."

"You can say that again!" came a gentle female voice.

Justin turned to see Laura, his sister-in-law, coming down the stairs with a chubby, red-haired toddler in her arms. Laura looked the same—a little wearier perhaps, but the same oblong face, high, narrow cheekbones with just a dash of color, and a long, regal nose. Her fine blonde hair was tied loosely at the back of her head. "Hello, Justin. Welcome home." In spite of her smile, her luminescent green eyes flashed muted glints of anxiety.

Justin wondered, *Is she unhappy that we've come home?*

"Hello, Laura," he said brightly. His eyes turned to the pudgy, squirming child she carried. Two large green eyes gazed at him from a round pixie face topped with a mass of thick, tousled carrot-orange curls. Little Rudy had a button nose with freckles galore, apple-red lips, and two large white teeth with a generous space between. Justin reached over and tickled Rudy's chin. "And who's this—my new little nephew?"

"Not so new. He'll be two in May," said Laura with a tentative chuckle. "In fact, it seems like we've had him forever. He runs the household with an iron fist."

"More like a fist full of applesauce," said Chris wryly. "One shake of his rattle and we all jump to attention."

Robyn went over and took the toddler in her arms. "He's darling!"

Rudy squirmed and began to bawl. Robyn bounced him a moment, and then handed the wailing youngster to Chris with an apologetic shrug. "I'm afraid I've forgotten the fine art of quieting a baby."

"Don't feel bad," said Laura. "So did I. But you learn again—fast."

"No, thanks. Not me," said Robyn with a firm smile.

"That's for sure. We did that bit once," said Justin.

"You should try *three* times," said Chris.

Justin glanced around. "Where are Scott and Lauralee?"

"Next door. Watching MTV with the neighbor girl."

"We don't see much of them these days," Laura added.

"They have their own lives. I suppose it's the same with you and Eric."

Justin met Eric's gaze and nodded. "Yes, you could say we travel in two different worlds. Eric, wouldn't you say—?"

Before he could finish, there was a rustling sound from the kitchen, and a voice, high, tremulous, mildly accusing: "Justin—Justin, my son, shame on you! Why didn't you tell me you were here?"

Justin turned to see his mother approaching, padding delicately, drying her hands on her apron. She looked lovely— her heart-shaped face glowing from the warmth of the stove, her brown, deep-set eyes snapping with her usual sprightliness and vigor. He noted with relief that while the fine network of lines had deepened around her mouth and eyes, they had simply carved more character into her face. "We just arrived, Mom," he said, wrapping her in his arms and kissing the top of her silvery head. She seemed smaller than he remembered; her body felt unexpectedly frail.

She looked around. "Well, my hearing's not so good anymore. Someone should have come and fetched me."

Justin gently turned her toward Robyn and Eric. "Here's Robyn, Mom, and take a look at your grandson."

More hugs and kisses.

"Why, I don't know this boy at all," Ellen Cahill marveled. "You're so tall, and looking more like your mother every day." She craned her neck at Eric. "The grandson I remember was no taller than I am, and he carried jelly beans in his pockets and fireflies in a mayonnaise jar, and he always had his nose in a book."

"I still like to read, and I like jelly beans—once in a while."

"You've been eating more than jelly beans. Why, you've shot up so, you're a regular string bean!" Laughing at her own inadvertent humor, she clasped Eric's hand. "My grandson—home again! You're going to be good for me, Eric. Come, are you hungry?"

"Always."

"Good. I've got homemade noodles and roast beef. They're your dad's favorites—or they used to be." Ellen looked from Justin to her younger son. "Chris, telephone next door and tell the children to come home and eat. Everything's ready and everyone's here . . . at last."

"What about Dad?" asked Justin. "Shouldn't I go up now and see him?"

"He's just had his pain medicine, dear. And Mrs. Pringle is with him. She's the nurse Chris insisted we hire. She's very good with Dad—turns him, monitors his condition, even makes him smile sometimes." Ellen removed her wire-rim glasses and looked up beseechingly. "Oh, son, he's missed you. You just don't know. It's been so long since we've seen you."

Justin's mouth was dry. He felt his throat closing up. "I know, Mom. I'm sorry. I should have come. Tell me—how are you?"

"I'm okay. It's not me I worry about."

"I know."

"He's bad, honey—"

"Dad?"

"Real bad. The doctor doesn't say much. You can't get a doctor to tell you anything."

"What does he say?"

"Oh, he's got a fancy name for it. Congestive heart failure. He says we've got to be prepared. It could be . . . any time."

"Then why isn't he in the hospital?"

"You know your father. He insisted on being home."

"Can't they do anything for him?"

She swallowed a sob. "Not anymore. This time his heart's just too weak." She removed a handkerchief from her apron pocket and dabbed her eyes. "If he just hadn't worked so hard all these years!"

Justin hugged his mother against him in a helpless gesture. "Listen, Mom, maybe I should go up and see him for just a minute."

She drew back and shook her head. "Wouldn't you rather eat first, relax a little, and then go up? It's been this long . . ." Her eyes registered pain and regret. "A little longer won't matter."

Justin emitted an unintentional sigh. He secretly welcomed the reprieve, however brief. Few things terrified him like the prospect of confronting his father, the indomitable Victor Cahill, on his deathbed.

But no. This was something he had to do. Now.

"I'm going upstairs, Mom. Before dinner. I want to start out on the right foot."

Ellen clasped his hand, her eyes moistening. "Then I'll come with you, son."

6

As Justin followed his mother up the stairs, his heart started hammering with a pounding fury—a hideous, palpitating sensation. He still felt unsettled after the long drive, but a new anxiety shot to the core of his feelings. He dreaded facing his father. His mind summoned images of a small, shame-faced boy trudging upstairs clutching a fresh switch from the old maple tree in his trembling hand. He could still feel the sting of that switch against his bare legs, the humiliation, the stormy disapproval in his father's expression as he meted out judgment and punishment. How Justin hated displeasing the mighty Victor Cahill!

And even now, as a grown man, he felt as if he were climbing these stairs with a switch in his hand, compelled to face his father's displeasure. Justin silently chastised himself for being so susceptible to a foolish anxiety attack. Where was his boldness, his strength of spirit? He was forty, a middle-aged man. Why couldn't he face his father as an equal?

Justin hesitated at the top of the stairs. The door to the master bedroom was ajar, the lamps casting out a muted glow. His mother entered and beckoned the nurse out. "We need a few moments alone with Victor, Mrs. Pringle." As the stout, sober-faced woman slipped by with a nod, Justin followed his mother quietly into the room and looked around. He'd been born here—an attractive but austere room with heavy, green velvet drapes, white cornices and antique wallpaper accented by sepia-tinted photos of generations past.

The air was stale, slightly medicinal. The gleaming mahogany furniture had been rearranged to accommodate a hospital bed and an oxygen tank. A urinal and bottles of medicine lined the bedside table.

Justin took several tentative steps over to the massive bed where Victor Cahill lay propped up with pillows. Shock numbed him as he stared at the fallen giant, his father. He couldn't recall ever having glimpsed his father from this vantage point; all of his life he had looked up to that towering, imposing figure. Now—now Justin shrank back instinctively, averted his gaze. He felt suddenly shaken, disoriented.

He forced his gaze back, allowed his eyes, his mind, to absorb this terrible new reality—his dying father. A gray pallor had replaced the once robust complexion; the furrows in his father's brow were deeper, his thinning hair whiter, his huge frame unnaturally shrunken. He was a ghost of the man Justin remembered.

"Hello, Dad," he said, taking the hand that lay impassively on the sheet. It was clammy, the veins distended.

His father took a labored breath and said throatily, "Justin—you're here—at last."

"Sure, Dad. You knew I'd come." He tried to sound light, casual.

The elderly man gestured toward Ellen. "My feet—they're cold."

Ellen smiled wanly. "Why, they're uncovered, dear. Just a moment."

Justin caught a glimpse of his father's swollen feet and ankles and his purplish toes. He looked away.

Ellen took the blankets and spread them gently across her husband's feet. "Is that better, dear?"

"I don't know—I suppose." Victor began to cough. Ellen fluffed his pillows, and then offered him a glass of water. He sipped awkwardly through the straw; then he jerked back his head. A trickle of water ran down his chin into the narrow folds of his neck.

Ellen adjusted her husband's sheet around his shoulders and straightened his pajama collar.

"Stop fussing," he snapped. "Wh—where's Robyn and the boy?"

"They're downstairs, dear. They'll come up and see you

soon." She walked to the door and looked back fondly at her husband and son. "I'll go now and let you two talk."

Justin pulled the overstuffed chair over to the bedside and sat down. He gazed around the room until the silence made him uneasy. He looked back at the broken figure in the bed. "How are you, Dad?" he asked, his voice uneven. *A stupid question, but it was all he could think to ask.*

"How does it look?" retorted the old man. "I'm dying— and I'm not about to go gracefully!"

Justin shifted in his chair. "I'm sorry, Dad," he murmured.

"Sorry, why?"

"I don't know—just sorry."

"Sorry I'm dying—or sorry I'm not going gracefully?"

I see dying hasn't diminished his caustic wit, Justin reflected ironically. He tried to think of an appropriate comeback, or some word of comfort, or even just some trifling bit of conversation to offer his father, but the harder he wracked his brain, the more powerless and immobilized he felt. He had no words—where were the words?—the right words!

Dear God in heaven, this isn't working! Why am I sitting here like an idiot, my mind blank, my palms sweating, feeling awkward and tongue-tied? What's wrong with me? Great Scott, I'm a pastor—a pastor! I've been trained for moments like this. I've sat by hundreds of deathbeds offering comfort and encouragement from the Scriptures. I've prayed with grieving parents and wordlessly embraced distraught widows. But now!—now as I face my own father, I feel like a bumbling school boy.

"I don't know what to say to you, Dad," he said at last.

His father coughed. "What's to say. Say nothing."

"Are you in pain?"

"No, not much. It's not the pain—"

"What? Not the pain? But something else—?"

"It's here—in my head." He gestured awkwardly.

"Then there is pain," said Justin.

"No, not physical. It's in my mind—my thoughts."

"I don't understand, Dad."

His father lay his head back on his pillow and closed his eyes. "How could you understand? You don't know how it is, boy."

"Tell me, Dad. I want to know. I want to help."

"Help? Hah! No one can help me now."

"Tell me what you're feeling, Dad."

"It's—it's just—I'm not finished with things. The business—you talked to Chris?—the business has hit some snags. I—I could have pulled it through."

Justin nodded. "You always could do whatever you set your mind to, Dad."

Victor eyed Justin grimly. "Life's not what it's cracked up to be, you know? You think it'll go on forever. Then one day— one day you wake up and people are saying, 'So long, old man. You've had your time. Now make room for someone else.'"

"No one's saying that, Dad."

"They might as well," he rasped. "It's over. I'm stuck in this bed. It's a blasted one-way trip."

"Dad, listen." *Find the right words,* Justin told himself silently. "Dad, there's more than this . . . more than the business, more than a mere handful of years."

"More for you maybe, not for me."

Justin sighed heavily. "Dad, I just wish I could help you find some peace."

"Peace?" Victor's fingers clutched the sheet. "You want me to die in peace?" he wheezed. "Then take my place in the business."

Justin recoiled. "Dad, please, not that again. You know I can't."

"I know no such thing!"

"Chris is handling the company just fine. He'll bring it through. I'm sure of it."

Victor's eyes narrowed bitterly. "What do you know about it? You haven't even been here for three years. We could have died, your mother and I. We could be dead and buried—"

"Dad, don't. I know I should have come home—I was going to, but then something would come up. Time just slipped away—"

Victor's nostrils flared; his ice-blue eyes sparked with fire. "Time slipped away? Didn't you stop to think it's slipping away for me too? What kept you so busy for three years, Justin? Tell me!"

"Dad, you're exerting yourself—"

"Don't you see, boy?" Victor's voice was rough, raspy. "Chris can't run Cahill Manufacturing. He's too easygoing. He's not the fighter you are."

"I think you've always underrated Chris."

"And overrated you?" Victor shot back heatedly, his face flushing.

Justin paused. "Not exactly, Dad. You—you just haven't understood my priorities."

Victor sucked in air and rested momentarily. Finally he said, "What I do understand—I understand that you have the drive, Justin—you have the resourcefulness the company needs." He managed a cynical smile. "And you—face it, son—you have my will of steel."

Justin almost returned the smile. "I won't argue with that, Dad. I-I've always suspected that you and I are more alike than either of us cares to admit."

His father was silent for a time.

Justin studied the old man's face—the immense forehead dotted with pale brown age spots, the perpetual scowl between his wide, bushy brows, the full jowls and pouch of sagging flesh beneath his generous chin. Victor Cahill was a formidable man even now, Justin realized; though stricken, he was no less a giant.

"Dad, since we are alike in so many ways, maybe . . ."

"Alike? Yes, we're alike." His father's expression hardened. "That's why I've never understood—"

"What, Dad? Understood what—?"

"Your preoccupation—"

"What—what do you mean?"

"Your preoccupation with—with religion."

"Dad, if you only knew how many times I've wanted to explain—"

"Explain? What's to explain. You made your choice."

"But if you could only understand . . ." Justin hesitated. *It's not going right*, he thought miserably. The words were there in his head, tumbling about like a child's alphabet blocks. But now, when he needed them, they were gone, scattered.

Justin leaned toward his father until the older man's

breathing and his own seemed to take on a similar rhythm. Quietly he said, "Dad, have you—have you given any thought to God?"

"God?" Victor's frosty-blue eyes pierced Justin's. "You mean now that I'm dying? Now that I'm standing at hell's gate?"

Justin flinched. "I didn't say that."

"But that's what you believe, isn't it—that I'm a damned sinner going straight to hell?"

"Dad, we're all sinners—"

The old man leaned forward, coughing fitfully. His eyes narrowed so that the whites were no longer visible. "You smug, audacious jackass!" he gasped. "Got all the answers, don't you! My son—my pompous son . . . the holy man of God!"

"Dad, you're getting too excited—"

"Why, you're nothing but a pampered, unweaned pup! What do you know about dying . . . or living!"

Justin drew back, the sting of his father's words sharper than any switch he'd known as a boy. His temples pulsed hotly as he countered, "I know more than you think, if you'd ever listen to me."

His father spit out the words venomously. "The only thing I want to hear you say is that you'll take over the business. If you can't say that, then get out of here and let me be!"

Justin rose abruptly and stalked out of the room without a backward glance, fleeing the old man's wrath. His hands trembled, his throat ached with unspoken retorts. He stood at the top of the stairs, in the familiar darkness, blinking back tears of frustration, his nails digging into the banister.

The realization struck him with the impact of physical pain that he would rather face a congregation of thousands than confront that cold, cryptic audience of one, his father.

I've botched it, he reprimanded himself severely. *What did I expect—a full-blown miracle like Moses and the Red Sea? Rabbits from a hat? Repentance on cue?* "Oh, Lord, Lord," he breathed aloud, more in dismay than prayerfulness, "will my father ever come around?"

7

"MOTHER CAHILL, is there anything I can do to help?" Robyn asked from the kitchen doorway.

Her mother-in-law turned from the ceramic counter where she was slicing a plump beef roast. "No, dear. Everything's under control. You go sit down and rest until dinner. You must be exhausted after that long drive."

"No, really, I'd like to help," Robyn insisted, but Ellen Cahill silenced her with an indulgent, peremptory little smile.

Robyn nodded and slipped quietly out of the kitchen, wondering why she always felt so inept around her mother-in-law. Certainly Ellen Cahill was capable and efficient, but there was something more about her—the imperious air of an empress, a certain queenly manner. She could have been born to royalty; yet she was never overbearing. In fact, Mother Cahill was invariably a courteous, genteel lady. So why did Robyn feel intimidated by her presence?

Robyn was straightening the silverware on the dining room table when her niece and nephew, Scott and Lauralee Cahill, came bursting in, filling the room with their youthful exuberance and energy. "We're here, everybody—the party can begin!" Lauralee sang out. Then: "Hi, Aunt Robyn. How's it going?"

Robyn smiled and said hello. She wouldn't have recognized either of the youngsters if she had met them on the street. Had her own son changed that much in three years?

Lauralee, at fifteen, had blossomed into an attractive young woman with a lean, wiry body, a perky face with expressive blue eyes, and chestnut-brown hair cut short in a casual boyish style. She was a natural, clean-scrubbed beauty with a Tom Sawyer feistiness about her. She looked over as Justin entered the room and said, "Hi, Unk. Long time no see."

"Same here, Lauralee," he managed, looking preoccupied.

Robyn sensed that it hadn't gone well with his father. "Are you all right, Justin?"

He nodded. "It was grueling, but . . . we'll talk later, okay?" He turned to his niece and said with forced enthusiasm, "Well, you've certainly grown up, Lauralee."

"Just Lee," she corrected.

"What?" said Justin.

"Lee. I want to be called Lee. Lauralee sounds too hifalutin."

"Call her Robert E. Lee," said Scott, pulling back a chair. "She goes around giving orders like a general."

Robyn looked over at Scott and smiled. He was a lean and lanky sixteen, a miniature version of his father—an angular face and jutting chin like Chris's, with features almost too sharply drawn, topped off with a mass of tangled, curly brown hair, giving his narrow face a slightly top-heavy look.

Mother Cahill appeared from the kitchen and set the platter of roast beef on the table. "Everyone come and sit down," she trilled. "Everything's ready." She looked around. "Justin, where's Eric?"

"In the family room setting up his keyboard."

"Tell him we eat on time here. We'll have music later. Now, where's Laura and the baby?"

"Right here, Mom Cahill." Laura came through the doorway bouncing little Rudy on her hip. She strapped him into his high chair, explaining, "We had some changes to make. Now maybe Rudy can get through dinner without needing his last Pampers."

As Scott and Lauralee took their seats, Chris cleared his throat and said in a sternly paternal voice, "It's about time you two got here. I told Kaylie's mother to send you right home. Another few minutes and the dinner would have been cold."

"We couldn't help it, Dad," said Lauralee. "Kaylie has this

chemistry exam tomorrow, and she was just going bananas over it, so she absolutely insisted that Scott help her study—"

"Scott? Help Kaylie with chemistry—our Scott?" echoed Chris.

"Right, Dad," said Scott. "So you can see how desperate she was. I told her I'm hardly getting a C in chemistry—"

Scott paused and everyone looked up as Eric ambled into the room and took his seat. His grandmother slipped over and placed her hand on his shoulder. "Eric, dear, I hope you'll remember that promptness is important. It's a trait well worth cultivating."

"Yeah, I know, Grandma Cahill. It's just that I—"

Laura nudged her son and daughter. "Scott, Lauralee, have you two said hello yet to your cousin? It's been three years since you've seen him."

The two looked over at Eric and flashed smiles that looked more like thinly disguised smirks.

Robyn, across the table, winced inwardly for her son. He looked like he would rather be anywhere but here.

"Hi, Eric," said Lauralee in a bright, singsong voice. "I wouldn't have known you. You look—great."

"You, too," said Eric, looking painfully self-conscious.

"Hey, Eric," said Scott, "remember the last time you were here—that summer—the Fourth of July—when we almost burned down the garage with all those neat fireworks?"

"Yeah, I remember." Eric glanced over at his father. "My dad hasn't let me shoot fireworks since."

"Mine neither."

"Are we ready to eat?" Chris asked his mother as she set a china gravy boat on the table.

"Yes, finally we are," she said, sitting down. "But you youngsters must remember to lower your voices. We mustn't disturb your grandfather upstairs." She looked over at Justin and smiled faintly. "Would you say grace, dear?"

Justin nodded and prayed, but Robyn knew that grace was a formality Mother Cahill observed only when her older son was home. Did Justin feel awkward speaking to God before his family who had no use for God, no time for spiritual things? Obviously he did, Robyn noted, for he kept his words brief and to the point, as if he were addressing a foreign dignitary, someone distant and remote, rather than the very personal Savior he and Robyn knew.

Afterward, Mother Cahill said, "That was very nice, Justin," as if he'd performed well in a class play back in grammar school.

He accepted the compliment with a subdued, "Thanks, Mom," but Robyn knew he felt ill at ease.

"Now everyone dig in and eat all you please," said Ellen Cahill expansively. "There's plenty more where this came from. I won't have anyone leaving my table hungry."

"Little chance of that, Mom," laughed Chris, as he scooped up a mountain of mashed potatoes. "No one puts on a spread like you do."

Robyn looked over and caught a grimace on Laura's face. "Your mother doesn't have three kids to chase after either, Chris."

"Give me a break, Laura. I didn't mean anything—"

"I know. That's just the trouble, Chris. You never mean—"

"Hey, Mom, Dad, pass the roast beef, okay?" Lauralee helped herself, and then handed the platter to Eric. "Hey, Eric, you wanna go over to Kaylie's after dinner with us?—you'll like her—she's weird but real nice. We're gonna watch a movie—"

Eric shrugged. "I—I don't know—"

"What movie?" said Scott, looking up from his plate.

"One I rented yesterday—with Richard Dreyfuss and Amy Irving—"

"Get real. We're watching Eddie Murphy," said Scott.

"Says who?"

"Says me. And Kaylie."

"Wanna bet? Maybe her folks won't even let her use the VCR."

"Hold it!" said Chris, raising his voice above the din. "I thought you said Kaylie has to study for a chemistry test."

"She does," said Lauralee. "But she can watch a movie too. She doesn't want to waste the whole evening just studying."

Ellen Cahill shook her head in bafflement. "I'll never

understand how anyone can study and watch a movie at the same time!"

"What's to understand, Grandma?" quizzed Scott. "Weren't you into movies and popular music when you were a teenager?"

Ellen smiled wistfully. "I was hopelessly in love with Frank Sinatra, if that answers your question. In fact, in my day teenage girls were called bobby-soxers and we all swooned over Sinatra, especially when he sang 'Night and Day' or 'I'll Never Smile Again.'"

Scott nodded triumphantly. "I rest my case, Grandma."

"Yes, those were wonderful days," she went on, reminiscing. "Swing was in, and the Big Bands, and the Andrews Sisters . . ."

Suddenly, Little Rudy—sitting quietly in his high chair longer than anyone had dared hope—began banging his spoon on his tray. "Mulk, Mama—I wan mulk!"

Laura handed him his plastic cup which he promptly spilled. His mouth puckered, and his chubby cheeks reddened as a shriek of dismay burst from his tiny lungs. Laura jumped up and grabbed a towel while Chris uttered soothing baby sounds in Rudy's direction. "There, there, big boy, it's okay. Come on, where's Rudy's happy face—?"

"Catch the spill, dear, before it goes on the rug," said Mother Cahill.

"I'm sorry," Laura fretted. "I shouldn't have given him the milk. I should have known better."

"Yes, you should have, Laura," said Chris thickly.

"Then next time you feed your son—if you think you can do it better."

"I didn't say that. I just know what he does with his milk."

Justin looked over and gave Robyn a knowing smile that said, *Thank goodness it's them and not us!* She nodded, but she couldn't help remembering that there was a time a few years back when she would have welcomed another child in their home, a brother or sister for Eric. But Justin had said, *Not now, maybe later, when life isn't so hectic, when we have time to enjoy a baby.* But somehow, later never came.

"Anything we can do to help, Laura?" Robyn asked, pushing from her mind the memory of a baby that never was.

Laura was near tears as she sopped up the milk. "No, thanks, Robyn. This is our regular routine at least once every meal. I wish just once—!"

Justin looked over at his mother. She was still eyeing her expensive carpet that had barely missed a dousing. "Any more beef and noodles, Mom?" he asked.

She reached over and patted his hand. "Of course. I made them just for you, you know." She pushed back her chair and stood up. The crystal chandelier overhead gave her silver hair a glowing halo. "Can I get anything else while I'm in the kitchen?"

"Mulk! I wan mulk, Gamma!" Rudy cried.

There was tittering laughter, but Chris and Laura weren't smiling.

While Ellen was in the kitchen, Lauralee turned entreatingly to her father. "Please, Dad, can't we go back over to Kaylie's? There's nothing to do here."

"There's plenty to do here," Chris returned sharply. "You could help your grandmother with the dishes—"

"Oh, Dad, you know how Grandma is about her good china."

"Then help Mom with little Rudy, or visit with your aunt and uncle."

Lauralee looked wide-eyed from Robyn to Justin. "Oh, it's not that I don't want to visit with you, Aunt Robyn and Uncle Justin. It's just that—well, you know, with Grandpa so sick, this place is as dreary as a morgue."

"Lauralee, that's enough!"

"Lee's right, Dad," said Scott. "Since Gramps got sick, you guys act like having fun is a crime."

"We just want you kids to show some consideration for your grandmother," said Laura.

"But we can't all just stop living and sit around waiting for Gramps to—"

Chris cut her off. "I said, that's enough, Lauralee!" He glanced at Eric, then at his son and daughter. "Why can't you two be polite and respectful like your cousin here?"

"Dad, be real!" said Scott.

"I bet Eric feels the same way we do if anyone gave him a chance to say so," Lauralee pouted.

"Stop, right now!" Chris's face was flushed, his eyes glinting with aggravation. He drew in a sharp breath. "I'm afraid you two are not making a very good impression on your aunt and uncle."

"Creepers, you should talk, Dad. Look at you and Mom."

"Don't give me any of your lip, young man, or I'll tan your hide! Your aunt and uncle have come a long way to see us, and I won't have you mouthing off—"

"Please, Chris," said Justin quickly, "don't bring us into this. The kids are fine. Let them go have their fun."

"See, Dad?" said Scott. "We don't have to cool it just because Uncle Justin's a preacher."

Chris looked sheepishly at Justin. "Kids!" He blotted his mouth nervously with his napkin. "Believe me, I'm not insisting on good behavior for your sake. It's for Mom too. She puts on a good facade, but she can't take much right now."

"I sensed that," replied Justin.

"That's why I hired Mrs. Pringle. Mom couldn't take care of Dad alone."

"But she's still working too hard," said Justin, "and she's so nervous underneath."

"I know. Mom flits. Like a bird. Never lands."

They were suddenly quiet as Ellen returned with a heaping platter of beef and noodles. "There's still more beef out there," she told them. "Eat it now or you'll get it on sandwiches tomorrow."

"Everything's delicious, Mother Cahill," said Robyn.

Everyone echoed Robyn's words—effusively; but they settled into a discomfiting silence as Ellen's stoic expression wavered and her eyes filled with tears. "I just wish your father could be down here with us," she said softly.

"We all wish that, Mom," said Chris.

As the silence at the table lengthened, Robyn scoured her mind for something of interest to chat about, and then sighed with relief when Justin filled the vacuum with a husky, "So how's business, Chris?"

His brother shrugged. "Fair." From his tone he might as well have said poor.

Justin nodded. "I suppose the economy—"

"The economy says it all," finished Chris. "No one trusts the future anymore—and why should they? You can't depend on the stock market, or the dollar, or even the government itself."

"So the shaky economy has affected business that much—?"

"Sure. People are cautious now. They aren't buying quality furniture like they used to. They buy particle board or pressed wood cheapies or laminated stuff with simulated wood veneers. Nobody even asks if it's wood anymore, so long as it *looks* like wood."

"I didn't realize it was that bad," said Justin.

"Well, it is. We all know that for over forty years the Cahills have made the best furniture in this state. But now sales are off . . . production is down. Dad and I have done what we could, but he's just pushed himself for too long." Chris caught himself and his tone changed. "How'd we get into this? I don't want to bore everybody with our business woes."

"You're not boring us," Justin assured him. "I just wish there was something I could do to help . . ." His voice trailed off.

Robyn met her husband's gaze and knew he was thinking that his father might not be dying if he'd accepted responsibility for the business. She wanted to tell him it wasn't so, that he shouldn't blame himself, that no one blamed him, but she could only say it with her eyes. Could he read them? Did he understand? Did he believe her?

"I'm managing okay," Chris said defensively. "The business is still solid. I'm in charge now, you know. Of course, Dad hasn't made my title official yet, but who else is there?"

Ellen spoke up, her voice tremulous. "Now, Chris, I don't want you fretting over the business like your father has all these years. It's nearly killed him. I won't have it killing you too."

"It won't, Mom. You know me. I take things in my stride."

"Do you, Chris?" Laura challenged quietly. "What about your ulcers?"

Chris forced a laugh. "You know me, babe. I'm the most laid-back guy around."

Laura's tone remained firm. "Not when it comes to your father, Chris. Then you're positively irrational."

"Come off it, sweetheart. You'll have my mom and big brother thinking we don't get along."

"Forget I said anything . . . like you always do. After all, I'm only a Cahill by marriage." Laura reached over and briskly wiped little Rudy's face. He squalled in protest.

Mother Cahill cast a disapproving glance at Laura; then she turned to Robyn and said pointedly, "Tell me, Robyn, dear, you do remember Alex Lanigan, don't you?"

Robyn looked up in surprise. Was her remarkable mother-in-law also omniscient? Did she guess how often Alex Lanigan had been on Robyn's mind lately? "Why, yes, I remember Alex," Robyn said guardedly.

"Well, he's been working for Cahill Manufacturing for some time now," said Ellen brightly. What's his position, Chris?"

Chris shifted a mouthful of food. "He's production manager, Mom."

"Oh, yes. And doing a fine job, according to your father." Ellen's expression clouded. "Poor fellow's had a hard time of it lately. His wife died about a year ago. Nice woman, she was."

"Yes, he wrote us about it," said Robyn. "We were very sorry—"

Eric perked up. "Who is this Lanigan guy, Grandma?"

"Someone your mother knew when she was your age," said Ellen.

"Oh, he was more than that," corrected Justin, a satirical note in his voice. "He's the guy who invited me to church years ago, and he had a pretty hot thing going with your mom—"

"Justin, please," Robyn protested.

"Tell me, Dad."

"Like I told you in the restaurant today, he was Mom's steady guy before she married me."

"Oh, yeah, that's where I heard his name." Eric's eyes sparked with interest. "Did you almost marry him, Mom?"

Robyn poked remotely at her roast beef. "No, Eric. We may have talked about it, but that's all."

"He still asks about you, Robyn," said Ellen. "He must have been very fond of you."

"He was a very nice person," she said vaguely.

"Perhaps you'll run into him at the factory while you're here." Ellen glanced around the table until her eyes settled on a small, linen-draped basket. "I have more biscuits and jelly if anyone wants them."

Chris took a biscuit and tore it open. "So how are things in your church?" he asked Justin offhandedly.

"All right," Justin said without looking up.

"I guess all you guys in the clergy are taking a beating these days, huh?" Chris persisted, then grew flustered when Justin only stared back solemnly. "I mean, you must get a lot of flack what with all the trouble these TV preachers have gotten themselves into. Of course, I know that's got nothing to do with you or your church, but still, there must be a lot of fallout—"

"Whenever people put their eyes on men instead of God, they'll be disappointed," said Justin.

Robyn sighed inwardly. She knew Justin hated being baited on this subject. It seemed to be a favorite topic of conversation these days, especially when people found out Justin was a minister.

"Well, sure, big brother," Chris went on in a faintly needling tone, "but if you can't expect more from a preacher—"

"Preachers are just as human as you are, Chris," Justin shot back. "Of course, that doesn't mean that we're to be excused—"

"Say, Justin," Laura interrupted with forced brightness, "didn't you write Mom Cahill about some promotion you were getting?"

Justin kept his knife and fork poised over his plate. "Yes," he said levelly, "but it didn't work out."

"Oh, really? Is that so?" She sounded genuinely sympathetic. "I'm sorry to hear it."

"Don't be," said Justin brusquely. "I simply assumed too much."

"But our church is really growing," said Robyn with more enthusiasm than she felt. "Justin recently set up a special visitation ministry—"

"They're not interested in that, Robyn," Justin snapped.

"Oh, certainly we are," replied Laura as she lifted Rudy out of his high chair onto her lap. "We hardly ever hear what goes on in your world, Justin." She smiled uneasily. "Why, it might as well be a foreign country."

"Well," Robyn went on tentatively, "about thirty of us meet together on Tuesday nights—"

Scott leaned over and whispered to Eric, "You must spend every night of the week in church!"

Eric chuckled politely. "Not quite. Sometimes it just seems that way."

"Well," noted Mother Cahill, "I think the good Lord should be satisfied with an hour a week. Heaven knows we're all busy people."

"Too busy sometimes," said Justin curtly.

Chris broke in with, "Speaking of busy people—" He sat back in his chair and folded his arms across his chest. "Mom, you're the busiest lady I know. Didn't I see you scooting around here baking pies this morning?"

Mother Cahill smiled. "Apple and pumpkin—my boys' favorites. They're ready any time you are."

"I'm ready and waiting!" said Chris. "And how about a smidgen of hot, black coffee?"

Before Ellen could reply, a sudden banging noise sounded from the front porch.

"Someone's at the door," said Chris.

"It sounds like someone's trying to break it down," said Justin.

"For heaven's sake, they'll wake your father!"

"I'll get it." Justin stood up and walked briskly down the hall. "I'm coming," he called as the pounding grew more insistent.

"Be careful, Justin," Robyn warned as a sudden chill of anxiety traveled the length of her spine.

8

JUSTIN OPENED the front door and stared into the face of a stocky, rough-hewn man with red puffy eyes, a swarthy complexion, and a mop of gray-black hair. "Yes?" said Justin, shivering against the blast of cold air.

The man stared blankly at him, his weathered, woebegone face lined with wrinkles. He wore a heavy plaid jacket, a wool scarf, and smelled of tobacco and cheap wine.

"What can I do for you, sir?" said Justin.

"Who are you?" the man asked, looking genuinely puzzled.

Justin studied the stranger. "Perhaps that should be my question."

The man looked around, bewildered. "I thought—I mean, isn't this the house—the place where old Cahill lives?"

"You mean Victor Cahill?"

"Yeah, that's him—that's who I'm looking for."

Justin sensed that it had been a mistake to open the door. "I'm sorry, Mister—?"

"No, this is the place, right?" the man said thickly. "Victor Cahill, uh—proud owner of Cahill Manu—uh, Manufacturing?"

"I'm sorry, Mr. Cahill is busy. If you'd like to leave your name, I'll tell him you stopped by."

"Forget it, buddy. He knows my name. Just let me talk to him."

"I'm sorry, I can't do that," said Justin. "Perhaps you should telephone ahead next time. Good night." Justin stepped back inside and began to close the door.

The man seized the knob firmly in one large hand. "Hold on, mister. I wanna see Cahill. Now!"

"He's not available," Justin declared. "If you don't leave now, I'll have to call the police."

"The devil you will! I want old man Cahill!" The man burst inside, shoving Justin out of the way, and stalked down the hall, a blur of volcanic anger and energy. "Cahill, you here? Where in blazes are you!"

Justin darted after the stranger, grasping his shoulder with a restraining hand. "Hold on, mister. That's far enough!"

The intruder flicked Justin's hand aside with a powerful shrug and bounded into the dining room. Everyone looked up from the table in stunned silence.

Chris had already scrambled to his feet and started for the hallway. He stared in astonishment at the man. "Bryden, what are you doing here?"

The man stood poised, legs spread, arms akimbo, as if to ward off attackers. His eyes flashed fire in his dark, runneled face; his voice erupted in anguish. "W-Where is he—old man Cahill?"

Ellen Cahill left the table, gesturing for the others to remain seated (humor this man; don't make waves), and slipped over beside Chris. "What do you want with my husband, Mr. Bryden?"

"I—I don't have no complaint with you, Mrs. Cahill. Like I said, it's your husband—"

"He can't see you, Mr. Bryden. You tell me what's on your mind."

The man's eyes darted about wildly. "Where is he—upstairs? I know he's here."

Ellen clenched her hands nervously but kept her eyes unflinchingly on Bryden. "I said, you tell me."

"I can't. You don't know. This is between him and me—"

"Then go home, Mr. Bryden, and contact my husband at the office."

"I tried that." He stared around the room, his eyes glazed with urgency. "They said he's here—he's sick—"

"That's right, Mr. Bryden—"

"But not too sick to hear what I gotta say—"

"Yes," said Ellen. "He's too ill. You must go now—"

"No, you listen—the whole bunch of you listen to me—" Bryden's words spilled out in an anguished sob. "Your old man—he—he killed her—just the same as if he'd murdered her—he killed my sweet baby, my little girl!"

Chris stepped forward and reached for Bryden's arm. "You're drunk, Bryden. Go home."

Bryden shook him off. "No, listen to me! I thought it out. For two hours I done nothing but think, and it's the only answer. Cahill's gotta pay! Don't you see? Nothing else makes sense!"

"You're crazy, Bryden," Chris shot back, his voice too shrill. "Get out, or I swear I'll have the cops after your hide—!"

Bryden took several lumbering steps backward, and then began to weep. "Please, let me—I'll just say my piece and go." He wiped his face with his wool scarf; then he shook his head as if to clear it. "I'll tell you—about Amy. My little angel. She was six. A smart little girl. Good grades in school. You listen and you'll see I'm right—it just hurts so bad—no one told me how bad it could hurt—"

"Bryden, listen—" said Chris.

"I saw her just this morning, held her in my arms. She was so soft and warm." Bryden's voice broke. "Then, tonight, just like that—gone! Tell me, how could it happen that quick?"

Ellen approached him. "You're talking about Amy, your little girl? She was ill?"

"They weren't even going to let me see her," Bryden went on doggedly, his eyes glistening with visions only he could see. "They said, 'We're sorry, she's gone—'"

"Amy—your daughter?" Ellen persisted. "Didn't I meet her once? You brought her to the company picnic—Are you saying she's—?"

Bryden's forehead settled into mournful furrows. "I went in anyway, pushed past them, went in and picked her up. She was cold and blue, looked like one of them ice statues in the park—"

"Your daughter's dead?" cried Ellen. "Is that what you're telling us?"

Bryden's chest heaved. "They couldn't save her. They said I waited too long—I should have brought her in sooner. How was I to know? I thought it was just a cold. But the cough kept getting worse—"

Justin gripped Bryden's shoulder. "I'm sorry—we're all sorry. Is there something we can do?"

"They said it was pneumonia," Bryden declared. "How could she die of pneumonia these days? They have miracle drugs—"

"Bryden," said Chris gently, "like my brother said, we're very sorry about your daughter. It's a terrible blow and we'd like to help you, . . . but what does it have to do with our father?"

The man's eyes riveted on Chris. "Everything! Your father fired me. You know that. You were there. You heard him."

"Listen, you know why my father fired you," said Chris. "He had no other choice, Bryden. You were caught red-handed—"

"He should have given me another chance . . . another chance." He shook his head imploringly, his shaggy brows furrowed over delirious, rabid eyes. "There was no money for heat, no money for medicine. The house was too cold and my little girl was sick."

Bryden glared around the room accusingly, his face contorted. "You don't care—none of you care that my life is over; my poor wife is crazy with grief. She's leaving me. She says she won't stay—won't live with a man who can't take care of his family."

"Bryden, listen—please!" Chris urged.

"I told her—I said over and over—it's Cahill's fault. He took my job away. He turned me in to the cops. Now no one in this town will give me a job. Did you know that? No one will hire me. Cahill saw to that. He shafted me good. See? Do you see? It's Victor Cahill—he wrecked my life, and now—" His voice throbbed with anguish. "—Now he's killed my baby!"

"Please, Mr. Bryden, try to calm down," said Justin. "You're not thinking straight tonight. Why don't you let me drive you home? You can get some sleep, and then come back tomorrow and we'll talk this out, help you deal with this—"

"My son's right," said Ellen, squaring her shoulders. "I'm sorry about your daughter's death, terribly sorry." She paused and breathed deeply. "But my Victor is not responsible. He's ill now and I won't have you upsetting him. So I'm afraid I must ask you to leave."

"Let Cahill tell me to go," said Bryden. "No one else."

"*I've* told you to leave, Mr. Bryden," Ellen returned testily.

His voice was raw with rage. "I'll go, but mark my words, Cahill's going to pay—!"

"Good night, Mr. Bryden. Please come back tomorrow when you're sober, and we'll try to help you with arrangements or whatever we can do—"

"My mother's right," said Justin. He could feel cold sweat on his skin, making rivulets on his forehead. "We'll do all we can to help, Mr. Bryden. Now if you'll give me your keys, I'll be glad to drive you—"

"The devil you will!" The angry man raked a calloused hand through his thatch of unruly hair. "It's too late for help! Too late for you, too late for me, too late for Amy!" He turned and lumbered to the door, tossing them a final backward glance. "You Cahills haven't seen the last of me."

He paused, his breathing labored, his voice husky, broken. "Cahill killed my daughter, and I swear on her grave—I swear I'll get even with him!"

◆

With a steady hand, Justin helped his mother over to the sofa. She sat down, visibly shaken, the color drained from her face.

"May I pour you a cup of tea, Mother Cahill?" Robyn asked.

"Please, dear. With a pinch of sugar."

Justin tucked a pillow behind his mother's head, and then looked up intently at Chris. "Tell me—who on earth was that man?"

Chris's breathing was ragged. "His name's Bryden. Richard Bryden. I've never seen him like that—I can't believe he—"

"I think he would have harmed Dad," his mother cried.

"He—he's crazed with grief," said Chris, "but violence?—you think he's capable of actual violence?"

"Great Scott," said Justin, "what I saw here tonight—I saw a man ready to explode, a man capable of—of—"

"Capable of murder," said his mother, her voice wavering.

Chris sat down beside his mother. "Mom, do you know what you're saying?"

"I know what I saw in that man's eyes—"

"I know Bryden's always been a troublemaker, but—"

"A troublemaker?" echoed Justin. "Or a man in deep trouble? Tell me, what's he done?"

Ellen took the cup of tea Robyn brought her. "Sit down, Justin, here, on the other side of the sofa. I want both my boys beside me."

Justin sat down while his mother sampled her tea. "It's good, Robyn," she said softly. "Just right."

Laura quietly approached the sofa with little Rudy in her arms. "Mom Cahill, I'm putting Rudy in his playpen to sleep until we're ready to go. And the kids have agreed to help Robyn and me clean the kitchen while you relax."

His mother reached up and patted Rudy's chubby knee. "Laura, dear, why don't you and Chris stay overnight? There's enough room."

"Thanks, Mom Cahill, but we'll just tidy up and leave. You need your rest." She leaned down and lightly kissed Ellen's forehead.

When Laura had gone, Justin coaxed, "Mom, what about Bryden?"

"Yes, I'll tell you all about it—the whole story, as much as I know." The golden lamplight lent a fragile, antique quality to his mother's troubled face. Fine creases marked her brows and gave definition to her thin, pursed lips. Gentle folds of flesh defined her delicate cheeks and chin.

With a shock, Justin saw that she was old.

Incredibly, he had never thought of his mother as old, had never really stopped to see the unrelenting handiwork of time in his mother's face. He winced a little, remembering the vibrant, invincible woman of his childhood—a youthful mother who was beyond aging, beyond mortality. He wondered, when had her ageless image yielded to death-bound reality?

"Justin, you're not listening to a word I've said," his mother scolded. "You asked me about Richard Bryden, and I'm trying to tell you."

"I'm sorry, Mom. Go on. What did you say?"

"I said, Bryden was your father's foreman for several years. He did rather a good job, in fact, didn't he, Chris?"

"Yes, Mom. I had no complaint with him."

"Nor did your father, until—"

"Until what, Mom?"

Between sips of tea, Ellen said, "One day your father caught Bryden doctoring the books. He was cheating the company out of money—charging Cahill Manufacturing for supplies and materials that were never purchased, or listing more expensive items than what he actually bought."

"How long had he been cheating the company?" asked Justin.

"Oh, months, maybe even years. Victor didn't want to talk about it." Ellen paused for another swallow of tea, her face etched with concern. "The point is, your father fired Bryden on the spot and informed the police."

Chris nodded. "There was an investigation, Justin, and a trial, but not enough evidence to bring a conviction."

"It was too bad," said his mother. "The man was obviously guilty."

"Right, Mom. Anyway, Justin, the publicity kept Bryden from getting work around here after that. I knew he was angry, but I never realized just how bitter he was until now."

"He's more than bitter," said Justin. "He may be suicidal. I wish there was some way to reach the man. Help him—"

Chris nodded somberly. "And now, with his daughter's death, who knows what insane thing he'll try—?"

"There must be something we can do," said Justin.

Chris shrugged. "What can we do? We'll just have to—we'll have to deal with it, whatever happens."

Justin managed a tight smile. "Speaking of dealing with things, I was impressed. You did okay, Chris—"

"What—you mean with Bryden?"

"Yeah, you stood up to him. You didn't back down."

Chris chuckled. "Back down? Like when we were kids, you mean?"

"Uh, right."

"Thanks, big brother. I hope I've learned something since those days, whether Dad thinks I have or not—"

Before Chris could finish, Scott entered the room and said, "Hey, Grandma Cahill, Mrs. Pringle says Gramps wants to know when you're coming up to say good night."

Ellen stood shakily. "I'd better go up now. Justin, do you want to go up again and say good night to Dad?"

Justin shook his head. "No, Mom. You go ahead. Have your time alone with Dad." Under his breath he murmured darkly, "I think Dad's seen enough of me for one night."

9

ALONE THAT night in Justin's boyhood room, he and Robyn undressed in remote silence by the dim light of the dresser lamp. Justin found the room eerie in its sameness—the same mauve curtains and dusky wallpaper of thirty years ago, the handmade eiderdown quilt on the bed (why did things in his mother's house never wear out?), the familiar paintings of ancient ships he had treasured at age ten, and the silver-framed photograph of Justin at five in a sailor suit.

Robyn, softly appealing in an apricot negligee, stood beside the dresser, gazing at the photo. "I wish I'd known you then," she murmured. "You were such a cute little boy."

He considered a faintly humorous comeback—*So what's wrong with me now?* But he was too spent tonight to indulge in even the mildest banter. He set his wallet and loose change on the night stand, and then sat down on the bed and flexed his shoulders in a useless attempt to relieve tension.

"You must be exhausted," said Robyn. "Driving all day . . . seeing your father . . . confronting that poor, crazed man who lost his daughter . . ." She poured a fragrant moisturizer into her palm and lightly patted her cheeks and forehead. Her skin glistened with a youthful translucence; without makeup her eyes looked as vulnerable and enormous as a child's.

"Yes, I am beat," Justin agreed. "My muscles are in knots."

"I'm not surprised. Sometimes that snow was absolutely blinding. I thought we'd never get here." She craned her neck and patted moisturizer under her chin. Then she moved in slow, graceful strides over to the bed. "Did you know Laura

77

offered to come over early in the morning and fix breakfast so we could all sleep in?"

"Did she really?"

"I said no, we'd be fine, but still, I'm glad she and Chris live just a few miles away . . . just in case."

Justin slowly massaged his neck muscles. "Yes, my dutiful younger brother never strayed far from the family nest."

"Justin, you're doing it again."

He looked at her, puzzled. "Doing what?"

"You know. Being sarcastic."

"I wasn't trying to be." He motioned toward his neck. "Sweetheart, give me a quick back rub, okay?—just a few minutes? The tightness is killing me."

She sat down and began to massage his neck with her long, tapered fingers. "Goodness, Justin, you *are* tight."

"I told you so." He drew in a deep breath, silently urging his body to relax, unwind. *Forget the tensions of the day; forget the anger and frustrations, the psychic jabs and blows, the wear and tear of simply trying to stay alive.* "Yeah, right there, Robyn, that's great—just above my shoulder blades. You've got the magic touch, hon."

"You used to tell me that all the time," she said with a hint of seductiveness.

He grimaced. "Yeah, those were my younger, better days."

"Really? I thought the saying was, 'You're not getting older, you're getting better.'"

He reached around and gently caught her hand. "That's true for you, darling; but the vote's still out on me."

"Justin, stop."

He looked around. "Stop what?"

"Listen to yourself—"

"Listen? Listen to what?"

"Your—your tone of voice, what you're saying—"

"I'm not saying anything. Tell me what I'm saying."

"It's your attitude, Justin." She sighed audibly. "I see it more and more, and it worries me."

He tried to sound nonchalant, patiently indulgent. "Come on, Robyn. What attitude?"

"This—this cynicism of yours, Justin. You've always been a very serious man, but never sarcastic."

"Is that what you think I'm doing—becoming a cynic?"

"I hope not. You're too good for that." She kissed the back of his neck. Then, in a slow, rhythmic gesture she moved her fingers up along the cords of his neck, and over his ear to his temple. "I know it's been hard on you, Justin, this whole thing with the church, and now your father so ill—"

"I'm not letting it get to me, if that's what you think."

"Aren't you?"

"No, I'm not. If I sound on edge, it's just that I'm dead tired, drained."

"I know. I'm sorry. I shouldn't have said anything."

"No, it's okay."

"I just want to help, honey. I know how concerned you are about your father." Robyn rubbed Justin's temples gently with a slow, hypnotizing rhythm

"Feels good," he murmured. He felt himself drifting, his mind pleasantly lulled toward sleep. Sweet oblivion.

"How do you think your father looked?" Robyn asked.

"Bad. You saw him after dinner." Justin didn't want to talk, didn't want to be brought back; he was drifting, his muscles unwinding . . .

"I only saw him a minute," said Robyn. "I didn't want to tire him. Besides, you're the one he wanted to see."

Justin's reverie snapped; he was back, reluctantly. He looked around at Robyn. "That's a laugh. My dad didn't want to see me. He wanted to badger me about the business."

"What do you mean?"

"He wants me to assume his position as head of Cahill Manufacturing."

Robyn's face registered surprise. "What about Chris? He thinks the job is his."

"I know. It would kill him to find out after all these years that Dad still doesn't trust him with the business."

"What did you tell your father?"

"Nothing—except that I can't do it. What could I say? I didn't want to argue with him. Any upset could be fatal."

They were both silent a moment before Robyn said, "I know you told your dad no, but . . . are you going to consider his offer?"

Justin heaved a sigh of frustration. "The irony is, I may have to consider it."

"Why, Justin?"

"You know the policy at Redeemer Christian. When a new senior pastor comes in, all people on staff automatically offer their resignation as a gesture of unity and support."

"Some unity!" Robyn mused darkly. "You lay your life on the line so the new pastor can bring in his own people without feeling guilty."

"Someone evidently thinks it's a good policy."

"It's lousy."

Justin shook his head somberly. "After all that's happened, I may not want to stay there anyway," he said, adding with forced lightness, "Redeemer isn't the only church around."

"No," Robyn said quietly, "but it's home."

Without reply Justin stood and flipped off the light. He and Robyn climbed into bed and lay back to back without speaking for several moments. Then she turned slightly and asked, "Justin, did you speak to your father about, you know, spiritual matters?"

"I tried."

"What happened?"

"He told me to get out—in stronger language, of course."

Robyn rolled over and put a comforting hand on Justin's arm. "Honey, I'm not just saying this. I really believe . . . soon he'll want to hear about God. I just know it."

Justin ground his jaw slightly and sighed, "I don't think he'll ever want to hear it from me."

"He will, darling, believe me." Robyn's arm circled Justin's waist. The warmth of her body next to his should have stirred desire within him. Instead, he felt vaguely annoyed; his muscles tensed.

It was strange. He never felt comfortable making love to his wife under his parents' roof, especially in this, his boyhood room. Perhaps there were too many memories of pubescent years of struggling with unchaste thoughts, of wrestling against his own burgeoning urges.

And there was the lingering, debilitating specter of his mother warning him, *Good boys don't do that.* The irrational fear that his parents might walk in on them short-circuited his passion, much to his consternation and Robyn's. But even after all these years he couldn't argue away the embarrassment and self-consciousness he felt in lovemaking when he knew his parents were in the next room.

But these days—tonight included—he found himself facing quite another problem. A lack of desire. Sometimes lately he actually experienced a revulsion deep in his loins when Robyn touched him. Occasionally he feigned interest for her sake, but he suspected he was fooling neither of them.

They had never talked about it. He was too baffled—he would not permit the word *frightened* to take shape in his thoughts—he was perplexed (yes, a word that still allowed him some control). He refused to ask the question, *If my career—my divine calling—caves in, will my manhood follow?*

Or was it gone already?

The question shattered in his mind as Robyn nestled closer. He could feel her warm, minty breath on the back of his neck.

"Justin, I love you," she whispered. "Are you asleep?"

He lay still, allowing his own breathing to take on the slow, steady rhythm of slumber.

"Justin?" she repeated softly. "Justin, are you awake?"

He didn't answer.

10

SEVEN A.M. *Shaving. Water too cold, whiskers wire-tough. Careful of that mole beneath your lip. Bathroom's dreary . . . shadows make you look as old as your father, Justin . . . Feel in some ways like you're dying too, going down the tubes, down for the last count . . . count three years since you stared into this mirror. You look haggard . . . too young to look so old. Why three years, Justin? You should have come sooner . . . It couldn't have been three years, three days maybe. Bathroom smells of Old Spice, rusty pipes, and Mentholatum. Mirror's still cracked where Chris pitched a football once. How long ago was that? Too long. Mirror's wearing away, amalgam backing showing through, reflection's distorted. Crack splits you in two ever so slightly, forehead to chin . . . image altered, halved . . . when did you start being two people, Justin? Man of the cloth, shredding piece by piece. Something's wrong . . . nausea starting again . . . another headache . . . anxiety attacks . . . ulcers maybe. God help me!*

"Justin, how long will you be in the bathroom?"

Robyn's voice outside the door. Concerned, slightly petulant. Angry with him for last night perhaps? Or had he actually convinced her he was asleep? "Just a minute, dear," he said in his husky, early-morning voice.

"I'm going on downstairs for some juice," she said.

"Fine, hon." Yes, fine. He wouldn't have to face her alone. If there was a question in her eyes about last night, it would be lost in the commotion of breakfast.

When Justin entered the kitchen ten minutes later, crisply attired in a casual shirt and slacks, and a smile in place, he found his mother already serving pancakes and sausages. He paused and glanced around, yielding momentarily to faint whispers of nostalgia. This was the same sunlit, aromatic room he had entered countless times since his earliest childhood. He couldn't imagine it ever changing. He couldn't envision his folks not being here, going about their comfortable, age-old routines. Weren't parents supposed to live forever?

"I hope you're good and hungry, son."

Justin shook off his bittersweet musings, walked over and kissed his mother's cheek. "I am, Mom, but you're not supposed to be fussing like this."

"I'm not fussing. I enjoy cooking for my family." She patted his cheek; her eyes glistened.

"But we're here now to help you, Mom," he persisted.

"She won't let me lift a finger," said Robyn.

Ellen set a pitcher of steaming maple syrup on the table. "I'll let you fix dinner tonight, dear."

"I'm going to hold you to that, Mom Cahill."

Justin sat down and unfolded his napkin. "Will Chris and Laura be here this evening?"

"Chris said they'd come over after dinner to see Dad."

Justin met his mother's gaze. "How is Dad this morning?"

Ellen shook her head. "He had a restless night. I think he's in a lot of pain."

Justin reached over and squeezed his mother's shoulder. He sorted mentally through a dozen comforting phrases—his stock in trade. They all seemed trite, inappropriate. "Mom, what can I do for you today?" he asked instead.

She absently curled the collar of her green-print housedress. "I need to see our lawyer, Richard Dobbs," she told him. "Dad wants me to make sure his papers are in order."

"All right. I'll drive you over."

"I want you to check everything thoroughly for me, dear. I just don't understand legal matters." She sighed and her voice faded to a whisper. "I don't know how I'll manage later. . . ."

"You'll be fine, Mom," he assured her, and winced at his own audacity. Who was he to say she would be fine? Who was he to pretend he could control the outcome of anyone's life when he had all he could handle with his own shaky future?

"I'm so glad I have you and Chris," she said, patting his hand. Her eyes were red-rimmed, her expression strained. "I'm so glad to have you home, son."

"It's good to be home," he murmured, and wondered guiltily at his own veracity. A phrase darted through his mind: *It was the best of times . . . it was the worst of times.* He was beginning to understand the meaning of those strangely haunting words.

Eric entered then with a chipper "Good morning," wearing scruffy Levi's and a pullover sweater, his dark hair sleep-tousled and tumbling over his forehead.

Justin, welcoming the diversion, moved his chair to make room for his son. "Sleep well, Eric?"

"Like a rock. Until I smelled the sausage and coffee. Then my nose just followed the aromas."

"A few minutes later and the food might have been gone," said Ellen as she filled his plate.

"Well, Grandma, I stopped in a minute to see Gramps."

"Oh? Is he awake?"

"Yes, but I didn't want to bother him, so mainly I just talked to Mrs. Pringle."

"Do you want me to take a tray up to Dad?" asked Robyn.

"I'll take it up shortly, dear. He doesn't eat much, I'm afraid."

"What's everyone doing today?" asked Eric as he scooped up a forkful of scrambled eggs.

"Your grandmother and I will be taking care of some business, son, but if you're worried about being bored, I'm sure Grandma can find something productive for you to do around the house."

"Bored? No way. I'll just kick around awhile. Besides, Scott and Lauralee are coming over after school, around three or so. They say I gotta meet this girl next door—Kaylie something—"

"Kaylie Hollis," said Ellen, bringing the coffeepot over from the stove. "She's a very nice young lady. A little unconventional in her dress, perhaps, but she always speaks very respectfully to me. And your grandad thinks the world of her."

They finished breakfast in relative silence. As Justin left the table, he said, "Mom, I think I'll run upstairs and check on Dad before we go see the lawyer."

"Fine, son. I'm sure Dad would like that."

As Justin scaled the stairs to his father's room, he grimaced inwardly. Did his mother really believe that his father would welcome his presence? She hadn't heard their volatile encounter last night. Justin himself wondered why he felt it necessary to subject himself to his father's wrath this morning. Hadn't he had enough already? Hadn't they both?

Still, he was drawn to the old man, obsessively, like a magnet, as if he believed this time could be different. This time perhaps they could talk like two rational adults. A fool's dream, maybe, but he had to try.

As he slipped into the darkened room, he felt as if he were entering a cave. The air was dank and scant, and the feeble sunlight fought its way through the narrow slots in the Venetian blinds.

Justin uttered an involuntary sigh of relief. There would be no confrontation this morning. The room was silent. Mrs. Pringle had stepped out and his father was asleep, his face relaxed, the muscles collapsed in blank, expressionless repose.

Justin stood for a long moment watching that sleeping giant, his father. He was drawn hypnotically to the familiar face, the aging, yet ageless features. His father. A man of power. A man who still held unspeakable powers over Justin, powers that could not be articulated, could not be fathomed. What were the powers that fathers had over sons? Did Justin hold the same power over his son? It hardly seemed so, and yet the powers were too elusive and too mysterious to be grasped by the conscious mind.

Slowly, Justin let his guard down, allowed memories and emotions to ease through the crevices of his mind—recollections of the invincible Victor Cahill, who had shown no weaknesses that Justin could recall, who had never wept or whined or asked for help of any kind; had instead given orders: "You, Justin, get off your duff and help with the chores. . . . Get your lazy bones out of bed and give me a hand with the car. . . . You give me any guff, boy, and I'll give you a fat upper lip!"

Justin had feared his father in those days, those callow, fleeting, bumptious days of childhood—days that struck him now as not quite real, improbable, preposterous, pages from a comic book, reels from an old-time movie. Surely not his own life, not something he had actually lived. What he remembered most: He had known better than to cross his father. What would his dad do if he disobeyed? Scold him? Ban him from the house? Beat him? What awful thing did Justin expect to happen if he disobeyed the great Victor Cahill?

Justin knew the answer now. His father would withhold his love, his approval. It had happened—in fact, the day Justin did disobey—no, not disobey—*disagree;* the day he had gathered the courage to say, *I can't live the life you've chosen for me, Dad. I can't take your place in the business. I've made another choice. I have a different master now. I'll always follow your principles, Dad, but I want to build lives, not furniture.*

He remembered that day like yesterday; it had burned into his mind like a branding iron, searing its imprint forever on his consciousness. No one had told Victor Cahill no before—not Chris, not their mother, not even Justin himself—until that day when he stood facing his father, a trembling, heart-pounding, terrified sixteen-year-old who knew God had other plans for him.

The elder Cahill had never forgiven Justin, had perhaps never forgiven God, for Justin's decision to go another way. But for Justin it had been a liberating experience. After the initial terror, a euphoria set in; he had told his father no and had survived; he had declared his independence and it felt good, satisfying, to realize that he was indeed a separate individual from his father, not just an extension of the old man. He could go his own way, make his own choices; he wasn't tied to his father anymore.

But, of course, at the time he didn't realize what his independence would cost him—the warm nest of his family, the approval of his mother and father, the admiration of his brother. He hadn't counted on becoming an outcast, on feeling like a stranger in his own home. Was the price too great? No, even now, in spite of everything, he knew he couldn't have made any other choice.

His father stirred.

Justin stepped back into the shadows; then he eased silently out the door. No sense in disturbing his father now. At least in slumber the old man looked nearly at peace.

When Justin arrived back downstairs, his mother was already standing by the front door, adjusting her hat in the hall mirror. Few women wore hats anymore, but his mother would never think of going to town without one.

"You look good, Mom," he said, kissing her cheek.

She looked up, smiled, and pinched his cheek like she did when he was seven. "You ready to go now, son?"

"Yeah. Give me a minute to grab my coat."

He went to the kitchen where Robyn was clearing the dishes and made a point of kissing her soundly on the lips.

She looked up in surprise. "What's that for?"

Assuaging my guilt, he thought. "Just a love peck," he said.

"You leaving now?"

"Yeah. Taking Mom to the lawyer's. We shouldn't be long."

Outside, the snow was falling gently like the fine, soft feathers from his mother's hand-stitched eiderdown quilts. As he helped his mother into the automobile, Justin wondered why everything in Southfield reminded him of the past. His senses were constantly bombarded by the sounds, sights, and smells of his boyhood. The sensations were at once pleasing and disturbing.

As Justin pulled out onto the snow-cloaked street, he realized his mother was talking to him. Always she spoke with a soft, precise articulation. He remembered that voice from the dusky chambers of childhood memory—that voice reading him *Uncle Remus* and *Poky Little Puppy* and—what was that title?—*The Little Engine That Could.*

I think I can I think I can I think I can . . .

Sometimes Justin's life seemed driven by that same rote compulsion, that same driving force in his mind, only the words were different: *You think you can you think you can . . . but you can't!*

"I worry about you, Justin," his mother was saying.

"Don't. I'm fine."

"You look drawn, tired. You work too hard, son."

"Don't worry about me, Mom. You've got enough on your mind."

"It's that church of yours—they expect too much of you."

Expect too much of me? he mused cynically. *Are you kidding? They don't even want me. All their expectations now are in the new man, William Bradford . . .*

"A man has more than his work, Justin. He has his family—"

"Mom, let's not get into—"

"They should give you regular time off, Justin, enough time to come home once in a while."

"They give me vacations, Mom." Ironically, they were willing now to give him a permanent vacation. He was—what was the polite word?—*expendable.* A civil word, yes, hardly conveying the devastation of being rejected, unwanted. What was it the pulpit committee chairman had told him? *You're terrific in the pulpit, Justin, but we want someone who's more of a people person, someone who can really identify with the needs of the congregation. Come down from your stained-glass tower, and let the people know you're human.* Human? That was the problem. If the church knew how terribly human he was, they surely wouldn't want him as their pastor. It was Catch-22, a no-win situation.

"When do they give you vacations, Justin?" his mother was asking. "Obviously they're not allowing you enough time to come back here to see your parents—"

His migraine was returning. "I could have come, Mom. It's just—" He groped for words. Why hadn't he come home in three years? He didn't know. What were the ties that bound and repelled him at the same time? The ties that he felt at this very moment in the warmth of this automobile with his mother beside him—cords of love and duty woven together—indestructible, oppressive, unfathomable. From his childhood he had loved his mother with a keen, deep, binding adulation, akin to worship. As a boy he considered his mother flawless, perfection itself, someone just a step above the earthbound masses, touched by the mysteries of the heavenlies. He had wanted nothing more than to please her, to gain her smile of approval. And how often he had secretly relished winning her favor—a feat his younger brother never quite managed.

"Then why, Justin? Why haven't you come home?" she was asking.

"I don't know, Mom."

"You knew what it would have meant to your dad and me."

He turned defensive. "What about you and Dad? Why haven't you ever come to California? You know you've had a standing invitation."

She nodded. "Yes, Robyn has said so time and again. But you know your father. I could never get him away from the business that long—"

"You could have come without him."

She paused, and then said, "I've thought about it, son, but your father would be helpless without me to see after him and fuss over him. You know how impossible he is if his meals aren't on time and his clothes laid out—"

"You spoiled him, Mom."

"Oh, I know. I've catered to him since our courting days. Back then women didn't think much about their own rights. Everything was geared to pleasing a man—"

"Still, Laura and Chris could have looked after Dad if you'd wanted to pay us a visit."

"I suppose," his mother said thoughtfully. "But I'm a homebody, Justin. I'm not much for traveling . . . especially without your father."

They were silent after that. What more was there to say? No matter what Justin said, he was left with the unmistakable sense that he had failed his mother. Yes. He had failed, and he didn't even know why.

It was the same with his church. Somehow, his people had preferred a stranger, were actually welcoming—opening their arms to a stranger, this William Bradford. After Justin's many years of devotion to Redeemer Christian, Bradford, not Justin, would shepherd them, minister to them, comfort them. It was tradition, they said, and he knew it was so; senior pastors were usually hired from outside the fold. And, of course, he was foolish to have allowed his hopes in the first place.

But there was more involved here, more than a lost promotion, more than a problem of bucking tradition. Justin was losing ground in every aspect of his life. It was a mystery, a painful conundrum that somehow held the answer to Justin's entire future. He was certain that if he could find the solution, unravel the mystery of his people's preference for William Bradford, he would somehow understand all the twists and turns and covert meanings of his own existence.

What had the pulpit chairman said? *You need to be more human, Justin . . . a people person . . . let folks know you hurt* . . . Hurt? Of course he hurt! But he wasn't about to spill his guts to a cold, callous world. Why should he humiliate himself by prattling sentimental drivel just to make people like him, or pity him? If they couldn't accept him as he was—

He realized with a start that his mother was talking to him. How long had she been speaking, blithely assuming she had his attention? ". . . and with all that's happened, Justin, I just don't know what I'm going to do."

"Do? What? You mean, about Dad?"

She looked at him. "Yes, of course, your dad. What else?"

"We'll take care of things, Mom—Chris and I. Dad has always kept his business matters up, hasn't he? And the lawyer will help—"

"I don't mean that."

"Then what—?"

"I—I'm not ready to give him up."

"I know, Mom. It's not easy. . . ." *Giving up is never easy. How well I know that.*

"Even knowing ahead of time, knowing what's coming—I can't think of it, can't imagine . . . I just can't let him go, son."

"We'll all be with you, Mom. We'll face it together."

She shook her head, and then stared out the window. "No, son, no one can face this with me. I'm alone. Even your father can't help me now. . . ."

"Have the two of you talked, you know, about all these things?"

His mother took a handkerchief from her purse. "No, Justin, not really. He's got enough to deal with. I'm afraid I can't help him and he can't help me."

"Mom, it doesn't have to be that way—"

"Oh, yes, that's the only way it can be." Her voice caught and she dabbed at her eyes and nose with her hanky. "Over forty years of my life will go with him, Justin. . . ."

"Mom, listen, you'll be okay—"

"Okay? How dare you say okay, Justin? Your father is my whole life!"

"I know, but you're a strong woman, Mother. You and Dad have had a long, happy marriage. Try to remember the good times."

"The good times? Of course, I'll remember the good times, and the bad times, and all the ordinary and uneventful times in between. They'll all be precious to me now."

"I know, Mom. I'll treasure the memories too, but you can't—we can't just live in the past either—"

"Live in the past?" His mother's voice was edged with indignation. "Please, Justin, don't tell me how to live or how to feel. You—you don't know anything about it—about what your father's dying means to me."

In a low, chastened voice he said, "I'm trying to understand, Mom." But how could he understand? He didn't even understand what his father's dying meant to him—to Justin, the dutiful, responsible elder son! How could he make sense of living, or dying, when his own life—his career, his calling—had been put on hold?

He heard his mother speaking, but her words seemed to be coming at him from a distance. "I'll tell you how it is for me, Justin. Maybe you need to hear this. Maybe I need to say it. What gnaws at me—and, oh, I admit it's a selfish ache, but it's there, and I need to tell someone. Look at me, Justin. I'm an old woman."

He glanced over and smiled distractedly. "You'll always look great to me, Mom."

"That's not the point, son. It's just—it's that no one else

remembers how I looked when I was young—only your father. He was the only person on earth who ever made me feel beautiful. Do you know what that means, Justin?"

He was listening, trying to listen, but somehow the meaning of her words evaded him. He concentrated on the road, on the chalky opaqueness of the snow-cloaked landscape, the pewter-gray sky, the faint, white, dancing flurries— "Yes, Mom, go on. . . ."

"This isn't easy, Justin, not easy for me to say. Do you know how it feels to realize I'll no longer exist in anyone's memory—me, Ellen Cahill, the young girl, the new wife and mother, the person I was years before you were born? Do you have any idea how it feels to realize that to all the important people in my life I've always been old?"

Justin was silent for a long moment. He was having a hard time focusing on his mother's words, on their exact meaning. Finally he said quietly, "I'm sorry, Mom. I wish I knew what to say. . . ."

"Someday you'll understand, Justin. You'll know what it's like to be old."

I already feel old, he reflected silently. Once time seemed open-ended, limitless, boundless, but now I see that it's deviously elusive, impossibly fleeting, totally inadequate. What did the Bible say?—life is but a vapor . . . a thousand years is as a day . . . what is man that Thou art mindful of him?

How can I cope with my father's dying and my mother's grief when I'm not sure how well I'm coping with my own mortality? Immortality—my eternal destiny—was settled long ago, but my earthly mortality, that's something I still struggle with. What if I die a failure? What if, ultimately, my life counts for nothing?—has no meaning, no impact, no significance? How can I give my mother trivial advice and pat answers when I haven't resolved my own deepest feelings about my father's dying, about my own inevitable dying?

And, as his mind churned darkly, from across a great gulf came his mother's voice like a tiny bird flying against the wind. "Are you listening to me, Justin? Are you listening?"

11

ERIC CAHILL rummaged through his grandmother's antique medicine cabinet looking for some Brut or Old Spice, whatever—just some nice smelly stuff to splash on his freshly shaved face. Surely Grandpa Cahill had some cologne lying around somewhere. Eric had sent him enough aftershave for Christmas over the years. What else could a guy send a grandfather who had everything?

But all Eric could find in this ancient cabinet were assorted medicine bottles, iodine, Preparation-H, and denture cream. Yuck! He would have to traipse upstairs and rifle through his overnight bag for some of his own Polo cologne.

He stepped back and scrutinized his face in the mirror. He hated old-fashioned bathrooms like this where the light was so dim and the mirror so decrepit it distorted his face. He had to stand just right or he looked like Godzilla from some horror movie. There. That was better. Now he looked at least half human.

He had been listening to his Walkman, but now he removed his earphones so he could comb his hair. Too bad he had to interrupt Whitney Houston. She was singing a soft, mellow ballad, one of his favorites. He liked her voice, liked her style. Maybe someday somebody would be listening to him, the popular Eric Cahill, and liking his voice, liking his style. It was possible. Anything was possible.

He ran his comb through his thick, ebony hair and carefully brushed several wisps over his forehead with a studied randomness, so the tendrils would look like they had fallen naturally in a rumpled tangle. He looked cool with his hair this way. Several girls had told him so. One girl told him he looked like James Dean and had Paul Newman eyes, but he wasn't sure that was a compliment since Dean had been dead nearly forever, and Paul Newman was probably old enough to be his grandfather. But Eric had seen the dudes in some old movies, and he liked Dean's hair, and Newman did have okay eyes.

Eric's eyes were a clear, cobalt blue, and he had a solid face with a sloping nose, high cheekbones, and good teeth. He wasn't sure he was handsome, but he liked to think so, and he liked the light he saw in girls' eyes when they looked at him. At seventeen, he wasn't exactly an expert on girls, but he pretended he was, and he figured he could bluff his way through just about any situation.

Like today. In an hour, he would be seeing his cousins, Scott and Lauralee, and the three of them would be going next door so he could meet this girl, Kaylie Hollis. Scott said she was a fox. And nice, a good personality; maybe a little off the wall, he said, but then maybe that was all right too.

Thinking of meeting someone new—a girl he might like, who might like him too—started Eric's adrenaline pumping. He liked the feeling, the sense of energy growing, gathering inside him, boundless and untapped. It gave him a feeling of power, like he could do anything, be anything. The whole world was open to him tonight; the idea charged him up, spun a sense of euphoria in his brain. He hadn't felt this good in days. For a few hours he would escape the somber mood, the oppressiveness of his grandparents' house. He could forget that death was imminent, that grief was inevitable. He could laugh and have fun without feeling guilty.

Guilty?

Come on now. Why shouldn't he feel guilty?

That's what his dad would tell him in his most controlled, sanctimonious voice. Eric could hear the words in his head, the exact inflections, the unspoken but implied condemnation.

Just look at yourself, Eric. Here your grandfather is upstairs dying, and all you can think about is having fun. What kind of insensitive jerk are you?

No, those weren't his dad's words. His dad might call him a headstrong son or a self-absorbed grandson, but not an insensitive jerk. Eric had come up with that phrase on his own. Maybe that's just what he was—an unfeeling, insensitive jerk. Somehow, he had a hard time concentrating on other people's problems, even his own family's, when he had so many concerns of his own to contend with. Grades. Girls. College. The future.

He ran his comb through his hair again, quickly, impatiently. It didn't look right. No matter how he coaxed the shock of hair over his forehead, it looked weird, nerdish.

He heaved a sigh of frustration and flipped his comb into the sink. It was crazy, the way his mood could flip-flop in a matter of seconds. One moment, he was feeling on top of the world; the next, he felt as if someone had dropped a rock on his chest.

It used to be he felt guilty only when he and his dad were at odds; his dad was terrific at laying a guilt trip on him. But lately, Eric could do the job all by himself, just by thinking of what his dad would say to him in any given circumstance. Like now: *Eric Cahill, where's your sense of compassion? Why are you gallivanting off to some girl's house when you could be home sitting with your sick grandfather or comforting your poor grandmother?*

Eric could feel all his energy and exuberance churning into a dark whirlpool of anger and anxiety. Stupid—he was stupid to think about his dad now. His dad had a way of playing mind games with his head, making him feel like dirt, like no matter what he did he could never make things right. Why was it? Everything Eric did seemed to irritate his dad—his taste in music, his clothes, his friends.

Eric didn't want to be a preacher—that was his real crime. His dad never came right out and said so, but Eric read it in his eyes and in his tone of voice more often than he cared to remember. It baffled Eric. Why should his dad want him to be a preacher? From the looks of things, his dad wasn't exactly crazy about the job himself.

Eric leaned forward into the mirror and examined the pores around his nose. Blast it—a zit! Why hadn't he noticed it before? It was practically sitting on his nose for all the world to see. How could he meet a new girl with a zit on his nose? He grabbed a jar of Noxzema and dabbed a glob of the cool white cream around his nostrils.

As he rubbed the cream into his skin, he couldn't stop thinking about his dad, about his dad's impossible expectations. A preacher! How could his father expect him to be a preacher? He hated speaking in front of groups. It just wasn't his thing. It never would be.

But his dad wasn't content to let the matter lie. The questions kept coming, always uttered in barely disguised exasperation. If Eric wasn't going to consider the ministry, then what was he going to do with his life? His dad asked him this question at least once a week, always phrasing it as though the question had just occurred to him for the first time: *How about it, son? Given any thought to what you're going to do with your life? It's never too soon to begin thinking about the future, you know.*

The future.

It was a catch-all word. It meant nothing. It meant everything. But his dad held it over his head like a threat.

As if Eric didn't already feel the pressures of facing his future, especially this year. After blithely sailing through eleven years of grade school, junior high, and even high school, he had suddenly been brought up short this year with the startling realization that his future was uncertain. Always before he had simply passed unquestioningly from one grade to the next, his future predetermined. He had no say about the school he would attend, the classes he would take; his choices were minimal, practically nonexistent.

But now! In a few short months, after his high school graduation, his future could take him in a hundred different directions. He had to make choices from a myriad of possibilities. The idea was terrifying and breathtaking at once.

Eric reached over and grabbed the hand towel, put one corner under the faucet, and washed the Noxzema from his face. The zit was still there but maybe not so noticeable. Chances were he wouldn't get close enough to this Kaylie Hollis for her to spot it anyway. But then, again, anything was possible.

Maybe that was the problem. With endless possibilities came endless choices.

And if Eric were going to be honest about it, he knew he wasn't ready to begin making life's big choices. He felt inadequate, unprepared. He could bluff his way through trig, conjugate a verb in Spanish, and find Yugoslavia on a map, but what did he know about carving out a career and earning a living, or finding a mate and setting up a home? He much preferred the sanctuary of the classroom or the solitary comfort of sitting alone in his room writing a song or playing his keyboard. Wasn't that good enough for now?

His dad would say no.

His dad would say, "You must be prepared to seize your opportunities." It sounded like a slogan Eric had read on some billboard. Maybe that's where his dad had seen it.

But how could Eric possibly make important decisions about his future when his life was one big question mark, a blank page, a book in a foreign language? He had no idea who he was, let alone who he should become—or what. He was a senior, about to embark on the roiling tides of life—the most wonderful time in his life, everyone claimed. But he was drowning in SAT tests and college applications and fears that his grades would not allow him to graduate with honors.

Where was he to go from here? Where was the road map for his life? The easy days were over when he could settle for the tag, "high school student." Now he must begin to become something—a professional, gainfully employed, a member of the team, part of the labor force, a citizen of the world. What a laugh! Never mind that he had no idea what he could do to warrant a weekly paycheck.

At least he knew what he *didn't* want to do. He didn't want to peddle junk food all his life like he'd done part-time at the Burger Hamlet back home. That was the real definition of failure—a thirty-year-old man still flipping fries at a burger joint.

Eric stepped back from the bathroom mirror and scrutinized his reflection. He tried on a couple of different expressions— cool guy, tough guy, brooding poet, and Romeo, with a lowered gaze and sensual half-smile. His idea of sensual, anyway. Would that look turn on Kaylie? He hadn't seen her yet, so maybe he wouldn't even want to impress her. But if she was a dog, he could always clam up and act like a nerd.

He worked some more with his hair, combing the back just so, and drawing his comb along each side so that the wave was finally perfect. But when he looked himself in the eye again, he realized he looked worried.

Maybe he was worried.

It worried him that he had no deep, driving ambition to carve out a career. Some guys had known since their childhood that they wanted to be doctors, lawyers, computer analysts, whatever. Not Eric. He loved music. He loved to sing, strum his guitar, play his keyboard. He loved writing songs and poems.

What was the going rate for a poem these days? A thousand dollars? A hundred? Or would he have to give them away? Poems for free—who on the green earth would want one of his poems? Not even his parents wanted to read them, except maybe politely, dutifully, as when he used to bring them his scrawled homework in grade school.

That wasn't exactly true. His mom admired his work and praised him for his scribblings. She was an artist; she knew what it was like to create something beautiful that had never existed before; she knew the struggle, the birth pangs. People said the creative process was like—what did they call it?—the *travail* of childbirth; he couldn't vouch for the childbirth thing, but he knew plenty about the labor pains of bringing a song or poem to life.

Eric met his own gaze again in the mirror with a slow, frank scrutiny. Well, maybe he wouldn't make a living writing songs, but his hair was perfect; he looked cool; he was ready for this Kaylie Hollis. Maybe this was just the beginning. Who knew what could develop over the next couple of weeks? He was stuck here in Southfield that long anyway, so why not make the best of things? A little romance might turn this cold, cruel world into a winter wonderland. He winced at his own clichés. If he ever wrote a song about Southfield in winter, he'd have to do better than that. And if he got something going with this Kaylie Hollis . . .

He let his thoughts wander, let the possibilities drift across his mind's eye. He could feel a surge of energy revitalizing his senses, that old euphoria coming back, sweet and tantalizing. He closed his eyes and created Kaylie in his imagination—her warm touch, the scent of her perfume, her kiss, her closeness. . . .

Then he caught himself and opened his eyes, chagrined, blinking his fantasies out of existence. His face felt hot; his pulse had quickened. What was he doing, imagining such things with a girl he hadn't even met yet?

Eric stepped back from the mirror and scowled at his reflection. He still didn't have quite the look he wanted, but it would have to do. He patted his back pocket for his wallet and arched his shoulders, trying to release the tension in his muscles. He drew in a deep breath and expelled the air slowly through his nostrils. You would think he was preparing for battle. Why did he always feel that so much was at stake? Why couldn't he simply wash his mind of worries and just go have fun?

Maybe he could. He strode out of the bathroom and down the hall, and grabbed his leather jacket off the tree rack by the door. He began to whistle. Who knew what the day held? The possibilities were tantalizing. Maybe this Kaylie Hollis was the girl of his dreams.

12

KAYLIE GREETED Eric, Scott, and Lauralee at the door in a hot pink, rhinestone-studded sweater and knit slacks. "Hi, guys," she said breezily, her voice throaty and yet pleasantly melodic.

Eric didn't believe in love at first sight, but from the moment he gazed at Kaylie Hollis, he knew he'd been hit. Kaylie was tall and willowy but round in all the right places; she had an oval face with skin as white as eggshell; her features were finely etched but not quite symmetrical—a long, narrow nose, dark snapping eyes spaced a little too close together, a wide red mouth, and perfect teeth. Kaylie's face reminded Eric of a Modigliani print that hung in his mother's art studio (actually a renovated corner of the garage). Her face possessed the same mysterious quality of the woman in the picture, except that Kaylie's face was framed with straw-blonde hair that spilled over her forehead and down her shoulders like a sun-spangled waterfall.

Sun-spangled? Yes, that was the phrase that came to Eric as he first gazed at Kaylie. He wished he had paper and pencil to write the phrase down. He sensed already that she was an irresistible mass of contradictions—child and woman, pouter and preener; a tantalizing mixture of beauty and homeliness, awkwardness and grace. He would write a poem about her—yes!

In fact, Eric knew he would write dozens of poems about Kaylie. He would pen songs, dream dreams, and struggle privately with his secret yearnings for her. And whether or not anything ever came of their relationship, he would never forget her. All this he knew and accepted in these first tentative moments.

"Kaylie, this is Eric. Eric, Kaylie," said Lauralee as the three stamped snow from their shoes and stepped inside the sprawling, marble-floored entryway.

"Hi," said Eric, a little breathless. His mind was still pin-wheeling.

"Hi, Eric." She touched his arm. "Uh, your shoes—"

He looked down. "What? My shoes?"

"Yeah. Take them off, okay? My mom's a bear about tracking in slush."

"Oh, yeah, sure." He quickly pulled off his shoes, tossing up a silent petition that he was wearing his good socks.

"Don't worry," she went on brightly. "We have carpet an inch thick in the rec room, so your feet won't freeze."

Eric noticed that Lauralee and Scott had already placed their shoes neatly beside an umbrella stand. Eric set his shoes beside theirs. He realized he hadn't even spoken an intelligible sentence yet to Kaylie, and already his mouth was dry.

With a jaunty casualness, Kaylie led the three of them downstairs to the basement, to a roomy, comfortable hideaway with oak paneling, overstuffed sofas and squat, bulky tables. Eric glanced around, taking in the expensive stereo system and CD player, the wide-screen TV and VCR, and across the room, a Ping-Pong table. And, sure enough, the carpet was plush and felt surprisingly good under Eric's stockinged feet.

"We can be as loud as we want down here," said Kaylie. "Upstairs, when I'm talking with my friends or playing my music, it drives my mother bananas. Like, she thinks I'm this noisy, scatterbrained person who keeps the whole house in an uproar. I mean, my mom's nice—she's not witchy or anything—but when she and my dad are in a bad mood, it's the pits, so I just come down here and turn on my tape deck, and it's cool, you know?"

Eric knew exactly. How often he escaped into the solace of his music when the world around him became too oppressive or demanding.

Kaylie walked over to a compact refrigerator beside a western-style wet bar. "Anyone want a Coke, Diet Coke, Sprite?"

"Diet Coke," said Lauralee, tossing her denim jacket over a chair. She ambled over to the stereo and began sorting through several cassette tapes. "Hey, Kaylie, where's your latest Randy Travis?"

"There somewhere." Kaylie handed her a can of Diet Coke, and then turned to Scott and Eric. "How about you guys?"

"Coke," they said at once.

She laughed lightly and handed them each a Coke. "Sit down, you guys. Throw your coats anywhere."

Eric set his Coke down, shrugged off his jacket, and then gazed around uncertainly. He waited until Kaylie sat down on the sofa, curling her legs under her; then he took the chair opposite her. He sat forward, resting his elbows on his knees and cracked his knuckles nervously. When he looked up he realized Kaylie was watching him with cool, complacent brown eyes—an expression of mild insouciance, skeptical but curious.

"Scott says you're from California," she said lightly, as if it might not actually be true.

He nodded. "Yeah, I am."

"Really? Like from Hollywood, somewhere terrific like that?"

"Not exactly. About an hour outside L.A."

"Oh, then you don't live where all the movie stars hang out." She sounded disappointed.

He sat back and cupped his hands behind his head. "No, I don't."

"But you go to Hollywood, right?"

"Yeah, sometimes." He was having a hard time relaxing under her scrutinizing gaze.

"Then you've seen movie stars," she said, her voice rising with excitement. "Who have you seen?"

"I don't know. I can't remember." What was this—the third degree?

"You're kidding! You've seen movie stars and you can't remember who? Be real!"

"Okay. I—I once saw Martin Sheen."

She didn't look impressed. "Okay. Who else?"

"He was in this restaurant eating dinner—"

"Did you talk to him?"

"Well, no, I mean, I wasn't going to just walk up and say—"

"All right, who else?"

"What?"

"Who else did you see—besides Martin Sheen?"

Eric glanced helplessly at his cousin. Scott, in turn, leaned over and nudged Eric's shoulder. In an exaggerated Three Stooges voice, Scott drawled, "Hey, man, I saw this dude, and he was totally cool. His name was Donald Duck. Does he count as somebody important? I saw him running around this place called Disneyland—"

"Oh, Scott, can it, will you, please?" said Lauralee in exasperation. "I want to hear who Eric saw too, so zip your lip."

"Yes, come on, tell us," urged Kaylie.

Eric cracked his knuckles again. He was tiring already of this silly game, but somehow he had to impress Kaylie! "Well, I saw Bruce Springsteen—"

"Really? In a concert? Did you hear him sing?"

"No. I saw him at the airport. Los Angeles International. He was running to catch a plane."

"Oh," said Kaylie. "Is that all?"

Eric blinked, feeling suddenly wounded; then he said rashly, "Ah, no, that's not all. I—I once spent an afternoon surfing with Richard Gere. . . ."

Kaylie swung her legs out from under her and bounced forward, clasping Eric's arms. She was beaming and breathy. "You don't mean it! Richard Gere? You actually went surfing with Richard Gere?"

Eric felt pleasantly warmed by Kaylie's touch and was tempted to elaborate on his little impromptu fabrication. But no, he couldn't. He shook his head. "I just said that, Kaylie. I never met Richard Gere."

She slapped his arm and sat back in a pout. "Boys! You're all alike. You'll say anything to get a girl's attention. Isn't that right, Lee?" she said plaintively, looking over at Lauralee.

Lauralee tipped her Coke can up and swallowed; then she gave Eric a wink. "I think what my handsome cousin said shows real progress. He's always been so stodgy, but he's finally starting to sound like a regular guy."

"Oh, that's right," said Kaylie, muffling a smile. "I forgot." She looked back at Eric. "Scott told me you're a preacher's kid. That must be a real drag, huh?"

Eric turned his Coke can in his hands. It was starting to feel warm. He hated warm Coke, but he drank it anyway because his throat felt dry, tight. "I—well, I—" His mind went blank. What had Kaylie asked? Something about being a preacher's kid?

Kaylie tittered, "You don't have to answer that, Eric. You can take the fifth—"

"No, it's okay. It's no big deal being a preacher's kid." He could taste the lie in his mouth even as he said it. Sure, it was a big deal wearing a label like that. It was a pain in the rear. No one in the church had the slightest idea who Eric Cahill was; he was just Rev. Cahill's son, a tag that separated him from all the other teenagers. Being a preacher's kid meant he couldn't just forget church for one Sunday and head for the mountains with his dad. Not that his dad would want to spend an entire weekend alone with Eric anyway. The two had never been close. They were only buddies for show, like when they sat together at the father-son banquet at church.

"Is that all you've got to say about it?" said Scott. "No horror stories about getting your halo tarnished or losing your wings? Doesn't your dad lean hard on you about setting a good example—?"

"No," snapped Eric. "My dad and I have an understanding. He goes his way, I go mine. That's how it is." He could see by their expressions that they didn't believe him. He knew he sounded defensive. He gave himself a mental swift kick. Why didn't he just keep his fat mouth shut?

"Oh, come on, Eric. I bet your folks expect you to be perfect all the time, huh?" quizzed Kaylie, absent-mindedly twisting a birthstone ring on her right hand. "I mean, my dad's a dentist and he expects perfection, so what chance does a preacher's kid have—?"

"It's not exactly unbearable or anything," said Eric, wishing he had the words to explain how he felt. How did he feel? The emotions were too deep, too complex. "I mean, it's like being on stage all your life, . . . like being a puppet with someone else pulling all the strings. But after a while you shut out the negative feelings and don't think about it anymore. So I guess you could say . . . I'm surviving."

"I know just how you feel," said Kaylie. "My parents hardly let me breathe. They'd live my whole life for me if I let 'em. Not that they've done so hot with their own lives—"

Scott spoke up. "My old man's got enough on his mind trying to work out his own problems, so he leaves Lauralee and me alone. Right, Sis?"

"Yeah, most of the time we come and go as we please," said Lauralee, "especially since little Rudy came along."

"Little Rudy?" Kaylie clapped her hands in delight. "Oh, I absolutely love your little baby brother. Someday I'm going to have a sweet baby of my own—"

Scott whistled teasingly. "Hey, Kaylie, you keeping something from us? You secretly married or got a lover on the side?"

Kaylie gave him a withering glance. "No, I'm not PG. I just like babies. They're more fun than some teenage boys I know—"

"Oh, wow, she got back at you, Scott," trilled Lauralee.

"It's not a joke," said Kaylie. "Sometimes I wish my mom had had more kids. It's a bummer being an only child—"

Eric nodded. "Yeah, I feel that way sometimes—"

Kaylie leaned forward impulsively and took Eric's hand. "See, we do have something in common! We're both an only child. We know what it's like to be alone—and lonely! Remember when you were a kid and had no one else to race you to the Christmas tree on Christmas morning, and no one to play with when your parents took you somewhere on vacation—?"

Eric laughed spontaneously. He suddenly felt more relaxed, at ease. He and Kaylie—this weird, wonderful, unpredictable girl—had something in common. "I never thought of it like that," he said.

"Oh, I do," said Kaylie earnestly. "Sometimes I lie in bed at night and think of all the things I can't do because I have no brother or sister to do them with."

"Like what?" asked Lauralee skeptically.

"Like fight," said Scott, jabbing his sister in the ribs.

Eric laughed politely, but his eyes were on Kaylie. He was pleased that she saw him as more than just a preacher's kid. They shared a bond. They both felt the pressure of overbearing parents, and they both had been lonely. He wondered with a keen sense of anticipation what other connections they would discover to draw them together.

13

FOR THE first time since her arrival in Southfield, Robyn Cahill was alone in the immense old Cahill homestead. Well, not quite alone. Victor Cahill, Justin's father, was sleeping soundly upstairs, with the day nurse at his bedside. But the others were off and gone—Eric to the neighbor's house with Scott and Lauralee (no telling when they would be back, especially if Eric liked this girl, Kaylie Hollis); and Justin—he had just telephoned to tell Robyn he and his mother would be delayed; they would be doing some banking and then talking with his father's insurance man, but they'd be home in plenty of time for dinner.

Dinner? Robyn refused to think about dinner now.

She had been given a special gift—time alone, the house to herself. What a delicious sense of relief she felt. She would savor this peacefulness and snatch an hour or so for herself without feeling guilty.

Like a child playing hooky, she got out her sketch book and pencils. Might as well get a little drawing in, she decided. She loved sketching the view from the kitchen window—the weathered, picturesque buildings nestled in a snow-draped wonderland, gnarled trees with naked limbs festooned with glittering icicles, the wintry sky gleaming with the opalescent sheen of porcelain. . . .

When she sketched, Robyn felt order returning to her world, no matter how chaotic or stressful her circumstances. She thrived on that sense of satisfaction and vitality that came when the drawing was going well, when the lines were exactly right and fresh, capturing some new truth she herself hadn't realized was there. Nothing else, except prayer, gave her quite this sense of joyous discovery.

When she wasn't sketching, Robyn found pleasure in studying the works of Andrew Wyeth, Winslow Homer, and Thomas Eakins. They were illustrators as well as painters, and with what natural beauty and simplicity they captured the exquisite, ordinary scenes of American life! Robyn dreamed of carving out such a career for herself, but it was unlikely, a fantasy without substance, a vain hope. No one took her work seriously; even Justin barely noticed; no one would imagine that she aspired to such lofty heights. She would blush with shame if Justin ever guessed how desperately she craved the taste of success, how she hungered for some recognition of Robyn Cahill, the artist. As far as Justin was concerned, her art was simply something to help her pass the time or calm her nerves—a diversion, a hobby, a mere distraction from what was truly important in life.

Justin had no idea how intertwined were her spiritual and creative energies, how one fed the other, how the very act of creating stirred within her a sense of her commonality with the Creator; yes, they had this in common—the act of loosing the imagination, igniting its power, to bring something out of nothing, beauty out of chaos, order out of disorder. Robyn felt sorry for those who had not discovered this truth for themselves—the miracle of being one with the Creator in the act of creating . . .

Robyn paused and cocked her head to one side. She had heard a noise. Was it from her father-in-law's room? Was he awake? Needing something? Was his nurse asleep? Out of the room? Robyn listened. Silence, except for the distant grating whine of a truck's wheels on icy pavement.

Perhaps she should check upstairs anyway. But if Victor was asleep, her footsteps on the creaking stairs might disturb him. And she was reluctant to relinquish these private moments alone. At noon, she had taken a steaming bowl of chicken soup up to her father-in-law. He had awakened from his slumber just long enough to look up at her and murmur, "Ah, it's my sweet little bird, Robyn, on a mission of mercy . . . or are you an angel? Have I died already?"

Victor always called her his little bird and spoke to her with a wry warmth, almost a gentle flirtation. He had never shown her his crusty, belligerent side, had never raised his voice to her, or belittled or intimidated her. He always made her feel special, as if he regarded her as some rare pet who required careful handling. How she wished Justin could experience the tenderness she managed to bring out in his father.

Strange. Sometimes she sensed more tenderness in the elder Cahill than she did in Justin himself. Victor opened a window of himself to her; he wasn't afraid to let her know he considered her an attractive woman. In fact, back down the dusky corridors of the past, when she and Justin were dating, Victor often told his son, "Don't let this one get away or you'll regret it all your life." Robyn had felt flattered, more so because she sensed that Victor Cahill meant every word he said. In fact, she was convinced that her marriage to Justin was the only thing Justin and Victor had ever agreed upon.

Justin . . .

She didn't want to think about Justin now.

She didn't want to think about last night, the sense of humiliation she had felt when her faltering advances were rebuffed.

Or was Justin really asleep?

No, she knew the difference, knew the deep, whistling sound he made when he was truly sleeping. Why had he pretended—he who preached truth and love to his congregation? Why had he deliberately deceived her and withheld his love?

It wasn't the first time. It had happened before, several times during these past few months, although she hadn't been so certain; she could have been mistaken before, could have misread the situation. But not last night. Last night she knew, and the reality of it burned in her heart even now.

She had tried to deny it.

Tried to rationalize her feelings away.

Tried to be loving and forgiving.

But she couldn't. She had to face it, had to acknowledge it, had to accept it. Oh, God forgive her, she couldn't help how she felt.

She was angry.

Not open, vocal, all-cards-on-the-table angry; not heart-pounding, throat-tight, hot-in-the-temples angry. That might have been easier—anger that erupted suddenly, had its say, loud and verbal, maybe even physical—a slap, a foot stomped, a door slammed. But no—this wasn't that kind of anger. This was something else, maybe not quite anger—was there another word?—resentment, disappointment, a wounded spirit?

She was angry—in a quiet, not-quite-realized, not-quite-verbalized way. It was there—a faint current under the skin, a sliver in the flesh too tiny to extricate with tweezers (bothersome, painful sometimes, but a pain one wasn't fully conscious of), an irritant like static on a radio not quite tuned in.

The problem was, she and Justin were not quite tuned in. Sometimes she felt the static between them, cutting off impulses of love and warmth, a noise in the background of their relationship obscuring their words, the meaning of their words.

It was worse whenever they were here in Southfield. Here, in the house of his parents, whatever subterranean conflicts existed between Justin and herself were dredged up and emblazoned like neon signs upon their relationship. Justin became an aloof stranger, remote and inscrutable; she felt herself becoming a nag, a dowdy middle-aged wife who had lost her appeal. Not a sex object—she had never been that!—but worse, a *sexless* object.

Without a word, with barely a glance, Justin made her feel ashamed that she needed him, wanted him. It wasn't supposed to be like this. Men were the great pursuers with their supposedly insatiable appetites for pleasure, and women—well, they could take it or leave it, so the saying went.

Justin was still a virile man, a handsome, sensual man, but he had made it clear that he no longer desired his wife. Oh, Robyn knew he still loved her; they had shared too much for too many years to lose the comfortable closeness that time and familiarity had bred. But he no longer found pleasure in touching her, caressing her, cherishing her. And if she was no longer attractive to the man who knew her best, how could she possibly be appealing to anyone?

Robyn put her sketchbook aside, stood, stretched, and then walked into the bathroom. She stared somberly in the mirror at herself, at her face and eyes, wondering what Justin saw, what others saw? Had some dreadful flaw escaped her? What did people see when they looked at Robyn Cahill?

She shook her head at the futility of it all.

Why couldn't she rise above the questions, the doubts, the disappointments? Why couldn't she just grow old gracefully?

No, she would go down fighting, greedily clasping every vestige of youth and beauty . . .

In fact, too often these days she stood and stared at her reflection in the mirror, analyzing her features—the tiny lines under her eyes, the slight softening of the flesh around her chin, the creases in her forehead and around her mouth. Slowly, with a painful scrutiny, she memorized this new self, absorbing with a sense of surprise and dismay this updated image of herself—no longer a schoolgirl with a child's glow of innocence, no longer a college student beaming with health and youthfulness, no longer even a young wife with a natural, unforced beauty.

These days she worked with care and precision to create the face Justin had fallen in love with; nothing came easy anymore; and each day it was harder to capture that look—the person she remembered in her mirror from a dozen distant years ago.

Was that why Justin no longer found her attractive? Did he see what she saw when she gazed in the mirror at her plain, scrubbed face every morning? He knew her so well, knew the planes and angles of her face and body as well as she did—how could there be mystery anymore? How could she recapture the mystery, the mystique and allure—the power and energy, and yes, euphoria—of being a sexual being again, of captivating—igniting!—another human being with that inexpressible fire and magic?

She had known only Justin. No other man.

Except.

She had almost known Alex Lanigan.

But that was another lifetime ago—nearly twenty years. She still recalled during rare moments of dream-steeped reverie the bittersweet passions and desperate yearnings they had shared, endured, and thankfully, not quite fully explored.

She was glad there had been only Justin. And she tried not to think what she would do if she must now forfeit his touch, the sweet, shared, familiar bliss of their physical union.

She was not truly angry with Justin.

Anger was too simple a word, too one-dimensional; it did not plumb the depths of her feelings toward her husband. Not anger. How could she be angry with a man whose father was dying, with a man facing the most traumatic career crisis of his life? It was her place to support Justin, encourage him, uphold him when he was most vulnerable.

But wasn't that the problem? Wasn't that essentially the issue? Justin was not vulnerable. He was not needy. He did not need her, rarely turned to her for solace. He was so bent on ministering to everybody else, but he wouldn't let anyone minister to him . . . not even his wife. At times Robyn wondered if he genuinely needed anyone, even God.

Still, she had vowed to be there for Justin, to stand beside him for better or worse, whether he needed her or not.

Yes, God helping her, she would always uphold her husband.

But (and the question persisted) . . . who, who would hold her?

14

SHORTLY AFTER 3:00 P.M., Laura Cahill arrived at the Cahill home with little Rudy in one arm and a shopping bag in the other. The chill wind had flushed her high cheekbones with color and brought tears to her luminous green eyes. Her breath escaped in little opaque clouds. "Hi, Robyn," she said with a tentative brightness as Robyn opened the storm door. "I hope you're ready for some company. It's freezing out here."

Robyn reached for Rudy. He was bundled like a little mummy. "Of course, Laura. Come in."

They went directly to the kitchen where Laura set her shopping bag on the table. "I made a meatloaf," she said as she removed a large Pyrex dish from the sack.

"Meatloaf? Oh, but, Laura, you didn't have to—"

"I know I didn't. I wanted to. I figured you could use some help with dinner tonight."

"You're right. Thanks. I—"

Laura walked over to the stove. "I'll just pop it in the oven now and it'll be ready by five."

"That'll be perfect."

"And I figured we could fix some mashed potatoes—or fried, if you prefer—"

"Oh, it doesn't matter to me. What does your family like?"

"Either one. Mashed would be good. I could peel the potatoes."

"No, listen," said Robyn, "you sit down here with Rudy and I'll get the potatoes. We can visit while I peel—"

They laughed. Robyn filled a huge mixing bowl with pota-

toes while Laura took a plastic bag from her purse and emp-
tied brightly colored cereal into a plastic bowl. "Froot Loops,"
she said. "Rudy loves them." She proceeded to unwrap Rudy
from his straightjacket of snowsuit, boots, and scarf.

His chubby, apple-red face broke into a grin as he spotted
the Froot Loops. "Wan fu-fu," he chirped.

Robyn watched with quiet amusement as Laura lifted
Rudy up on her lap and handed him the bowl of Froot Loops.
He sat munching them one at a time. With tiny, precise gestures he speared the little doughnut shapes on his index finger, raised the tidbits to his mouth and made an exaggerated
display of biting them off. He crunched noisily, and then
grinned squint-eyed, baring his teeth, as if inviting congratu-
lations for his mighty accomplishment. When Laura failed to
acknowledge his deed, he squirmed and whined until she
said absently, "That's wonderful, Rudy. You're such a smart
little boy."

"It must be quite an adjustment having a little one in the
house again," said Robyn.

"Really!" said Laura as Rudy leaned back and pushed a
Froot Loop between her lips. "He keeps me running all the
time. I never saw such a little ball of energy. I don't remember
what it feels like not to be tired."

Robyn finished one potato and picked up another. "I suppose you don't have much time anymore to help out in the
Cahill office."

"Yeah, I still get in once in a while if they need a secretary
or clerk-typist, but it's so hard finding good baby-sitters. It's
easier for Chris to get temporary office help from one of those
agencies."

They were silent a few moments; then Robyn said, "Justin
and I are so glad the folks have had the two of you close by. I
know you've been a real comfort to them, especially these
past few months. . . ."

Laura gave her an odd glance, as if weighing the sincerity
of her remark, and then said doubtfully, "Yeah, I suppose."

"I'm sure it's true," said Robyn, somehow feeling the need to
defend her comment. "I know how supportive you and Chris
have always tried to be to them. I've seen your devotion—"

Laura played absently with one of Rudy's silky tangerine-bright curls. Her voice came out in a low monotone. "We've tried, Robyn, but I—I don't think we've been much help."

"How can you say that, Laura? You've both stuck by Mom and Dad Cahill all these years. You must realize how much that means to them."

Laura looked blankly at Robyn. Her mouth turned down slightly in a queer little grimace. "Really, Robyn, surely you know. It's never been us they wanted."

Robyn flinched. "Not you? What do you mean?"

"You know. Say it, Robyn. All these years—why haven't we ever had the courage to say it before?"

Robyn shifted uneasily. The paring knife in her hand slipped from the moist white potato, nearly grazing her finger. "I'm not sure what you're getting at, Laura."

"Oh, come on, Robyn! We can talk, you and I. There are no hard feelings. We can say it. It's just the two of us. None of the Cahills are here now."

"All right, Laura. I'm listening."

Laura's tone was brittle. "It's you—you and Justin Mom and Dad Cahill have always wanted." Laura rubbed her cheek, pushing back a stray wisp of wheat-colored hair. "You've known that. You must have. I've always known."

"I—I—"

"You watch them, Robyn. Watch what they do and say, what they don't say. They won't let Chris or me comfort them. They shut us out." Laura mindlessly picked up a Froot Loop and fed it to Rudy. Her expression took on the tenuousness of fragile china, as if at any moment her composure might shatter. "Don't you think Chris could have run Mom Cahill on all her errands—the lawyer, the banks?" she rushed on, her voice edged with bitterness. "But she didn't want Chris. She insisted on waiting for Justin. It's always been Justin."

Robyn shook her head slowly. "I suppose I've sensed . . . something. . . ."

Laura's mouth twisted slightly; her chin puckered. "Sometimes I think they resent us because we're not you. At least, Chris isn't Justin. Justin's the one they've always wanted."

She went back to Rudy's curl, twisting it around her finger. "Ironic, isn't it? Chris would do anything for his folks. He's devoted to them. He would do anything in this world to please them . . ."

"Oh, Laura, surely he—"

". . . But he never will, Robyn; he'll never be able to please them, because no matter what he does, he's not Justin."

Robyn set the bowl of potatoes on the table. Gently she reached over and touched Laura's arm. "I'm so sorry, Laura. I didn't realize—"

Laura was fighting tears. "It's just that I'm so—so fed up with us trying to live up to this impossible standard. Sometimes I just—"

Before Laura could finish, Rudy lunged forward and grasped Robyn's hand, turned it palm up and dropped a Froot Loop into it. Then he grinned proudly.

"Thank you, Rudy," said Robyn with a smile. "You're a very generous boy." She looked back at her sister-in-law. "Laura, I really want to help if I can."

Laura shifted the toddler on her lap, bouncing him as if trying to quiet him. He looked up contentedly and patted her cheek. She didn't notice. She had already lapsed back into their conversation, picking up the thread where she left off. "Sometimes, Robyn, I just want to scream. Honestly. Sometimes I do scream—I lock myself in the laundry room and turn up the radio full blast and scream until my throat hurts, but it doesn't help."

"Then why?" countered Robyn. "Why do you stay here? Why does Chris stay on at Cahill Manufacturing? If he doesn't feel appreciated, why doesn't he go somewhere else and do what he wants to do?"

Laura nuzzled her head against Rudy's hair. For a long minute she was silent, moving her mouth slightly as if composing the right words in her mind. Finally she looked up frankly at Robyn and said, "Leave? I've asked Chris that a thousand times. But he'll never leave. Because the only thing Chris really wants to do is please his father."

"Oh, Laura . . ."

She rushed on. "But that old man is so stingy with his

favors." Laura's face flushed crimson; her expression grew animated with unleashed emotion. "He gives Chris the crumbs of his affection, and Chris is willing to settle for crumbs, so what can I do? I mean, we've got three kids, a big mortgage, and too many years together to throw away, so what can I do but live with it and keep my mouth shut?— most of the time anyway."

"Has Chris actually told you that's how he feels—that he's willing to devote his life to win his father's favor?"

Laura laughed derisively. "Oh, no, are you kidding? In fact, when I accuse him of always kowtowing to his dad, he comes unglued. He denies everything. He hates it when I tell him he's sacrificing his life for a man he can never please."

Robyn gathered her words carefully. "Then this whole— this situation has been a sore spot between you for a long time?"

Laura tilted her head and lifted her chin in a nervous, defensive gesture. "Oh, wow, Robyn, if you only knew. I think if anything was ever going to break us up, it would be this thing with his folks. They can do no wrong in his eyes, and he can do no right."

Laura twisted one of Rudy's carrot-orange curls too tightly and he emitted a sudden, piercing shriek. She lifted him up and hugged him against her shoulder and patted his back. Then she gazed forlornly at Robyn and shrugged. "What can I do? It's a no-win situation, no matter how you look at it. . . . Sometimes I think I can't take it any longer."

15

AS HE sat down at the dinner table that evening, Justin felt more relaxed than he had since arriving in Southfield. That afternoon he had successfully attended to his mother's financial matters at the bank and her legal affairs with the attorney, and now, knowing that things were in order gave him a surprising sense of accomplishment.

As if reading his thoughts, Chris, sitting across the table, said, "So you got everything squared away at the bank today, Justin?"

Justin gave his mother a fleeting glance and nodded. "Yes, I think Mom has a pretty good handle on things now. And we had a long talk with the lawyer and ironed out a few problems. I don't think there should be any surprises."

His mother flashed him a tight little smile. "It still baffles me, all of the complexities and legalities. I don't know what I would have done, Justin, if you hadn't been there to sort things out for me. But it's such a relief to be finished with it at last."

Chris made an odd little sound in his throat, not quite clearing it. "Well, Mom, I've been after you for months to get things settled. I would have taken you any time—"

"Oh, of course you would, Chris. But you've got all you can handle with the company. I didn't want to burden you with more. Besides, the time just never seemed right. Now it's done and we can all breathe a little easier."

Justin glanced over warily at his brother. "Is there a problem, Chris?"

"No, no problem. You've seen to that, Justin."

"I was just trying to tie up a few loose ends around here."

"I said, no problem. Forget it, okay?"

"Sure." Justin swallowed a forkful of meatloaf, and then washed it down with several gulps of coffee, but he still felt a tightness in his throat. He tried for a lighter note in his voice. "Chris, you'll never believe who I talked with at the bank. He's a manager now."

"Someone from high school?" Chris managed.

"Before that."

"Grade school? Who do I remember from grade school who's still in town?"

"He lived over on Mulberry Drive, and his parents owned that antique store we used to browse in on Saturdays. Remember? Sometimes his old man gave us horseshoes and junk for our fort—"

Chris's tone brightened. "Wait, you don't mean—you're not talking about old Hermy—little bookworm Hermy, the Owl!"

"That's him—good old Herman Grousenek, the kid we voted the Buster Brown look-alike of the year, with his horn-rimmed glasses and funny suits. He used to talk with a nasal twang—"

"I remember," said Chris. "Boy, what a hoot we had teasing him. He was the most gullible kid I ever saw."

"Remember when we convinced him we were in contact with Martians," said Justin, "and he called the National Guard on us?"

"Boy, did we have a time explaining that one to Dad."

"And the time—" Justin was chuckling now, "—the time we told him we found pirates' treasure—"

Chris broke into a grin. "They were plastic doubloons we got from a cereal box—"

"Right. Hermy thought they were real gold—"

"We told him he could have them if he could find them—"

"Boy, did we have him going!"

"Hermy nearly died when you threw those coins in the swamp," said Chris. "In fact, so did I!"

Justin rubbed his eyes. "I sure never thought old Hermy would go slogging in after them."

"I never saw anyone so caked with mud," said Chris. "I bet his mama never got over it either, him in his fancy duds, looking like a chocolate Doughboy."

"He hasn't forgotten," Justin smiled. "He told me today it's a good thing I'm a minister or he'd have some rather choice words for me."

The smiles faded after that. Justin wondered if it was because he'd mentioned being a minister. Was that enough to silence his family—or was he being paranoid?

Robyn came to his rescue and said, "Laura, your meatloaf is delicious. You'll have to give me your recipe."

Laura smiled, pleased. "It's nothing—I just throw everything together and pop it in the oven."

"Really? Mine always tastes so bland."

"It's the onions and spices," said Laura. She looked over at Justin's mother. "Mom Cahill, do you think Dad would like some?"

"Oh, no thank you, dear. He's not supposed to have onions. I'll take him some soup and toast after dinner."

"Oh, that's right. Chris, why didn't you remind me your dad can't have onions? I could have fixed it plain—"

"How am I supposed to know?" said Chris, sounding exasperated. "I don't keep track of Dad's diet."

"It's all right, children. I don't mind fixing something for your father. I've done it practically every day for over forty years."

"But I wanted to spare you from kitchen duties tonight," said Laura. "You never let us do for you, Mom Cahill—"

"Well, why should I, dear, as long as I can do for myself?"

Robyn smiled at Laura. "I welcome kitchen help wherever I can get it."

"Me too," said Laura. "Lauralee shrieks when I mention washing a few dishes. To her, cooking means popping a TV dinner in the oven. I don't know what she'll do when she gets married."

"She'll eat fast food on paper plates," said Chris.

"Speaking of the children," said Justin's mother, "shouldn't they be home soon?"

"They're okay, Mom. They're having pizza at Kaylie's,"

said Chris. "Then they'll probably watch a movie or something. I told them to be home by nine since there's school tomorrow."

"Speaking of tomorrow," said Chris, "Justin, why don't you and Robyn drop by the plant in the morning and I'll give you the grand tour. We have a few innovations I think you'd like to see."

"Sounds good to me," said Justin. "Robyn?"

"Yes. That'd be fine."

"Great," said Chris. "Alex Lanigan told me to be sure and have you stop by his office, Robyn, and say hello."

Robyn flushed slightly. "I haven't seen Alex in so long—"

Chris looked over at Justin. "That's okay with you, isn't it?"

"Sure. It's a little late to get jealous after eighteen years of marriage."

"Oh, Justin, there's no reason to be jealous anyway. I married you, didn't I?"

"One more thing," said Chris. There was a guarded note in his voice. "We had a little problem at the factory."

"A problem?" asked his mother with alarm. "What sort of problem?"

"Dooley, the night watchman, discovered a couple broken windows in the main plant. It doesn't look like anyone broke in, but—"

"You think it was vandals?" said Ellen.

"Probably some kids playing pranks," said Chris.

His mother didn't look convinced. "You don't think it was Richard Bryden stirring up trouble, do you?"

"No, it's happened before. I don't think it's anything to worry about."

"Did you call the police?" asked Justin.

"No, it wasn't that big a deal. I just told Dooley to keep an eye on things. But I thought you should know, Mom."

"Well, I won't tell your father. He worries enough about the company without fretting over vandals. We've got to keep him calm."

"Right, Mom. Don't worry, please."

After dinner, Justin and Chris settled down in the living

room with their coffee while the women cleared the table. Chris turned on the TV and flipped through the channels with the remote control. "You in the mood for a Clint Eastwood movie, Justin?"

"No. You watch what you like. I'm not much for movies."

Chris looked over at him. "Against your religion?"

"What's that supposed to mean?"

"I thought maybe your church didn't approve of TV."

"We have a television set. I just don't care much for movies."

"You did once," said Chris. "Remember when we were kids? We sat right here, cross-legged on the floor, our eyes glued to the old boob tube, watching Superman and Davy Crockett and pigging out on M&M's—"

"I remember," Justin admitted. "We fought over the red ones."

"You always won," said Chris. "Man, how I wanted to win just once."

"Come on. I let you win sometimes."

"Yeah, that's just it."Chris settled back on the sofa. "Remember our James Dean phase? When we combed our hair in those massive duck-tails?"

"Do I ever. We must have used a pound of Butch Wax."

"Odd thing is, Dean had already been dead for years."

"Yeah, it was a cult hero thing. Everybody wore their hair that way—and walked with a swagger."

Chris laughed. "We had some pretty good times back then."

Justin nodded, but it seemed like another lifetime, another man's memories. He felt far removed from those days.

Chris sat forward and gazed at Justin, his blond brows lowering over his crinkly, smoky-gray eyes. His face seemed leaner than usual. "It's different this time, big brother," he said solemnly.

Justin flinched. He didn't know why. "What's different?" he asked guardedly.

"Everything. The other times you've come home, Dad was his usual self—the Rock of Gibraltar with a pit bull personality. You breezed in, did your duty, paid your respects, and were on your way. But it's not like that this time."

Justin straightened his back. "I don't like the way you put that, Chris. You think I'm—what?—calloused and unconcerned?"

"No, I don't mean—well, yes, maybe that's what I do mean. Maybe this time we can't get by with all the politeness and pat phrases. Maybe we've gotta talk, Justin, brother to brother."

"I'm always willing to talk," said Justin.

"Are you? Are you ready to talk about Dad?"

"What about Dad?"

"Man, he's dying, that's what!"

Justin drew in a deep breath. "I'm aware of Dad's condition, Chris. And if you think it's not tearing me apart inside—"

"Sure, it's tearing me apart too. Dad's getting weaker every day. His heart is ready to give out, stop. That's why we've gotta talk."

"All right. What's on your mind?"

Chris lowered his voice. "You've got to give him some peace of mind. You're the only one who can do it."

"Peace of mind?" Justin thought immediately of his father's soul, but he knew Chris wasn't talking about his dad's spiritual condition. "What do you mean, Chris?"

Chris shook his head ponderously. "I'm no good at putting things into words. I don't even know what I mean. It's just that Dad will listen to you. If you could reassure him about the company, about, you know, my taking his place."

Justin shrugged. "I don't have anything to do with that, Chris. What can I say?"

"Don't do this, Justin." Chris's voice was shrill, edged with emotion. He ran his fingers through his thatch of straw-blond hair. His eyes seemed more recessed than usual, his expression more vulnerable.

It hit Justin with a sickening thud in his stomach: Chris was flying apart inside. Walking an emotional tightrope. *Not tonight*, Justin vowed. *I can't deal with this tonight.* "Don't do what, Chris?" he asked quietly.

"Distance yourself. Pretend you're not involved with the rest of us, that what happens to us doesn't affect you."

"Is that what you think I'm doing?"

"It's what you've always done, Justin."

Justin reeled inwardly, as if his brother had delivered a powerful blow to his midsection. His anger rose, red-hot. "Go on, Chris. Spill it out. You blame me for walking out on Dad. I've always known. It was just a matter of time before you found the guts to tell me to my face."

"Oh, man, why did I start this?" said Chris, rubbing his temples with a slow, circular motion. "I should have known. You can't see this through anyone's eyes but your own."

"See what?"

"You know what. Dad. You and me. Us."

"Maybe you'd better spell it out, Chris."

"Don't make light of it, Justin. Don't act like nothing's been going on here for the last twenty years, because I've had to live with it every day, and, by heaven, you'd better have lived with it too. And if it hasn't eaten out your guts like it's eaten mine—"

Justin reached out for his brother's shoulder. "Listen, Chris, what's the point of dredging things up now? It's going to be over—"

"Is it? Not for me. You'll pick up and leave, run back to your church. But it'll never be over for me."

"All right, Chris, tell me. You think I owe you something? You think I was wrong to leave home years ago? Come on, put it all on the line. You think I failed Dad by going into the ministry instead of taking over the business. Isn't that what we're talking about?"

"Is that all you think it is?—that I'm angry because you didn't stay home and take over the business? Or maybe you think I'm jealous because Dad wanted you to run the business instead of me!"

"I wouldn't blame you for being angry—or jealous."

Chris stood up and walked over to the window, his back to Justin. "Okay, maybe I am angry. Maybe I'm jealous too. Maybe I don't even know who's right anymore, but this thing is too big for me to handle. I can't keep the lid on anymore. Especially now, with Dad up there helpless and—"

"Then tell me, Chris. Say what's on your mind."

Chris turned to Justin and raised his hands in a gesture of frustration and despair. His words came out jagged and halting. "It's Dad. It's always Dad. I've been with him all these years, Justin. Where've you been? I've stood by that man day after day after day. I killed myself—broke my back for him and the business, and all the while, what do you think he was telling me? He was saying, Oh, if only Justin were here; think where this company would be if we had Justin working with us."

Justin's temples were throbbing. "I—I'm sorry, Chris. I never wanted it to be that way."

Chris ambled back over to the sofa and sat down. His eyes were moist, his hair mussed. "But that's just how it was, Justin. It was always you, and you weren't even around. You didn't know the first thing about Dad or what we were going through here, or what I was going through."

"Chris, I—"

"I busted my back trying to keep Dad's dream alive, being his sounding board, his flogging post, his whipping boy." Chris searched Justin's eyes for a long, painful moment; then he buried his head in his hands. "I haven't lived my own life, Justin; I've lived his life, the life he wanted *you* to lead, and what thanks do you think I got for it?"

"I understand what you're saying, Chris—"

"I got nothing! A big zero! All Dad gave me were his complaints because I didn't do things the way he figured you'd do them. You say you understand? I wonder! I was condemned for not being you, Justin."

Justin reached over and clasped his brother's arm. "Would you listen to me? I never asked a thing of you. Never told you how to live your life. You had the same choices I had—"

Chris shook off Justin's hand. "You know what really gets me? You have the gall to walk in here, the big man, with all the answers. The prodigal son home for the fatted pig. You run Mom around and take care of business I was ready to help her with months ago. But you're the miracle man, not me."

"That's not fair, Chris, and you know—"

"You wanna talk about fair?" The veins pulsated along

Chris's temple. His breathing was ragged. "I've got a question for you, Justin. Where were you when I was spilling my guts for our father? What were you doing when I let my marriage go down the tubes and shelved my own dreams so Dad could have his? Where were you when Dad and I needed you?"

Justin shot to his feet and glared down at his brother. "You listen to me, Chris. No one told you to shelve your dreams or bust your back for Dad. No one twisted your arm. You did it because you wanted Dad's love and approval as much as I did. You feel cheated because Dad wanted me here instead of you. Well, I feel cheated too."

Chris looked puzzled. "You? Cheated? How?"

Justin spoke over raw, rushing emotion. "Dad never gave either of us any real love, Chris. It was always conditional—if you want my love, you do what I say. Oh, not in so many words, but the message came through loud and clear. You dealt with it your way, by falling all over yourself to please Dad. I handled it the only way I could, by distancing myself from Dad. I couldn't be his cookie-cutter son, a carbon copy of the old man; and I couldn't stick around and live under his silent condemnation." Justin drew in a deep, shuddering breath. "You want to know why I haven't been home in three years? Because I can only stomach so much guilt and then I get the dry heaves." Justin slowly massaged his temples. "And now he's dying. Dear God, Chris, he's dying. And I can't bridge the distance back to him."

Chris sank back against the sofa. He took a handkerchief from his pocket and blotted his forehead, his eyes, his nose. He shook his head as if emerging from a great weariness. "What's the answer, Justin? Tell me, what's the answer?"

"I don't know."

In a small, anguished voice, Chris asked, "How am I going to get along without him? I don't want to let him go."

"The choice isn't ours, Chris. It's not in our hands."

"But what's life going to be like without him? What's the meaning of anything? Oh, if I could have pleased him just once!"

"Please yourself, Chris."

"Myself?" Chris gazed absently out the window. "Who am I? Nothing. Pleasing Dad—now that was a goal. He was bigger than life. He was someone worth trying to please."

They were both silent a moment. Then Justin said softly, "You may not want to hear this, Chris, but I've got to say it anyway."

"Say what?"

"I know Someone bigger than life, Someone you could please with nothing more than your love and devotion."

Chris eyed Justin intently. "Who?"

Justin answered in barely a whisper. "God the Father. He's bigger than Victor Cahill."

16

AT TEN the next morning, Robyn and Justin drove over to Cahill Manufacturing for the "grand tour" Chris had promised them. Robyn, not sure she wanted to go, had thought of several excuses to stay home, and then dismissed them all as implausible or suspect. How could she tell Justin that she didn't want to accompany him to the plant because Alex Lanigan was there? Surely, if he guessed the nervousness she felt even now as they parked the car and walked toward the main office, he would laugh, or stare at her in astonishment. It would not occur to him that she might have residual feelings for this man she had once loved and almost married—this man, Alex Lanigan.

At times it irritated Robyn that, for Justin, everything was inevitably black or white; there was no middle ground, no gray areas, no subtle gradations of truth. Thus, in his mind, his devoted wife could not possibly be attracted to another man.

Perhaps it was true. Perhaps Robyn would see Alex again and realize at once that there was nothing left of what they once shared. Perhaps she would feel nothing—nothing except relief to be free of the lingering shadow of the man she had rejected so many years ago.

But what if—? What if she, a minister's wife—?

No, she refused even to consider the possibility. As a matter of courtesy, she would pay Alex a brief, dutiful visit, as he had requested, and then she would leave promptly, putting all her memories of him behind her forever.

Or perhaps Alex had changed so dramatically over the

years that she would feel only profound gratitude that she had married Justin instead. Perhaps Alex was bald now, or grossly overweight, or prematurely gray, or old beyond his years, or simply boring. Perhaps she would look into his eyes and realize that he was a stranger to her, that somehow she had exaggerated the emotional bond they once shared. Whatever happened when she faced him again, she was not the sort of woman to allow her emotions to control her, not the sort to be confused by her emotions . . .

"Well, my darling," said Justin as he held open the door for her, "you certainly look deep in thought. I hope I'm not the cause of that perplexing frown."

She looked up, startled. "No, of course not, Justin. My mind just strayed for a moment."

He touched her elbow lightly. "Listen, Robyn, I'm going on to Dad's office—uh, I mean, Chris's office. Why don't you go say hello to Alex?"

"Oh, Justin, I'll just come with you—"

"No, you go on. Please. Chris and I had some words last night, and I'd like some time to smooth things over. You understand, don't you?"

"Well, yes, I suppose, but I—I thought we could go see Alex together."

Justin chuckled with amusement. "Listen, hon, Alex doesn't want to see me. He wants to see you. Frankly, I don't think he's ever forgiven himself for inviting me to church when I was sixteen. After all, that's where I discovered you."

"That's ridiculous," Robyn scoffed. "You didn't notice me for another five years."

"True. But if it weren't for Alex, I might have missed you entirely. So tell him thanks for me, okay?"

"I'll let you tell him yourself."

Justin gave her a love pat and walked on, leaving Robyn alone to cope with her mushrooming panic. She walked on down the hall, her knees unexpectedly weak, and chided herself for feeling like a moonstruck teenager. Somehow she found the door with Alex's name on it and knocked lightly.

She thought he would call, "Come in," but instead, the door opened suddenly and there Alex stood, taller, more imposing than she remembered. She stared up at him in momentary bewilderment, and then managed to utter, "Hello, Alex. You, uh, wanted me to stop by."

"Robyn!" He grasped both of her hands in his. "Come in. Come right in!" As she stepped into the room, he gestured expansively. "Please, sit down here—the comfortable chair by my desk."

She glanced around at the plush, masculine office with its polished cherry wood furniture, leather chairs, and stunning oil paintings. It was impressive, but understated—just what she would have expected of Alex.

They sat down and gazed at each other. Robyn could see immediately that Alex was the man she remembered—the same twinkling hazel eyes, square face and generous jawline, forehead almost too high, especially now that his fine blond hair was thinning on top. She remembered when he was younger, people told him he looked like a movie star, someone familiar, although no one could ever recall the name. Alex was still a handsome man, with a broad nose, pronounced but not unattractive, and feathery brows so blond they seemed nonexistent. He had put on a few extra pounds, but on his large frame they looked good.

After a moment, Alex sat forward, folded his hands on his desk, and said in his deep, familiar voice, "How've you been, Robyn?"

"Fine," she said quickly, smiling, wondering suddenly whether he held it against her that she hadn't married him nineteen years ago. Had he forgiven her for marrying another? She hadn't considered the fact that he might still hold a grudge.

"You look great," he said approvingly, his warm eyes echoing the sentiment. "As beautiful as ever."

She felt a sweeping relief. Obviously he held no grudge. "You look great too," she said. "You haven't changed a bit."

"Neither have you." He laughed. "It sounds trite, I know, but I mean it. This could be twenty years ago, the way you look."

She felt herself blushing. "You're too kind, Alex. But then, you always were."

"You were easy to be kind to."

She paused, not wanting to sound singsong and silly. He was silent too. Finally she said, "I was sorry to hear about your wife."

For the first time his smile tumbled and his brow furrowed. Now she could see that he was indeed older, no longer the hollow, happy, laughing boy. Time had stamped its image on his face.

Alex took so long responding that she wondered if she had spoken out of turn. Perhaps his grief was still too fresh, the wound too deep. "I'm sorry," she murmured. "I shouldn't have mentioned it."

He smiled again. "No, of course you should. I'm grateful for your words. It's just—I don't know—it's been a year. It should be behind me by now."

"No, I understand. Something like that—it's such a loss—it takes time."

His voice softened. "I knew you'd understand, Robyn. It's one of the things I loved about you."

She shifted uneasily in her chair. "I—I probably shouldn't stay long. Justin's here to see Chris—"

"Really? Well, tell him to stop by. In fact, we're looking forward to seeing him in church on Sunday."

"We?"

"Yes. I'm on the deacon board at Southfield Community. I suppose that surprises you."

It did surprise her. Alex had rarely taken a deep interest in spiritual things. He was out to conquer the world, not serve God. It was the issue that ultimately divided them, that prompted her to turn to Justin, a man headed for the ministry.

"You are surprised, aren't you?" Alex repeated.

"What? No—I mean, I always hoped—well, you know what I mean."

He grinned. "You always hoped I'd get my life straightened around, my priorities in order—is that what you're trying to say?"

"Yes, I suppose it is."

"Well, you can thank my wife for that. Deanna was a lovely woman, and a devoted Christian. I learned a lot from her."

Robyn lowered her gaze. "I'm glad you found someone like Deanna."

Alex nodded. "I admit, life was empty after you married Justin. I wasn't sure I'd ever find anyone else. Still, being a bachelor didn't appeal to me either. Then things just sort of fell into place with Deanna. No lightning bolts exactly, but we were very comfortable with each other. It just seemed right." Alex pushed back his chair and stood up. "Tell you what, Robyn. You haven't been around here for a few years, have you? Let me show you around the place."

"You're right. It's been ages."

"Then let's go. I'm proud of what we've done with the company."

She followed him out of the office and down the hall toward the main plant. She had forgotten how large the facilities were, and how impressive. Striding with an easy confidence, Alex led her into a sprawling, noisy, high-ceilinged room smelling fragrantly of oak and cherry wood and bustling with activity. Raw, unfinished furniture stood in endless rows like bleached-white, disjointed skeletons. Men in wool plaid shirts, baggy trousers, and carpenter's aprons hovered over the varied pieces, working artfully with glinting tools.

"We have several new designers and artisans who worked in Europe before they came here," Alex told her proudly. "Our craftsmen and cabinetmakers are the best you can find."

Robyn gazed around in wonder. "It's all so impressive."

"How long has it been since you last visited the plant?"

"Oh, several years ago. I'd forgotten how big the plant is."

"We use only solid woods," Alex explained as if she were a customer to be won over. "The best wild cherry, the finest white and red oak, the choicest white pine. And they're all kiln-dried."

"You've sold me," Robyn smiled.

"That's only the beginning, my lady," he said with mock seriousness. "Our woods go through a meticulous operation of staining, lacquering, sanding, highlighting—"

She laughed. "You sound like a born Cahill."

"Don't interrupt please; I'm on a roll. As I was saying, our process involves antiquing and distressing, sealing and hand rubbing. Tell me quickly! Have I forgotten anything?"

"Not a word." Robyn reached out and touched the smooth, unfinished back of a wing chair. "I'd forgotten how much work is involved in making fine furniture."

"Beautiful things require tender loving care," Alex murmured.

She realized with alarm that he was gazing intently at her. Her pulse quickened and she averted her eyes, suddenly self-conscious.

"Come, let's visit the showroom," he said, taking her elbow.

She shivered involuntarily at his touch, welcoming it and fearing it at once.

They left the noise and sawdust din of the factory for the thick-carpeted, luxuriant silence of the immense showroom. As Robyn's eyes moved with pleasure over the attractive furniture groupings, she savored the rich mellow-browns of maple, the red burnished glow of cherry wood, and the polished, fine-grained sienna tones of pine and oak. "I love it," she told Alex.

"What—the maples or oak—?"

"All of it. I simply love fine wood. Some women like crystal and china. I adore wood."

He laughed. "Then you've come to the right place." He stretched his arms out expansively. "Take your pick, my dear. As you see, we have Early American tea wagons, Queen Anne wing chairs, Chippendale love seats, Lincoln rockers, Colonial trestle tables—"

"I'll take one of each." She looked slyly at him. "I'll wait while you wrap them, Alex."

"A sale like this may bring me a much needed promotion," he mused, "although I must admit I haven't considered sales my forte." He paused, their eyes locking, and said solemnly, "After all, Robyn, I was never able to sell you . . . on us."

17

ALL AFTERNOON Eric Cahill kept his eye on the house next door, watching for Kaylie Hollis. He couldn't wait to see her again. He had spent a half hour combing his hair, splashed his face with aftershave, and was wearing the aqua sweater his old girlfriend Julie liked so well. She said it brought out the blue in his eyes.

Scott had told Eric that Kaylie got home from school around three. But it was 3:30 before Eric spotted her ambling up the sidewalk with an armload of books. She looked as incredible as he remembered—all bright and blonde and beautiful as spun sunshine.

Eric stepped outside and took several quick strides to the mailbox. He pretended to be checking for mail just as Kaylie turned into her yard. "Hey, Kaylie," he called, trying to sound genuinely surprised to see her.

She turned and smiled. "Hi, Eric! How's it going?"

"Okay. How about you?"

"So-so. How's your grandfather?"

He shrugged. "About the same."

She gestured toward her house. "Come on over!"

"Now?"

"Sure."

"Okay." Before she could change her mind, he dashed over and, in an attempt at gallantry, took her books. "You sure your mom won't mind?"

"She's not home."

"Oh?"

"She's into this charity thing on Fridays. Usually gets home about six, just in time to throw something in the microwave for Daddy's dinner." She unlocked the door and stepped in. "Come on. The place is ours."

He entered with a tentative glance around. "Your mom won't get mad—you know—you having a guy in when no one's home?"

She shrugged off her beige, fur-trimmed coat. "Oh, Eric, be real. How will she even know?"

"Yeah, okay." He followed her to the family room.

"Toss the books over there," she said, nodding toward the coffee table. She turned on the tape deck and slipped in a cassette. "Okay, you're not into punk and heavy metal, right?"

"Right. Pop. Soft rock."

"Then you should like this. Fleetwood Mac." She drifted over to the sofa and sat down, curling her legs under her. She was wearing another of those soft, luscious cotton candy sweaters and a short skirt. "This was our last day of school," she murmured.

"What?" His mind was still on the sweater.

"I said, our last day. We're out now for Christmas vacation. I didn't think I'd survive it. Hey, are you gonna sit down or what?"

"Right." He sat down beside her, not too close, not too far. He could smell her perfume. It was sweeter than the stuff Julie used to wear. He liked it.

"So you must be bored out of your skull," Kaylie mused, fluffing her hair. "Lauralee says it's the pits over there, like pure gloom."

"Yeah. It's not much fun."

"Do you know how long you're staying? Through Christmas?"

He shrugged. "Nobody knows."

She eyed him carefully. "I guess it depends on your grandfather, huh?"

He nodded.

"Do you—like, does it bother you?—you know, talking about him? Scott says he's not—not going to get well."

Eric averted his eyes. This wasn't something he wanted to talk about with Kaylie. "That's what they say. But who knows? Miracles happen."

"Then there's a chance? He's not actually dying?"

Eric frowned. "I didn't say that."

Kaylie examined one long polished fingernail. "Wanna know something? I was always scared of your grandfather. I mean, he was nice to me and all, but he had such a big booming voice. When I was a kid, I figured that's how God must sound—sort of stern and scolding even when you weren't doing something wrong."

"God's not that way," said Eric.

Kaylie nudged him playfully. "How do you know? You ever hear God speak?"

"Uh, not with an actual voice."

"But you've heard Him some other way? Is that what you're saying? Tell me. You've actually heard Him?"

"Maybe I have. What's the big deal?"

"Come on, just because you're a preacher's kid, don't tell me you've got an inside track—"

"Listen, it doesn't have anything to do with my dad being a preacher, you got that? I hear God . . . I hear Him in my head when I pray."

"How does He sound?"

"I don't know. I just—like I sense Him there, talking to me in my thoughts."

Kaylie looked curious. "What does He say—in your thoughts?"

"He lets me know when I'm doing things right . . . or wrong. He makes me feel like I'm not alone, like how I feel counts for something . . . like I count for something."

"That's neat." Kaylie twisted a small birthstone ring on her little finger. "I go to church too, you know."

"Which one?"

"Good Shepherd, over on Edinger."

"Do you like it?"

"It's okay. My folks go off and on. I go with them."

"Then maybe you've heard God too."

"Maybe. I'm not sure. When I was a little kid, I raised my hand in a Good News Club. Someone prayed with me, but I'm not sure what it meant, if it meant anything."

"Did you ask Jesus into your life?"

She shifted uneasily. "Yes, but nothing real dramatic happened. I mean, everything was the same. I was the same."

"Maybe you just didn't know how to listen to Him. Maybe He's there right now waiting to talk to you, waiting for you to listen."

She bit at her nail. "You're weird, you know."

He shrugged. "I just know if you ask Jesus into your life, He'll come in."

She laughed self-consciously. "So maybe He's there, who knows?"

"He's not just some stained-glass God in a church, Kaylie. He's real. He wants to walk with you down the halls at school and sit with you in your classes and always be with you—"

"Even my best friends don't do that."

"Mine neither."

She studied him for a moment. "Do you do this often?"

"Do what?"

"Talk about Jesus like He's your buddy, like the two of you are real tight."

He slipped his arm around the back of the sofa and lightly touched her hair. "I'm not a religious freak, if that's what you mean."

"I didn't say that."

"I know. I just don't want you getting the wrong idea. I'm no Holy Joe."

"But you are big on religion. You like going to church and all that stuff."

He wound a strand of her hair around his finger. "Not really."

"What? Come on."

"I'm saying, I feel close to Jesus. Like when I'm alone I can talk to Him better than I can talk to my old man. It's like, I know He accepts me. I can say what I want and He won't come down on me. He loves me even when I fall flat on my face."

"Okay, then if Jesus is so cool, how come you don't like church?"

Eric gazed off into space. "Church doesn't have anything to do with how I feel about Jesus. Church is where my dad works."

"Like, they expect you to be perfect, right?"

"Yeah, that's me. Mr. Perfect. Eric Cahill, preacher's kid. People don't see me; they see my dad. They think I should be just like him, a carbon copy." He hesitated. "Oh, they don't say it, but I see it in their faces. I hear it in their voices. It's like I've got to be this shining example of a Christian or the church roof will fall in."

"It's that bad?"

"I don't know. Maybe it's just me. I feel like my dad's career is on the line if I cuss or take a punch at some guy or get fresh with a girl. Know what I mean? It's like if I blow it, my dad's reputation goes down the tubes."

"So why don't you just stop going to church?"

"I've tried. My dad nearly split a gut. 'What will people think?' he said. He gave me his if-I-can't-run-my-own-house-hold-how-can-I-run-a-church routine."

"Laid a real guilt trip on you, huh?"

"Yeah. That's why sometimes I go to another church, a place where no one ever heard of my dad, where I can be me and not have to carry around all the baggage of being a preacher's kid."

"What does he think of that?"

"I'm not sure he knows. Suspects, probably." Eric moved his hand over to Kaylie's shoulder and said, "What I wanna know is . . ."

She met his gaze. "What?"

"Why we're wasting this time alone talking about my dad." Slowly he drew her against him and kissed her lips. He was surprised. Some girls just sat impassively when he kissed them, but Kaylie was already responding, kissing him back. He drew back slightly and whispered into her hair, "I like you, Kaylie. I like you a lot."

"I like you too, Eric."

She laid her head on his shoulder. For a minute, neither

spoke. Then she said in a soft, breathy voice, "You ever done *it*, Eric?"

"It?"

"You know. Made it with someone."

He chuckled self-consciously. "You don't beat around the bush, do you?"

"Why should I? I figure if I'm straight with you, you'll be straight with me. Right?"

"Yeah, I guess so."

"So?"

"You first."

She laughed lightly. "No, I haven't. Not officially."

"Not officially? What's that mean? Either you did or you didn't."

"I mean, like there was this guy, and he was really pressuring me, you know, but I knew he'd been around, so I said, 'no way, mister!'"

"That's smart," said Eric. "And he bought it?"

"Yeah. He was totally teed off, but I said no way am I risking AIDS and all that stuff. I know what they say about how if you sleep with someone you're really sleeping with everyone that dude slept with and then everyone *they* slept with, and pretty soon it's like you're sleeping with the whole world, and man, I don't need trouble like that. That's why I'm looking for a special guy—"

"Special?"

"Yeah, you know, like a guy who hasn't done it yet. Then, maybe, if the vibes are right, and we're both virgins, well—you know, it'll be safe—"

Eric shook his head. "Kaylie, what if the guy tells you that just so he can make it with you?"

"I—I don't know." She looked up at Eric with a small, pouty smile. "You still didn't tell me. How about you? Have you ever—?"

"No, Kaylie, I haven't."

She eyed him with mock exasperation. "Eric Cahill, are you saying that just so I'll—"

"No, I promise. I haven't."

"How come? You're a neat guy. I figure a lot of girls would—"

He shrugged. "I haven't had much time for dating, what with school and all."

She reached up and ran her fingers through his hair. "You're too good to be true, Eric. But tell me honestly— haven't you had plenty of chances?"

Eric heaved a sigh. He was having a hard time dealing with her closeness. "Yeah, sure, I've had chances."

"Well, then?"

"Okay, so it's been my choice."

"Your choice?"

"Not to have sex. Not yet. Not until I . . ." Why was it so hard to say? ". . . until I get married."

She stared open-mouthed at him. "You're not one of them? Abstainers? People who don't believe in sex?"

"No way. I'm all for sex. I just want it to be something special. For one person. My wife someday."

"Oh, Eric, I never heard a guy talk like you do. You're unreal — to think about your future wife!"

Eric shifted uncomfortably. "It's not just my idea, Kaylie. It's the way God wants things too. It's His plan—"

Kaylie sighed invitingly. "Oh, Eric, I love the way you talk." Languidly she wound her arms around his neck and drew his face close to hers. Her breath was warm and minty.

His heart started hammering. "Kaylie, I meant what I said. I'm not into casual sex."

"That's what I love about you, Eric. You talk about God and sex all in one breath, like they're connected somehow—"

"They are, Kaylie."

"I know. God made sex to be beautiful . . ."

". . . In marriage," Eric managed.

"Is that what you believe or what your Sunday school teaches?"

"Both."

She kissed him with a slow, delicious dreaminess.

All too swiftly his words were short-circuited. All of his impulses were traveling another route now—not the coolly calculated boulevard of his mind but the careening, helter-skelter roller-coaster of his passions.

As he and Kaylie eased down onto the sofa, only the small,

distant voice of cold reason pulled him back on track. He released her and sat up, stunned to realize how far he had gone in just a few short minutes since his dispassionate announcement of his own purity.

He was breathing hard, the heat in his veins at the boiling point. "I'm sorry, Kaylie. We can't—I shouldn't have—"

She sat up and smoothed her clothes. "Like be real, Eric. We didn't do anything. Come on, don't get bummed out over a little messing around. Besides, I liked it—"

He moved away with a scrambling, little-boy awkwardness. "I gotta go, Kaylie. Listen, I'll see you later, okay?"

"Call me, Eric."

"Uh, sure. Maybe tomorrow."

"I'll be thinking about you, Eric. I'll be remembering every moment we just spent together."

He choked out the words in a nervous, froglike croak. "Yeah, Kaylie. I'll be remembering too . . ."

In fact, as he darted out the door, he doubted if he'd be able to think of anything else in the days—and nights—ahead.

18

"THIS PLACE needs a Christmas tree!" declared Eric as he gazed around his grandmother's living room, gray with gloom in the pale winter morning light. "What about it, cousins? Don't you agree?"

Scott and Lauralee had arrived only moments before on this chill Saturday morning and were sitting now by the fireplace sipping hot chocolate. "If you're suggesting we go chop down a tree, give me a few minutes to let my fingers defrost," said Scott.

"Is it that cold outside?" asked Eric. "Didn't you drive over?"

"It wasn't the drive—"

"My industrious brother was up at dawn chopping firewood for Dad," said Lauralee. "I think he deserves a medal or something."

Scott nodded. "Yeah, right, Lee. Rub it in. I didn't see you out there getting your pretty fingernails dirty."

"I do my share, brother, dear. I was up late last night helping Mom with the fruitcakes—"

"That fits," said Scott, his dark eyes glinting with mischief. Before she could offer a retort, he looked back at Eric. "Now that school's out for the holidays, our parents don't want us getting bored, so they pile the work on. Can you believe it?"

"Yeah, I can," said Eric. "Sounds like my dad. He'd have a coronary if he thought I was lazing around wasting time."

Scott winked knowingly. "From what I hear, you aren't wasting any time, cousin, at least as far as Kaylie Hollis is concerned."

Eric cuffed Scott's arm. "You been talking to Kaylie? What'd she tell you?"

"Nothing much. Just that she thinks you're pretty hot."

"Hey, guys, back to the tree," said Lauralee. "You think Grandma will go for it . . . a Christmas tree . . . with Gramps so sick?"

"Why not?" said Scott. "We'll talk her into it. After all, there's nothing here of Christmas, other than a handful of unopened greeting cards on the table. A tree will cheer her up."

"Usually Grams does this place up in style for the holidays," said Lauralee, her voice animated. "Christmas wreaths on the doors, holly and mistletoe everywhere, and a tree clear up to the ceiling."

"Sounds great," said Eric. "But do you think she'll feel like celebrating this year?"

"Then we'll do it for her, right, Lee?"

Lauralee nodded. "Why not? You guys can go out and cut down a tree. We can all decorate it. We can even bring over some of our presents from home." She grinned, gesturing playfully toward the mantle. "And we can hang our stockings by the chimney with care—"

"In hopes that St. Nicholas soon will be there!" the boys chanted in unison.

Grandmother Cahill entered the room with a quizzical little smile. "What have we here? The makings of a choir?"

"No way, Grams," said Scott, raising his hands in protest.

"Actually, we were just talking about getting you a Christmas tree," Eric ventured. "Would you mind, Grandma?"

She sat down on the sofa and tucked her lace handkerchief into her sweater sleeve at the wrist. "Christmas," she mused, aloud. "Why, I haven't given it a thought this year."

"Well, we just figured—you know—a tree would be cool—"

She looked thoughtful, and then brightened. "Yes, you're absolutely right, Eric. We're all together this Christmas. We're a family again. Certainly we should have a tree. The Cahills always celebrate Christmas."

Scott gripped Eric's shoulder. "We can use my dad's truck—"

Grandma Cahill was smiling now. "You boys go get both your fathers and tell them I want a tree. Have them drive you to the tree farm and chop down a big one."

Lauralee gave her grandmother an impulsive hug. "Thanks, Grams! You're terrific!"

Early that afternoon the troop returned from the tree farm, laughing and shivering and stomping through the crunchy snow, sporting the most magnificent blue spruce Eric had ever seen. "I'm not sure we can get this baby in the front door," Uncle Chris said as they lifted the tree from the truck bed. "We might have to trim her a bit."

"No way," said Eric, giving his dad and Uncle Chris a hand. "This tree's perfect as is. All ten feet of it!"

They stood the tree up in the front yard and cleaned out the dead branches; then somehow they managed to lug the huge tree inside. Its sprawling branches dwarfed the living room and its top nudged the ceiling. "We'll have to cut a little off or the star won't fit," Eric's dad told Uncle Chris. "That's if Mom still has that big tin star she had when we were kids."

"She does. Along with every misshapen ornament we ever made her in school. Come on. We'd better get this beauty in a bucket of water before her pores close."

It took another hour of work before the tree was at last properly positioned by the living room window. But it was worth it. The tree was a beauty. Eric felt warm and good inside just gazing at it. For the first time this season it really felt like Christmas. The drifting snow outside and the crackling flames in the fireplace helped too. Eric couldn't remember when he'd last seen snow for Christmas. Probably when his parents took him to the mountains, but that was different. Mountain snow didn't count when your house was still surrounded by green grass and palm trees. No question about it—Christmas was better with snow.

As Eric's mother and Aunt Laura brought out the garlands and decorations, Eric turned to his grandmother. "What did you decorate Christmas trees with when you were little?"

She laughed lightly, her expression softening with memories. "Oh, goodness, we strung popcorn and cranberries and lit lots and lots of candles. It's a wonder we didn't burn the house down."

"Now the stores have all these weird flocked trees that come in pink or white or blue," said Eric.

"That's right, dear. Times have changed, but not the fragrance of a real Christmas tree. That stays the same, thank goodness."

"Yeah, that's for sure."

Once the adults had the lights on the tree, Eric, Scott and Lauralee hung the garlands and bulbs and tinsel. Little Rudy sat in his plastic walker, sucking on a bottle of apple juice, watching intently. When Uncle Chris plugged in the lights, Rudy jumped up and down and squealed with delight.

Eric smiled with satisfaction. The tree did look terrific. As beautiful as any he'd ever seen.

"I love it!" cried Lauralee, clasping her hands.

Grandma Cahill dabbed at her eyes. "I wish Victor could see it. It would lift his spirits."

"Listen, Grams," said Eric, "couldn't Dad and Uncle Chris carry Gramps down so he could see the tree for himself?"

"I'm afraid not, dear. The strain might be too much on your grandfather." She glanced sadly toward the stairwell. "Besides, your grandfather vowed that he wouldn't come downstairs until he could walk. He's a very proud and stubborn man, children."

"Then how about if Scott and Lauralee and I set up a little tree on Grandpa's dresser and maybe string some lights around his window?"

"I suppose we could ask him, Eric. Yes, he might like that."

A thumping sound drew Eric's attention back to the tree. Little Rudy had pushed his walker into the tree and was gleefully grabbing handfuls of tinsel.

"Rudy, no!" cried Aunt Laura. She dashed over and yanked him out of the walker and pried the glittering tinsel from his fists. His face turned as red as his curls as he bawled and screamed and flailed his arms.

In desperation Aunt Laura handed Rudy to Uncle Chris. "Stop it, Rudy," he demanded, bouncing the howling child up and down. "Come on, big boy. You stop crying this

minute. We can't have you upsetting your Grandpa Cahill."
But when Rudy's shriek rose another decibel, he promptly
handed him back to Aunt Laura.

"Man, the lungs that kid has," Scott told Eric under his
breath.

Finally, in what Eric surmised as a brilliant strategic move,
Aunt Laura stuck the bottle of apple juice into Rudy's open
mouth. He blinked in surprise, sputtered a moment, and then
clutched the bottle in his hands and sucked happily.
Everyone heaved a sigh of relief.

Scott elbowed Eric and murmured, "You know, I'm crazy
about that pint-size brother of mine, but the fact is, he's
spoiled rotten. He's got this whole family in his sticky little
fist and he knows it!"

"Including you," laughed Eric.

"Yeah. Including me." Scott hooked his thumbs on his
jeans pockets and looked over at his sister. "How about it,
Lee? You wanna see if Gramps wants us to do his room up
for Christmas?"

"You go ask him, okay? If he thinks it's a lousy idea, I'd
rather hear it from you than him."

"Aw, he won't bite. Come on."

"No, I gotta help Mom watch Rudy."

"Chicken!"

As the two boys headed for the stairs, Grandma Cahill
called, "Don't wake your grandfather if he's sleeping."

When Eric peered into his grandfather's room, Mrs.
Pringle motioned him inside with a grim little smile. "How
about you boys keeping your grandfather company while I
fix myself a cup of tea?"

Eric nodded uncertainly. He looked over at the large hospital bed. Gramps appeared to be asleep, but when the floor
creaked under Eric's feet, Gramps looked over with a glimmer of recognition in his eyes. "Don't just stand there," he
said huskily. "Either come in or stay out."

With dutiful reverence Eric and Scott approached the bed.
Eric wasn't sure what to say or whether to look serious or
smile. He opted for the smile and said, "Guess what we've
been doing, Gramps."

"I'm no good at games, boy."

"We got the biggest Christmas tree you ever saw," Scott said in a rush of words. "Goes clear to the ceiling and you should see the lights—"

Gramps was silent for a minute, the lines in his face shifting slightly. Eric wondered whether their words had upset him. Finally Eric asked, "Gramps, are you too tired to talk? How do you feel?"

"Never mind how I feel. Tell me more about . . . the tree."

Scott drew closer to the bed. "That's what we came up for. We want to decorate your room too, Gramps. Put a little tree on your dresser. Some lights on the window. What do you think?"

Their grandfather stared at the ice-glazed window for several long moments, his breathing labored. Eric wasn't sure but he thought he saw tears glisten in the old man's eyes. Then, in little more than a whisper, Gramps said, "When I was a boy . . . I always looked for the tallest tree in the forest. Went out with my father every year. Helped him chop it down. What a man he was—strong, powerful. When the snow was too deep . . . I walked in his footsteps." The ancient eyes smiled faintly. "Those were big footprints to fill . . . my father's."

"I guess you and your dad had a lot of fun together," said Scott.

Gramps swallowed hard and licked his lips. His lips looked cracked and dry. "Fun? No. My father was a hard taskmaster. Didn't believe in fun. But we had our times. Never enough of those times though, boy. Never enough."

I guess that's just how families are," said Eric. He couldn't think of anything else to say.

Gramps looked over, his shaggy brows arching with curiosity. "Did your dad go with you boys, Eric? For the tree?"

"Yeah, he did, Gramps. I think he had a good time."

"Good." With trembling hand their grandfather reached for his water glass on the table and took a halting sip through the straw. Then he looked back intently at Scott and Eric. "You boys go ahead. String up some lights. Set up a tree.

Bring some life to this old room." He let his hand fall back limply on the sheet. His voice broke in a raspy tremor as he uttered, "Heaven knows, this is the last Christmas these old eyes will see."

19

ROBYN ROSE early Sunday morning and fixed a quick breakfast of toast, oatmeal, and coffee. Justin was already up and dressed, sitting at the dining room table reading his Bible. He was always up at dawn on Sundays to study the Word before assuming his pastoral duties at Redeemer Christian. Today, of course, there would be no pastoral duties. Robyn and Justin would be visiting Southfield Community, the church they had attended in their youth, the place where, after a long, rocky relationship with Alex, Robyn had pledged her love instead to Justin.

Even now Robyn felt unsettled, recalling the memories, the buried feelings, the conflicting emotions. She had loved both men—Alex first and then Justin. She had sensed in Justin a commitment to ministry that she had never found in Alex. But that wasn't the only reason she had turned to Justin. He had possessed a magnetism, an energy, a dedication that mesmerized her, convinced her that he alone was the man for her.

Alex, on the other hand, had always seemed a bit too laid back, will o' the wisp, impassive, as if content to let life simply slip by, taking him where it would. Robyn had found that trait irritating; she wanted a take-charge man who knew where he was going. But now that Alex was older and in a responsible position at Cahill Manufacturing, he no longer seemed so passive and easygoing. The years—and his wife's death—had no doubt toughened him, strengthened him, and perhaps even increased his compassion. Robyn wondered, on the other hand, whether the years and Justin's trials had strengthened him or just made him more brittle and unapproachable.

"Is the coffee ready?" Justin called from the dining room.

"Yes, dear. I'll bring it right in."

She served the coffee, and then the toast and oatmeal.

He pushed his Bible aside and looked at her. "Is Eric up yet?"

"I called him. I think he's showering."

"Good. I want to be on time this morning."

Robyn sat down across from him and poured milk on her cereal. "Are you, you know, nervous about today?"

He looked blankly at her. "Should I be?"

"We haven't been at the church for over three years."

"I suppose I have some reservations. I'm not exactly coming home the conquering hero."

"Really, Justin, no one asks you to."

He smiled wryly. "How about you? Excited to be back?"

"I have a few butterflies in my stomach," she admitted.

Justin cleared his throat. "I may try to talk to Joe if he has time today."

"Rev. Wyden? What about?"

"I don't know. My situation. The future. Everything."

"I think that's a good idea. I've always considered him a wise man."

Justin smiled. "Sure. He married us, didn't he?"

"You remember," she teased.

"It wasn't that long ago."

"Eric would say it was the Stone Ages."

"It was one of the best days of my life."

"Really?"

"You doubt it? Come on, Robyn—fishing for a compliment?"

She smiled. "What do you think?"

"I think it was a great day—our wedding day. I remember like it was yesterday. And I'd do it again in a second."

"Would you? Honestly?"

"Of course. Wouldn't you?"

"Yes, I would." But a small voice nagged, *Are you sure?*

Justin swallowed the last of his coffee and pushed back his chair. "Listen, honey, did I tell you Alex wants to take us out for lunch after church? His treat. I said okay."

Robyn's pulse quickened. "Lunch with Alex? You never told me."

"Sorry, hon. I forgot. He mentioned it when we were at the plant Friday. You don't mind, do you? He's lonely . . . you know."

Robyn nodded. "You're right, Justin. It's fine." She absently touched the back of her hair. "I'd better go upstairs and get ready."

"Right." He came around the table and squeezed her shoulder. "I'd like to get there early enough to greet Joe before the service."

In fact, Justin pulled into the church parking lot with a half hour to spare. He went directly to the pastor's office while Robyn and Eric entered the auditorium and sat down near the front. It was the same as Robyn remembered, except for new seat coverings on the pews and beige carpeting instead of brown. The walls were decorated with silver garlands and wreaths, and a lush Christmas tree stood on the platform with tiny blinking red and green lights. Perhaps the choir would be doing a cantata this morning, Robyn mused. She welcomed the thought; she needed these quiet moments in church to refresh her spirit.

Justin sat down beside her just as the choir entered singing, "Joy to the World." He leaned over and whispered, "I'll be seeing Joe right after the service."

"But what about lunch with Alex?"

"You two go on. I'll join you as soon as I can."

"No, Justin. We can't—"

"Sure you can. Alex will welcome the time with you."

The service began, so Robyn swallowed her protests, but she couldn't ignore the uneasiness she felt at the idea of being alone with Alex. She felt guilty too. Would Justin encourage her to spend time with Alex if he knew how ambivalent she felt about him?

When it was time for announcements and recognition of visitors, Rev. Wyden took the pulpit and opened his arms expansively. "My friends, we are honored to have with us some dear friends of mine. They practically grew up in this church and I even had the privilege of marrying them. Let's welcome Rev. Justin Cahill, his wife Robyn, and their son Eric, all the way from California!"

The congregation applauded.

Rev. Wyden continued, "Perhaps we'll get Rev. Cahill into the pulpit while he's in town. Have him share his testimony. He's associate pastor of a large southern California church, out where the sun shines year-around. Sounds like a welcome change to all this ice and snow, doesn't it, folks?"

Everyone laughed. Robyn looked over at Justin. His face was reddening. Under different circumstances, he would be pleased by this attention; but now, with their future uncertain and his career up for grabs, she knew he hated being put on the spot. What kind of testimony could he give? *I'm serving at a great church . . . where I've just tendered my resignation . . . ?*

In the hour that followed, Robyn struggled to keep her mind on the sermon, but her thoughts kept ricocheting between Justin and Alex. Should she just cancel lunch with Alex? No, he wouldn't understand. His feelings would be hurt. Besides, it was silly of her to fret over what was obviously just her imagination. There was nothing between Alex and her anymore, nothing but the lingering vestiges of a long-departed teenage romance. They were mature adults now, settled into very different lives. Why should she let her schoolgirl fantasies destroy a pleasant, rewarding friendship? She would go to lunch with Alex and have a very good, guilt-free time.

After church, while Justin met with Rev. Joe and Eric joined the youth group for pizza at the local Pizza Hut, Robyn and Alex drove over to a nearby steak house for lunch.

"Justin will be joining us shortly," Robyn assured Alex after a waitress seated them at a corner booth. "He just wanted to catch Rev. Wyden for a few minutes after church."

Alex smiled tolerantly. "I know. He told me. It's no problem."

"I know, but I just thought—"

"Actually, it'll give us a chance to talk . . ."

"Talk? Yes, I suppose it will." Robyn slipped out of her coat and sat back. She was still cold, her blood too thin for zero-degree weather. Or was it her nerves that were chilling her now? Somehow she sensed that more was at stake here than a mere Sunday lunch. Why hadn't Justin come with her? Then she wouldn't feel this sudden, sheer panic.

"You okay, Robyn?" He was eyeing her with a mixture of curiosity and concern. He was the old Alex—it might have been twenty years ago, the two of them sitting in this very restaurant, only teenagers, but so in love. Was it possible to erase twenty years so easily?

"What, Alex?" she asked, realizing he was waiting for an answer.

"I said, are you okay?"

"Oh, yes, I'm fine. Just cold." She pulled her coat back up around her shoulders. "I'm not used to this frigid weather yet."

"Yeah, you're a California girl, all right. All sunshine and light." He paused. "But you're still the girl I remember—the golden redhead with a face full of freckles and a terrific smile."

She felt her face flushing. "Really, Alex. You make me sound like a—a teenage girl."

His hazel eyes grew crinkly at the corners. "That's how you look to me. That's the picture I've carried in my mind of you all these years."

A sensation of pleasure and alarm stirred deep within Robyn's breast. She wanted to flee; she wanted to stay. She turned her gaze away momentarily, then back to Alex's solid face, his generous grin, the laughing half-moons of his eyes.

"Don't tell me I've embarrassed you," he said.

She shook her head. "Of course not. It's just—"

He finished for her. "It's just nice to sit here talking like this after all these years."

"Yes, it is." She turned her attention to her menu. Steaks, chops, Sunday brunch specials—what did she want? Anything, except this unsettling encounter . . .

A waitress—a small, pixie-faced girl hardly older than Eric—came to take their order. "Just coffee for now," said Robyn. "Someone else will be joining us in a few minutes." Silently, she added, *Hurry, Justin. I'm not handling this well.*

They were silent as the waitress served their coffee. Then Alex offered her sugar and cream. "You take both, as I recall."

"I'm amazed that you remember."

"I remember you took the same as Deanna. Cream and sugar. Heavy on the cream."

"It must be very difficult for you," said Robyn quietly.

He averted his gaze. "It's been . . . very hard. There aren't words—"

"I—I didn't mean to bring it up, Alex."

"No, it's all right. I'm doing better."

"Do you feel like talking about her? Deanna?"

He grimaced slightly, but recovered with a grim little smile. "You mean our life together . . . or her death?"

"Both."

Alex cupped his hands around his coffee mug. The lines in his forehead deepened. "She was like you . . . but different. There was never quite that—what would you say?—that abandonment we felt as teenagers. You and I, Robyn, remember how it was? With Deanna and I, it was more . . . settled, but very rich. Deep." He sipped his coffee. "She was solid . . . always there when I needed her. And wise, so wise—" He stopped, blinked, glanced away, thumbed the table, and then forced his gaze back at her. "I haven't talked about it. There's no one—family, friends, colleagues—uh-uh, I can't dump on them—"

Robyn sat forward, her hands clasped on the table. "I want to listen, Alex. Please, go on. If I can help at all—"

He ran his fingers through his thinning hair and chuckled self-consciously. "This is—this is so—exactly what I need, Robyn. Talking to you. Now if I can just—if I can say what I feel—"

"You can, Alex."

"That's just it. For nearly a year now—since it happened—I haven't felt . . . anything. I've been numb. Not pleasantly numb, not anesthetized, just dead numb. Like I died with her. Like maybe I was really in the crypt with her. I know this sounds bizarre, but I've got to say it—like I was buried in the ground and just this shell was out walking around and talking like nothing had ever happened. It sounds weird, I know, but it's how I've felt."

"Grief takes many forms, Alex. It's all normal, natural."

"I know. That's what they say. But when you're going through it, you think you're the only one. You become very self-absorbed."

Instinctively she squeezed his hand. "I think you're being very hard on yourself."

He put his other hand over hers. "And you're being wonderfully kind, as always."

"I wish there was more I could do—"

He studied her intently for a long moment. "You're doing more than you know, being here now. I'm glad we have this time alone."

Robyn drew her hand back slowly. "Justin is your friend too, Alex."

"I know. Of course he is. Do you think I'd forget?"

"No. It's just—"

"I'm making you uncomfortable, aren't I?"

"No, Alex."

"I'm sorry. It's the last thing I want to do." He sat forward, his voice growing confidential. "If you only knew what you've done for me, Robyn—"

"I've done nothing."

"Oh, but you have. Since I saw you Friday—when you walked into my office and I saw you after all these years—"

"Please, Alex, don't say it—"

"I've got to, Robyn. For a year I've been dead inside. Do you know what it's like to feel nothing, to feel like your heart has turned to wood or stone? To feel no emotional response to anything or anyone? It's worse than death, Robyn. But when I saw you, it all came back—"

"No, Alex, please don't." Robyn shifted in her seat, looked around, as if she might jump up and run, as if there might be some way of escape without embarrassing herself or Alex. But no. She was being foolish, reading too much into a poor man's grief.

"I'm not asking anything of you, Robyn," he was saying earnestly. "I'm just telling you how I felt. Don't you see what it means? I actually *felt* something. I didn't think I could. I didn't think I'd ever feel anything again."

Robyn drew in a deep breath. "I'm glad for you, Alex."

"I experienced those old feelings, Robyn—the warmth, the tenderness, the excitement—all the things we meant to each other—"

"But those days—they're gone, Alex."

"Yes, certainly they are." His tone grew reflective, somber. "We're different people. Everything's different. I know that. I know you don't feel the same. I wouldn't expect you to—wouldn't want you to. What we had is gone. But I had to let you know you're still special to me, Robyn. I—I'll always care—"

Robyn felt her mouth go dry. She felt light-headed, as if she were acting out some scene from the past, or reliving some moment from a dream. An old, disturbing question resurfaced. *What if I still love Alex?*

"Have I upset you?" he asked.

"No. Yes. I don't know."

"I wouldn't for the world—"

"I just don't know what to say—"

The waitress returned, smiling. Justin was with her. "Your other party is here," she said brightly.

Justin slid into the seat beside her. "Hi, hon." He kissed her cheek. "Hope I didn't keep you two waiting long."

"No, of course not. We were just talking," she said in a rush.

"We haven't even ordered yet," said Alex. "Just had coffee."

"Great." Justin smiled benevolently at her. "Then I haven't missed a thing, have I?"

With reluctance Robyn met Alex's gaze, and then looked away. "No, Justin," she said softly. "You haven't missed a thing."

20

As JUSTIN buttoned his pajamas, he watched Robyn from the corner of his eye. She was patting moisturizer on her face as she did every night before bed; they both performed their familiar rituals even here in his parents' home. There was something vaguely reassuring about following timeworn routines.

He wanted to talk to Robyn about his conversation with Rev. Wyden, wanted to articulate aloud what he was feeling now, but Robyn seemed so preoccupied. Usually she was the one trying to draw him out, prodding him to share his feelings, but tonight she was the silent one, moving about in an aura of remoteness. When she did speak, it was in short, curt monosyllables. Justin recognized that visiting his parents was always a trying experience for both of them; maybe Robyn's nerves were just showing signs of wear.

He sat down on the bed. "Want me to set the alarm, hon?"

She approached the bed and drew the covers back. "The alarm? Do we need to?"

"No. Not as far as I'm concerned. I'd just as soon sleep in."

"Your mother will be stirring at dawn, working on breakfast."

"I know. Let her. She loves to putter."

"I'll feel guilty if I don't help her."

"She loves that too—making people feel guilty."

"Justin!"

"I'm kidding—no, I'm not. But she doesn't realize that's how she makes people feel."

"Set the alarm," said Robyn. "I need to be up early anyway."

163

"No, you don't."

"All right," she said, sounding peeved. "Don't set it."

He climbed into bed and pulled the covers up around his chest. The sheets were cold. "You never asked about my talk with Joe."

"Didn't I? At lunch?"

"No. You and Alex were both quiet. But I guess it's hard knowing what to say to him."

Robyn gave him a startled glance. "Why do you say that?"

"Why? The man's wife died. What can you say to someone with a loss like that? Even with a strong faith, it's got to be tough."

"He's managing," said Robyn. "I just wish I could help him."

"You are. I can tell. It's done him a world of good just to see you again."

Robyn sat on the edge of the bed. "It doesn't mean anything—"

"I didn't say it did. I just think it's nice if we can cheer him up a little. He was always a good friend . . . to both of us."

"Yes, he was." Robyn examined one fingernail, then worked with the cuticle. "He'll always be a good friend, won't he, Justin? Isn't that what you want too?"

"Yes, of course. If it weren't for Alex, I might never have come to the Lord." He eyed her carefully. "I might never have found you either."

She met his gaze momentarily; then she looked away, busying herself with her nails.

He put his hands behind his head and stared at the ceiling. "I didn't say much to Joe this morning."

"Why not?"

"I let him do most of the talking."

"And—?"

"Joe's looking for someone to take his place."

Robyn eyed him quizzically. "You mean he's retiring?"

"In a way. He wants to step down from the pulpit. Have a more hands-on ministry with the people. He wants someone else to preach." Justin paused meaningfully. "He asked if I'd be interested."

Robyn's tone was wary. "What did you say?"

"Nothing. I just listened."

"Are you saying you'd actually consider coming back to Southfield? Permanently?"

"Right now I don't know where God wants me, Robyn. If you're asking, do I want to come back, the answer is no. There's too much emotional baggage for me here." He sighed. "Trouble is, there's not much left for me at Redeemer Christian either. I don't know where I belong, Robyn."

"I thought you were going to ask Joe for his advice."

"I planned to. I wanted to spill my guts, but I just couldn't. Especially after he talked about my taking his place. Joe sees me as this successful California preacher coming home in victory, so what could I say? He wants me to get up and tell the congregation how the Lord is blessing my life. He expects me to be an inspiration to people. How can I *take* from him when he's expecting me to *give*?"

Robyn looked mildly perturbed. "You can't give forever, Justin. Sometimes you have to take. Sometimes you have to admit you're not invincible, you have feet of clay—we all have feet of clay—"

They were silent for a moment. He reached for her hand. "Right now I have feet of ice, not clay. Get in here, hon, and warm these babies up."

She grimaced. "Then what?"

He caught her drift and promptly retreated. "Then we both get a good night's sleep."

"Just what we need," she said dryly.

"Don't we?"

"I suppose." She flipped off the bedside lamp and climbed in beside him. He could feel her warmth along the length of his body, close, but not quite touching. They used to lie in each other's arms and pray before drifting off to sleep, but lately . . .

Justin wondered if he would ever find the courage or the words to confess his fear to her—his *problem*. Perhaps there was no problem. Perhaps it was entirely his imagination, and if he gave it a chance, everything would be okay, normal again. But he was afraid to find out, afraid to try, afraid to fail. How could he tell Robyn what he refused to verbalize in his own mind? He was okay, certainly he was okay; he wouldn't think about it tonight, wouldn't risk putting his manhood on the line, even though now, in the darkness, in this heavy silence, with Robyn breathing quietly beside him, he yearned for her tenderness, her closeness.

Aloud, he said, "Robyn? Are you awake?"

"Yes." She didn't move.

"Are you okay?"

"Why do you ask?"

"I don't know. You seemed . . . troubled today."

"It's nothing, Justin."

"Is it me?"

A long silence, then: "Partly."

"Tell me."

She sighed. "I can't."

"Why not?"

"I don't have the words."

"Try."

"I don't have the energy."

In the dark, where he didn't have to meet her gaze, he found the courage to ask, "Is it too late for us?"

Her voice faltered. "I hope not."

"Me too." He knew he should gather her into his arms to reassure her, but he kept his hands locked under his head. His body was tense, his heart pounding. He wanted to draw her against him as much as he wanted to flee. Maybe this was the first wave of insanity washing over him, throwing his mind into confusion, putting him at odds with himself. "I don't know what's wrong," he uttered in desperation.

Her voice softened. "I don't either, Justin. I just know I don't know you anymore."

"You know me, Robyn."

"Do I?" She turned over on her side so that her face was close to his. "Then why don't I know what to expect from you anymore, Justin? Why don't I know what you're thinking or how you're feeling?" The words came out in a whispered sob. "Why don't I know why you turn away from me?"

"I don't mean to turn away—"

Robyn uttered a hard, ironic laugh and sat up. "But you do, Justin. You turn away."

He sat up too. He was glad he couldn't see her face, the hurt in her eyes. It was bad enough that it was all there in her voice. "You know how troubled I am, Robyn—about Dad, the church—"

"This isn't about your dad or the church, Justin. . . . It's about us."

"Us? I don't know what you want from me, Robyn. I'm sorry—"

"Sorry? What good does sorry do? Will it change anything?"

"I don't know." He shook his head. "Maybe the problem's spiritual."

She lay back down abruptly. "Oh, great. Blame it on God."

"What's that supposed to mean?"

"It means when you don't want to face something, you put on your sanctimonious mask and no one can get near you."

"That's not fair, Robyn. You know the problems I face."

"What problems?"

"Come on. It's the age-old story. Just because I'm a minister people think I have a direct pipeline to God, some secret code between the Almighty and myself. Well, I don't." He heaved a sigh. "Do you know what it does to me when I realize some little kid who talks about trusting Jesus has more faith than I do, or some old lady who's never been to seminary and who's too blind to study the Scriptures has seen Jesus more clearly than I ever will? It's just as hard for me to make Jesus real in my life as it is for anyone else, maybe even harder, because people expect it of me, expect me to be this spiritual saint walking two feet above the earth. The truth is, Robyn, I have spiritual struggles just like anyone else."

"So do I, Justin. So do I." She began to weep.

He reached across her and turned on the lamp. "What's wrong, Robyn? Why are you crying?"

She got out of bed and walked over to the bureau. "I can't tell you, Justin." She took a Kleenex and blew her nose. "I don't have the words. Everything's all jumbled—"

"Everything?"

"Life. You . . . me . . . everything."

"I don't understand. What happened?"

She shivered in her pale pink satin gown. She looked like a fragile doll with porcelain skin and dark, teary eyes.

"What happened?" he said again.

"Nothing happened." She dabbed her eyes. "Maybe you're right. Maybe our problem is spiritual. Maybe God's trying to tell us something."

"What?"

She threw up her hands in perplexity. "How should I know? How can I understand God when I can't even understand the people close to me?"

"Robyn—"

"And how can I understand the people I love when I can't even understand myself?"

"Robyn, listen—"

She glared at him. "Don't give me that patronizing look, like you think it's that time of month. It's not. I'm not just being emotional, Justin."

"I didn't say you were."

"You asked me what's wrong. I'm trying to put it into words. I'm trying to express what's going on inside me." She came over to his side of the bed and sat down. She was trembling.

He slipped his arm around her. "Tell me, Robyn. I want to hear."

She shook her head in bafflement. "I can't. It's so—so crazy. I shouldn't even get into it."

"Get into what? You're talking in riddles, sweetheart."

"I know. It is a riddle, Justin. You talk about your problems being a minister. Well, I have problems too. Just when I think I know who I am and what I can expect of myself, it changes—I change. And I realize there are vast landscapes of myself I've never even glimpsed."

"Yes, I've felt that way—"

"I realize more all the time, Justin, that all I can count on is God, and even He doesn't give any advance signals. He makes me take Him by faith, and I see Him only in rare, infrequent glimpses, like looking through a—a kaleidoscope, or a prism, or a funhouse mirror."

"Honey, I understand. That's just what I was trying to say."

Robyn drew in a deep breath. She was twisting her tissue into a ragged snake. "There's so much clutter in my life, Justin. I have to strain to look around it or under it, or through cracks and fissures of myself before I see Him. And even then it's not like looking through clear glass, because the amalgam of my sins darkens the image so that when I think I'm seeing Christ, I'm really seeing myself, and my own image obscures His."

"Robyn, I know. I feel that way too—"

"I know you do, Justin." She sank against him, her head resting in the hollow of his shoulder.

He nuzzled his chin against the top of her head. She felt wonderfully good to him. For a few brief moments he was her protector, her comforter. He wanted to tell her he loved her. He wanted to confess why he had kept her at arm's length for so long—the secret fear that tormented him to his very marrow—but he stifled the words before they reached his lips.

Softly Robyn said, "We came home, Justin, to bring Christ to your family. But sometimes we lose sight of Him ourselves. I do. I feel it. I distance myself from Him. Make wrong choices. But I don't want to grieve Him, Justin."

Soothingly he told her, "How could you possibly grieve Him, Robyn? You have the purest heart of anyone I know."

She looked up at him with a tearful urgency, her voice hardly more than a whisper. "Oh, Justin, I wish it were true. I really want to please Him—"

For several minutes they sat together in the semi-darkness, their heads together and arms entwined, sharing a rare and special closeness. But privately, Justin felt strangely unsettled. He had a feeling there was something of momentous importance that Robyn wasn't saying.

21

ERIC ROSE early Monday morning and went straight to the window. Fresh snow. Clear skies. A perfect day to spend outside skating or sledding. Since Scott and Lauralee were on vacation now, maybe the three of them could make plans. Wait, what was he thinking? The *four* of them! No day would be complete without Kaylie. Just thinking of her now, savoring the memory of her kisses, Eric could feel a delicious warmth radiate through his whole body. He couldn't wait to be with Kaylie again.

Things were definitely looking up here in Southfield. Eric didn't mind if his folks stayed through Christmas—and New Year's too! In fact, if his relationship with Kaylie developed the way he hoped, he might stay through Easter.

He dressed quickly, paused by the hall mirror to comb his hair, and then stopped by his grandfather's room to say good morning. But Gramps was asleep. Eric stood by the big hospital bed, listening to his grandfather's strangulated breathing. The old man's eyes fluttered restlessly and perspiration dotted his forehead. Eric wanted to reach out and touch him, but he was afraid he'd feel cold. The nurse, sitting nearby, caught Eric's gaze and smiled faintly. Eric gave her a twisted grin and left the room, heading downstairs.

Grandma Cahill was just setting a platter of pancakes on the table as Eric slipped quietly into the room and took his seat. Everyone was already there, including Uncle Chris, who was hovering by the table, eyeing the pancakes. "Sit down, Chris," said Grams. "There's plenty for everybody."

Chris took the nearest chair and reached for the platter. "I really didn't come to eat, Mom," he said between mouthfuls. "I came to talk to Justin."

Eric looked over as his dad straightened and said, "What's up, Chris? Problems?"

"Looks like it. At the plant. I got a call from Dooley, the night watchman, this morning. He says somebody broke in last night."

"Oh, no," said Grams, her hand fluttering to her mouth. "Was it a robbery?"

"No, Mom. Someone set a fire in a trash bin. Dooley caught it promptly or it could have spelled big trouble."

"How does he know it was deliberately set?"

Uncle Chris didn't answer for a moment. Then he said, "Someone painted a warning on the wall."

They all stared at him. "What warning?" Eric's dad asked.

"It was probably the same kids who broke the windows last week. A bunch of smart-alecks."

"What was the warning, son?" asked Grams.

Uncle Chris squirmed a little. "Someone painted the words *death* and *blood on your hands* on the wall."

Grams's face paled. "Oh, Chris, no. Who would do such a thing?"

"Search me. Like I said, probably a bunch of hoodlums."

Eric's dad spoke up. "What about that foreman of yours? The guy who stormed in here? Bryden, wasn't it? Do you think he could have done it?"

"Oh, I don't think so," said Uncle Chris. "Bryden's a boozer and a big mouth, but he wouldn't destroy property like that." He helped himself to some more pancakes. "I told Dooley to keep a sharp eye out tonight and if he sees any sign of trouble, call the police. They'll take care of any rowdies who show up tonight."

"It wouldn't hurt to have the police look around today," said Grams. "Chris, will you call them?"

"Sure, Mom, I'll call them from the office. But I doubt if they'll do anything."

"Still, I'll feel better if they know what happened. But not a word about this to your father. I don't want him upset."

While the family talked on about the vandalism, Eric

wolfed down three pancakes and two slices of ham; then he drained a glass of milk and stood up.

"Through already, Eric?" asked his mother.

"Yeah. I want to call Scott and Lauralee. We're going skating."

"Well, it's mighty cold out," said Grams. "Dress warmly."

"You bet."

Eric telephoned Scott. They agreed to get together at ten. Eric could rent skates at the outdoor rink. Lauralee would call Kaylie. The four of them would have a really great time.

Their plan went like clockwork. They spent several hours at the rink, until Eric thought his fingers and toes would drop off with frostbite. Then they headed for Kaylie's house where they gathered around the warmth of the fireplace and savored mugs of hot chocolate and devoured bowls of buttery popcorn. In Eric's mind, it was a perfect day, with a warm, magical touch reminiscent of the Currier and Ives Christmas cards his mother placed on the mantel each December. Yes, it was a "White Christmas" in the best sense—snow flurries outside the window, a roaring fire inside, the girl of his dreams in his arms.

That evening the four of them went out for pizza, and then came back to Eric's grandparents' home for hot cider and doughnuts around the Christmas tree. He was feeling fine, real fine. It was as if he were no longer touched by the worries and concerns of his family, no longer weighed down by the terrible specter of his grandfather's dying. At Kaylie's insistence, he got out his keyboard and played several of his own compositions and basked in her effusive admiration.

Late in the evening, after Eric's family had gone to bed, the four teenagers sat around the fireplace swapping stories. *What was your most embarrassing moment? What's the worst thing that ever happened to you? Spill all the juicy details about your first kiss.* As they confided their secrets, they laughed so hard Eric had to warn them to quiet down before they woke his grandfather upstairs.

Shortly after midnight, as Eric's cousins and Kaylie were gathering their things to leave, the telephone rang. "I bet it's my dad wondering where we are," said Scott as Eric picked up the receiver.

"Hello?" said Eric lightly.

For a moment there was silence on the other end of the line; then a deep voice said huskily, "Tell Victor Cahill to get over to the plant fast. If he's not there in a half hour, the whole place goes up in smoke!"

"What? Who is this?" Eric demanded.

The line went dead.

"Who was it?" asked Kaylie, coming over beside him.

"Must have been an obscene phone call by the look on your face," quipped Scott.

Eric shook his head. "Man, that was weird."

"Was it a crank call?" asked Lauralee.

"I don't know. It was about the factory. This guy said if Gramps doesn't get over there fast, the whole place will go up in smoke."

Scott's eyes widened in disbelief. "You're kidding!"

"That's what he said. But Gramps—he's too sick to go anywhere."

"You'd better call the police," said Kaylie.

"And tell them what?" said Scott. "Maybe it was just a practical joke. What do we have to go on?"

"Well, then call the fire department," said Lauralee.

"So they can rush to a fire that's not even there?" scoffed Scott.

"Listen, I'll go wake my dad," said Eric. "He'll know what to do."

Scott shook his head. "What can he do in the middle of the night?—except maybe knock our heads together for waking him up."

"Well, we've got to do something," said Lauralee.

"What about the night watchman?" said Eric.

Scott nodded. "Yeah, we can call Dooley. No, wait, he's probably not by a phone. But I know where he usually is. We can go over there ourselves."

"Go over to the factory?" cried Lauralee.

"Sure, why not?" said Scott. "We go tell Dooley about the call, he takes care of things, and nobody's sleep is disturbed."

"Well, I'm not going over to any spooky factory in the middle of the night," said Lauralee, folding her arms decisively.

"Aw, we'll take you girls home first," said Scott. "Get your coat, Eric. We'll be back before anybody even misses us."

Eric glanced back at the phone. He wasn't sure he liked Scott's idea, but then again, why shouldn't they handle this thing themselves? His dad told him often enough that he should take more responsibility and not keep "running home to Mama" when he needed help. "Okay, I'll get my coat," he told Scott.

Scott dropped the girls off. Then he and Eric headed for Cahill Manufacturing, taking Arbor Road to Main Street, and then heading four blocks south. Eric shivered as he gazed at the huge brick structure. It stood like a monstrous shadow against the glittering backdrop of new-fallen snow. Only a few random pinpoints of light beamed out to welcome them.

"Looks awfully dark," said Eric.

"Yeah, Dooley must be falling down on the job. But I know where he camps out." Scott swerved into a parking space beside the building and turned off the ignition. "Come on, Eric. Get the flashlight out of the glove compartment and follow me."

"How are we getting in if Dooley's not here?"

"Easy. Dad gave me my own key for emergencies. I even know how to fix it so the alarm won't go off."

They entered the silent building by a side door that led directly into the lobby. Scott whistled.

"What's that for?" whispered Eric.

"My signal for Dooley. Lets him know I'm here. We've done this before."

"I'm glad you have," said Eric. "This isn't my idea of fun."

Scott whistled again. "Strange. Usually Dooley whistles back."

"Hey, Scott, what do you say? Maybe we should call the police."

"Let me think a minute, buddy. Old Dooley's gotta be around here somewhere."

"Let's turn on the lights and see."

"No, lights on in the middle of the night might bring the cops. They'd call my dad and we'd be in hot water for sure."

"Why? Just because we're doing a good deed?"

"Yeah, right. Listen, Eric. Did you hear something?"

"Like what?"

"I don't know. A groan maybe. I heard it over this way."

They inched along the wall to the opposite side of the lobby near the reception desk. Suddenly Scott let out a low, startled exclamation.

"What's wrong?" demanded Eric.

Scott was kneeling over something. "Look at this, man!"

Eric knelt down beside his cousin. "What is it?" He squinted through the shadows at a twisted form on the floor.

"A body," said Scott, running his flashlight over the length of the torso and legs. It was a man in a leather jacket and slacks. Scott reached out and turned the head slightly. "Oh, man, no. It's Dooley."

"Is he—?"

Scott held his hand under the bright oval from his flashlight. "Oh, gross me out—there's blood on my hand, man. Blood on my hand!"

Eric's heart started pounding like a jackhammer. "Is he dead, Scott? Check! See if he's dead!"

Scott placed his hand gingerly on Dooley's chest. "I don't know, Eric. His clothes are too thick. I can't feel a thing!"

Eric felt the man's forehead. "He's cold—man, I bet he's dead!"

Scott scrambled to his feet. "We gotta get help—"

Eric jumped up too and stopped abruptly. He heard something—a creaking sound, a click somewhere in an adjacent office. "What was that?" he whispered urgently.

"What?" said Scott under his breath. "Wait. I hear it too."

"Let's get out of here!" declared Eric, his voice shrill with alarm.

They started for the door, but the crack of gunfire brought them up short. A guttural, menacing voice from the doorway demanded, "You boys stay where you are or you're both dead meat!"

22

THE PHONE was ringing.

The sound seemed to be coming from a great distance. Justin wasn't sure how many times it rang before he realized the shrill sound wasn't part of his dream, but something separate—an ominous noise repeating itself in the dark, chill silence of the night. He stumbled out of bed and fumbled for the receiver on the bureau. He muttered hello even as he tried to unscramble his groggy thoughts from the lingering cobweb of his dreams.

A muffled voice said, "Victor Cahill, I have your grandsons."

"What?" said Justin. The words made no sense. Had he heard right?

More ominously now: "I said, I have your grandsons."

"Who is this?" asked Justin.

The gravelly voice continued, "And I swear on my daughter's grave, they'll be dead by morning . . . just like my precious Amy." And then it hit—like a sudden jab in the stomach. Justin was coldly, terrifyingly awake, and he knew exactly who was speaking on the other end of the line. "Bryden? Richard Bryden? That's you, isn't it?" When there was no response, Justin demanded, "What are you doing, Bryden? Why are you making such a threat? Do you hear me, Bryden?"

The line went dead.

Justin stood unmoving in the dark room. He felt a shiver like an icy hand travel the length of his spine. He spoke Robyn's name, but his mouth felt like cotton.

177

She stirred and said, "Did you call, Justin?"

"The phone—did you hear it?"

She sat up attentively. "No, who was it?"

"That man—Richard Bryden—the foreman Dad fired."

"What did he want?"

"He threatened the boys—Victor Cahill's grandsons, he said."

"Oh, Justin, no!" Robyn got up and slipped on her robe. "Was he drunk?"

"No, I don't think so. He sounded . . . dead serious."

"Well, I think you should call the police."

"I will. In the morning. It's barely 4:00 A.M. No sense in waking the household now."

Robyn touched Justin's arm. "Do you think we should tell the boys about the phone call?"

"I don't know. I hate to alarm them. . . ."

"Well, I'm going to look in on Eric. I'll feel better . . ."

Robyn was gone only a few moments. When she returned she rushed into Justin's arms, frantic. "He's not there, Justin. His bed hasn't been slept in!"

Justin held her close. "It's unlikely, but maybe he's still downstairs with his cousins."

They went promptly downstairs, but everything was dark.

"All right, don't panic," said Justin. "He probably went over to Scott and Lauralee's. Or maybe he's next door at Kaylie's. You know how crazy he is about that girl."

Robyn was already turning on a lamp and reaching for the phonebook. She dialed and, after several long moments, said, "Hello, Mrs. Hollis? This is Eric Cahill's mother. I'm sorry to wake you, but I wondered—is Kaylie there? She is? Is Eric with her? What? Kaylie's asleep? Oh, I see. Yes. Then Eric must have gone to his cousins' house. Thank you. Good night."

Justin took the phone from her. "I'll call Chris. Eric must be there."

"I pray to God he is."

After half a dozen rings, Chris answered sleepily, "Uh, Cahill here."

"Chris, it's me, Justin. Are the kids there?"

"The kids? You mean Scott and Lauralee?"

"And Eric. He's not here. Is he there?"

"I don't know, Justin. Everything's dark here. Let me check their rooms."

There was a long silence; then Chris was back, his voice tinged with alarm. "Listen, Justin, Lauralee's here. I woke her out of a sound sleep, so I can't get a sensible word out of her. She's mumbling something about the boys getting a phone call and going over to the factory."

"The factory? Why the factory?"

"I don't know, Justin. Hold on. Let me ask her." A minute later Chris returned and said urgently, "Lauralee says the boys got a call at your place—someone threatened to burn down the factory, so—would you believe it?—they went over to warn Dooley."

"Oh, no," Justin groaned. "We've got trouble, Chris. I just got a call from Richard Bryden. He says he's got our boys."

"Got them? You mean, holding them hostage? At the factory?"

"Looks that way." Justin repeated Bryden's deadly threat.

"The man's become a raving lunatic," said Chris.

"I'm calling the police," said Justin, "then we'd better go to the factory."

"I'll pick you up in five minutes."

Ten minutes later they pulled into the parking lot at Cahill Manufacturing. A police car pulled up just behind them. Two officers got out. One came over to the driver's side of Chris's blue BMW. "You Mr. Cahill?" When Chris nodded, he said, "I'm Sgt. Perez. That's my partner, Sgt. Zigler. We got a call about an arson threat and a man holding some kids hostage—"

Justin quickly told him what he knew.

Sgt. Perez nodded to Sgt. Zigler. "Let's go in."

Justin and Chris sprang from their vehicle, but Sgt. Perez waved them back. "Let us check it out first. You two wait here."

"Let me come," said Chris. "I'll turn off the alarm."

Sgt. Zigler shrugged. "All right, but you both be careful."

They entered the lobby from the side door. "Looks quiet so

far," Chris whispered to Justin. "Dooley should be here some-where."

They heard a low moan. The first rays of dawn streaming through the Venetian blinds on the plate-glass windows illu-minated a crumpled form beside the reception desk. The offi-cers approached cautiously, their weapons drawn.

"It's Dooley, my night watchman!" said Chris. He bent down beside the wiry, gray-haired man. Dooley's hands and feet were tied, and a gag was stuffed in his mouth. Chris removed the gag while the officers untied the ropes. "Dooley, can you hear me? Are you okay? What happened, Dooley?"

Dooley choked out the words. "Your old foreman—Bryden—he's gone loco. Knocked me out. When I came to, he had your boys. I couldn't stop him—"

Justin knelt beside Dooley. "Where'd he take them?"

"To Mr. Cahill's office. Said he was waiting there to have it out with Victor Cahill." Dooley's face drooped with despair. "One more thing, Sergeant."

"What's that, sir?"

"Bryden has a gun."

"Let's go," said Sgt. Perez.

They filed down the hall to the double doors of Victor Cahill's luxury office. Sgt. Perez motioned for Justin and Chris to stay back, and then he knocked soundly on the door. When there was no answer, he shouted, "Open up, Mr. Bryden. Police!"

After a moment, a muffled voice inside replied, "Get outta here. I'm not talking to anybody but Victor Cahill!"

"That's Bryden, all right," said Chris.

"Come on, Mr. Bryden," Sgt. Zigler called back. "We just want to talk to you. Open the door."

The response was immediate. "Leave me alone! I'll talk when I hear Victor Cahill's voice! Not before!"

"Find out if he has the boys," said Justin.

Sgt. Perez nodded. "Hey, Mr. Bryden, we got a couple of worried fathers here. They're looking for their sons. You seen a couple of teenage boys around here?"

Suddenly, Scott's voice rang out shrilly, "We're here, Dad. He won't let us go!"

"Oh, no," cried Chris. "He has them!"

Sgt. Perez's voice took on a sharp edge as he approached the closed doors. "Mr. Bryden, we don't want any trouble here. You send the boys out and we'll let you have your say."

Silence. Sgt. Perez repeated his demand.

Then Bryden's voice: "Maybe one of these boys should die—like my Amy!"

Justin flinched, as if he'd been struck hard. He strode to the office doors and hammered sharply. "Mr. Bryden, I'm Rev. Cahill. Let me talk to you. We can work this out—"

Silence again. Then Bryden replied, "I got no business with you, Rev. Cahill. You go home and get your father. I got a score to settle with Victor Cahill, no one else."

Sgt. Perez spoke up. "Mr. Bryden, if you don't open that door for us, we'll have to enter by force. You don't want trouble like that. Be reasonable and let us in—"

A gunshot exploded in the Cahill office. Justin sprang back reflexively. Bryden shouted from inside, "That's just a warning, officers. The ceiling took that bullet. The next two are for these boys if you touch those doors!"

Sgt. Zigler motioned for Justin and Chris to back off. "I'll call for backups," he said as he ushered them back through the lobby and out to the squad car.

Dazed, Justin and Chris listened as Zigler radioed for reinforcements. "We have two teenage boys being held by an armed man down here at Cahill's furniture factory. I repeat, he's armed and dangerous. We talked to him, but no deal. Right! If we antagonize him, he could go over the edge and do something violent. That's what I figure. It's going to be a waiting game."

Justin met his brother's gaze and read his own desperate sense of helplessness. Quietly he said, "We'd better call home, Chris."

His brother nodded, his lean jaw sagging with resignation. "We can't call from inside, but there's a phone in the Rexall drugstore across the street. They open early for the factory workers."

They walked through the chill early-morning air, their shoes crunching in the fresh, clean snow. The wind whipped through Justin's California-thin overcoat. He shivered, but it was more from shock than the freezing temperature.

"They'll be all right," he heard himself assuring Chris. "The police will know how to talk Bryden out of there. They handle this sort of thing all the time. It'll be okay." Even as he spoke the words, he heard the hollowness in his voice.

Chris gave him a grudging glance as they entered the drugstore. "Justin, our sons could be killed."

Justin heaved a sigh and squeezed his brother's arm. Chris returned the gesture.

In the phone booth, Justin dialed with stiff, cold fingers, praying that Robyn would answer instead of his mother. How could he begin to explain this bizarre situation to his mother? But when he heard Robyn's voice, he thought for a moment that he would break down. Actually weep. He groped for words, spilled out the details unceremoniously. He could hear the stunned disbelief in Robyn's voice as she asked, "Are you sure that man has the boys?"

"Yes. Scott called out, said Bryden's holding them both. It sounds impossible—"

"Laura and I will be right over," said Robyn.

"No, hon, there's nothing you can do—"

"I can be there with you. I can be near our son."

"All right," Justin conceded. "But be careful." He grimaced inwardly. It was Eric who must be careful. Silently he wondered, *What chance do a couple of young, clean-scrubbed kids have against a grief-crazed man with a gun?*

23

ERIC FELT a sinking sensation in his chest as he realized his father and the policemen were no longer outside the double doors of his grandfather's office. He had hoped against hope that this deranged man would release them and surrender to the police. But the gruff, seedy-looking Bryden had only become more incensed by the officer's demands that he open the door. Now Eric was terrified that Bryden would turn his weapon on them. He had fired impulsively at the ceiling, and even now he was pacing the room, fingering his gun nervously.

Eric looked over at Scott who sat on the opposite end of the plush leather sofa, his hands tied at the wrist like Eric's. Scott's eyes were round with fear and he chewed anxiously on his lower lip. Eric tried to force a smile to let Scott know they would be okay; somehow they would get out of this, and it would be something they would look back on and maybe even chuckle over someday. But he couldn't smile; his lips felt tight and stiff. He realized he wasn't half as calm as he pretended to be.

Bryden stopped pacing and lowered his bulky frame into the swivel chair at Grandpa Cahill's desk. He sprawled his legs out in front of him and set his gun on the desk. He didn't look so ominous now; he looked like a weary, defeated man.

Eric studied the gun on the desk. He wondered what kind it was—a revolver, an automatic, a semi-automatic? He had never thought much about guns, never liked them anyway, not even a shotgun for hunting. All he could be sure of was that that gun was real; it had blown half the plaster off the ceiling.

Scott was watching the gun too, no doubt contemplating how they might distract Bryden and grab it, but that sort of thing was straight out of the movies. It didn't always work out in real life, with the good guys winning and the bad guys getting their comeuppance. Eric had a feeling if he tried to get the gun, he and Scott would end up dead.

Dead? The idea struck Eric suddenly with a sickening jolt. He had never thought seriously about being dead. Oh, dying someday when he was old and gray like Grandpa Cahill, and too old to care—maybe. But dead, as in right this minute, this hour, this day—the idea was more than he could handle. There was a choking sound in his throat. His mouth was dry; he couldn't swallow. Did fear do this to a person? He looked desperately at Scott. Scott's face was pale, and his eyes had the wild look of a cornered animal. Eric wanted to say something, reach out to his cousin, but he was terrified himself, and Bryden was sitting there watching them, silencing them with his gaze.

For a long while Bryden chewed silently on a toothpick, his eyes steady on them. It wasn't exactly a cruel expression—more curious than anything. Finally he said, "Listen, you guys, I'm sorry about this. I don't have anything against you two. It's Victor Cahill I want. He brought this on himself. He did a terrible thing. I tried to talk to him, but they wouldn't let me. So I had to do something. He can't get away with what he did. You understand?"

"What did my grandfather do?" asked Eric.

Bryden's lined face sagged. His eyes began to tear. He fumbled in his pocket for his wallet and removed a dog-eared photograph. "This is Amy," he said, holding the picture out for Eric to see. "My little girl."

"She's very pretty," said Eric dutifully.

Bryden leaned over, holding the photo out to Scott. Scott nodded. "Yeah, real cute."

"She *was*," said Bryden. "Like they say, the good die young." Huskily, he launched into a rambling, impassioned account of his daughter's illness and tragic death. It was the same story Eric and Scott had heard the night Bryden burst in on their family dinner.

"Now it's almost Christmas," he said as he fingered the gun on the desk. He seemed to be talking more now to himself than to the boys. "I was going to buy her a doll. She saw it in the window at Sears. She loved that doll. I promised I'd get it for her soon as I got a job." His voice hardened as he looked back at Eric. "Only I couldn't get a job—thanks to your grandfather."

"I'm real sorry about your little girl," said Eric.

"Yeah, me too," said Scott. "Only there's nothing we can do to change anything—"

"So why don't you just let us go on home?" Eric finished.

"Yeah," said Scott. "In fact, if you let us go, we'll go talk to our grandfather for you. I bet you anything he'll give you back your job, or lend you some money, or something."

"Then let him come here and tell me," said Bryden.

"He can't," said Eric. "He's real sick. He can't even get out of bed."

Bryden wrapped his fingers around the handle of his gun. "That's an excuse. That old man can do anything he pleases."

"Not anymore," said Scott. "Gramps is never getting well. He's dying."

"Dying?" Bryden looked sharply at Scott, his brows furrowed. "Now you're really feeding me a story. That old man is too stubborn to die." He scowled at the boys. "Besides, he can't die, not until I've paid him back and done to him what he's done to me."

"It won't bring your little girl back," said Eric cautiously.

Bryden's eyes glinted with fire. "No, but your grandfather took my child from me. I vowed to do the same to him. An eye for an eye. Take his children . . ." His lips twisted menacingly. "And if not his children, then his grandchildren!"

Eric read the mute terror in Scott's eyes and felt his own heart pounding furiously. How could they argue with a madman, a man convinced that revenge was his right? *Dear God, where are our dads, the police?* he wondered, sweat beading on his forehead.

Eric became aware of the clock ticking on the wall, a steady heartbeat sound. They had been in this room for several hours now, and it had been over a half hour since the police arrived and ordered Bryden to open the door. *Where are the police now?* Eric wondered. *Everything is too quiet. Dad and Uncle Chris wouldn't give up and go home. But what are they doing? How do they feel, knowing their sons are being held prisoner by a crazy man?*

Eric winced, thinking about how his mom would react when she learned what had happened. She might cry. Eric hated to see her cry, hated to see anything hurt her. And what if Bryden actually shot the two of them? What if Scott and Eric died today? Eric imagined the grisly scene—his family gathered at the cemetery, everyone weeping and telling one another what wonderful boys they had lost, and how would they ever manage without them? And Kaylie—would she care? Would she cry?

Eric felt some comfort in thinking about how everyone would appreciate them when they were gone. Even his dad—the great, perfect Rev. Justin Cahill. He would wish he had treated Eric with more kindness and respect, been more tolerant of their differences, maybe even taken pride in Eric's accomplishments, even if they weren't the achievements he had planned for Eric. Eric fought back tears as he pictured his dad weeping over his grave, regretting that he hadn't been closer to his son.

Eric thought about his own regrets too. He would regret not graduating from high school, and not getting to know Kaylie better, and not becoming a recognized, first-rate musician. But at least he knew the Lord and, as far as he knew, everything was okay there. Not perfect, of course, but he was forgiven. He had never quite figured out what to do with his passions, his lusts, but at least he had kept them in check so far. Sure, it had been a close call with Kaylie the other night, but even then he had ultimately managed to be true to his convictions. So, okay, if he had to die today, he was ready to meet the Lord.

But I'm not all that eager to join You today, God, he admitted silently. *If You want the truth, I'd just as soon stay around here a few more years. There's a lot I still want to do, like have a singing career, and get married, and make love, and have a family of my own. Please, don't let it all be over yet . . . but if it is, I know I'll be in heaven with You . . .*

Another thought struck Eric. He stole a glance at Scott. His eyes were closed, his mouth set in a grimace. Did Scott know the Lord? As far as Eric knew, his cousin had no interest in God. None of the Cahills did. Eric had never bothered to talk to Scott about spiritual things; it just didn't seem like the cool thing to do. They had talked a little about dying, about their grandfather's dying, but not of eternity, of heaven. So Eric had no idea whether Scott had ever asked Jesus to be his own personal Savior. If he hadn't, that meant—Eric dreaded thinking about it—it meant if they both died today, Scott would go to hell.

Scott stirred, shifted in his seat, and then stared down at the floor, mindlessly twisting his bound hands. Eric cleared his throat. Their gaze met for a moment and Eric felt a stab of guilt. *Man, why didn't I talk to you sooner, Scott? Why didn't I give you a chance to know Jesus?* Now maybe it was too late. Maybe they would both die and Eric would always kick himself for not talking to Scott. Or would Eric even remember the chance he'd missed? Would he recall in heaven that he'd ever known a guy named Scott Cahill, his own cousin, who maybe never made it to heaven because of him?

The idea was mind-boggling. But maybe there was still a chance. Maybe he could talk to Scott right here, right now. What else did they have to do? But what should he say? How should he begin? With the Four Spiritual Laws? John 3:16? He tried out a couple of possibilities in his mind, but nothing sounded right. He couldn't just come right out and say, *Listen, Scott, just in case this guy shoots us dead, how about praying the sinner's prayer?* Might as well come out with a slick advertising slogan—*For eternal life insurance, try Jesus!*

No, there had to be another way. Oh, if only he'd brought up the subject before, when their lives weren't hanging in the balance!

Eric looked over at Bryden. He was sitting forward, his elbows on the desk, his head in his hands. His gun lay beside his right elbow. Eric had the feeling Bryden's eyes were closed, but he couldn't be sure. Maybe the man was dozing off. Why not? They had all been up all night. Eric could feel the weariness radiating through his own back. He felt the urge to go to the john too, but feared asking. And Scott—Scott look tired too; the usual twinkle in his eyes had been replaced by dark shadows.

Eric caught Scott's gaze and rolled his eyes toward the gun, as if to say, maybe there's a way we can get it. Scott blinked agreement. Slowly, painstakingly Eric extended one leg out toward the desk. Then he would spring forward with his other foot and grab up the gun. If he moved fast enough, he could do it even with his hands tied. Eric kept his eyes riveted on Bryden's head. The man's large, squarish hands nearly covered his face. If only Eric could see his eyes!

Just as Eric was ready to pounce on the unattended weapon, a noise outside the window startled Bryden into alertness. He sat bolt upright and glared at Eric. "What was that?" he demanded.

Eric sank back against the sofa in mute frustration.

"What noise?" Scott asked.

"Outside. I heard something." He stood, picked up his gun, and lumbered over to the window. Glancing back at the boys, he said, "Don't move a muscle, you two." He peered out the window, and then swore under his breath. "Cops everywhere! And would you believe? The TV reporters are even out there!"

"What?" said Eric. "What TV reporters?"

Bryden ambled back to his chair. "The local Channel 5 news team, that's who. They must think this is a big story. Well, we'll give them headlines, all right."

"What do you mean?" Eric asked, his voice sounding shrill and uneven.

Bryden looked from Scott to Eric. His rumpled face looked almost apologetic. "Like I said, I don't have anything against you boys. You seem nice enough, better than most, maybe. But your grandfather is forcing my hand."

"Yeah? How?" ventured Scott.

Bryden sat back and shook his head somberly. "Victor Cahill had his chance to meet me face to face. But he didn't have the guts. So now I've got to take things into my own hands, mete out my own justice."

Eric flinched. "Justice?"

"A life for a life." Bryden's tone turned sinister. "Looks like I've got no choice . . . but to kill one of you boys."

24

On her way to the factory, Robyn stopped by and picked up Laura. Neither woman wanted to be alone now, although neither knew what to say to the other. Laura sat gripping her hands tensely, staring out the windshield, murmuring over and over, "This can't be happening. This can't possibly be happening."

Robyn didn't reply. She was afraid she would burst into tears if she spoke. Even now, as she turned onto Main Street, she felt a knot of panic twist in her stomach. Her temples throbbed with sheer dread, belying the first pastel pink glimmer of dawn bathing the deep purple skyline. After a moment, she realized she was saying aloud, "Dear God, let them be all right. Please let them be all right."

Laura looked over at her with tears in her eyes and said, "Oh, Robyn, I'd give anything now to have your faith."

Robyn blinked back her own tears and reached for Laura's hand. "I just pray that God won't let anything happen to our boys," Laura went on compulsively. "He'll protect them, won't He, Robyn? You believe it, don't you?" She wiped her eyes with a tissue. "Please tell me you believe it."

Robyn nodded. She believed it, but she knew what Laura didn't know—that she had turned her son over to God since before his birth. How could she explain to Laura that she had asked for God's will above her own wishes, above all else—and now, in this terrible, fateful moment, she was afraid that God would hold her to it.

Minutes later, as Robyn approached Cahill Manufacturing, she caught her breath in surprise. "Oh, Laura, look. The place is surrounded by police cars."

Laura covered her mouth with her hand. "Do you suppose it means—oh, Robyn, it can't be—"

"Don't even think it, Laura. Maybe they've caught Bryden. Maybe the boys are free."

Oh, God, please—!

Robyn pulled into the Cahill parking lot, braking so quickly that her vehicle almost skidded into a nearby squad car. Her eyes scoured the landscape for some glimpse of Justin and Chris; they were nowhere in sight.

But suddenly Alex Lanigan was there, opening the car door for Laura and then coming around and helping Robyn out. "I'll take you ladies to your husbands," he said.

"Is there any word on the boys?" Robyn implored.

"Nothing yet."

Alex took their arms and guided them against the frigid early morning wind toward a barrier of squad cars where Justin and Chris stood talking with several officers. Robyn broke free from Alex's grip and rushed into Justin's arms. They clung to each other for a long moment. "What about Eric?" she cried.

"The boys are still in Dad's office with Bryden," Justin said, loud enough for Laura to hear too. "The police ordered us to stay back while they assess the situation."

"Stay back? Can't we go inside—do something to help?"

"We'd just get in the way," said Chris. "Nobody's sure what we're dealing with."

"Bryden's behavior is unpredictable," Justin added. "We don't know whether he's crazy or just acting out his grief. The wrong move could force his hand—"

Laura began to weep. "I can't bear this—I can't! There must be something we can do!"

Justin nodded at Chris. "We'll talk with Sgt. Perez and see what they've decided to do. You two stay here."

Robyn watched the two men cross in front of the squad cars, stepping carefully over patches of ice and clumps of dirty snow. They inched their way to the front of Cahill Manufacturing and spoke with two officers standing by the door. After a moment they returned. Justin spoke first. "They're trying to reason with Bryden. They hope he'll send the boys out. If that doesn't work—"

Robyn forced herself to ask, "What will they do?"

"Use force of some kind, I suppose."

"Do they think the boys are all right?" asked Laura.

Chris nodded. "There's no reason to think they're not. Bryden hasn't fired his gun since that earlier warning shot."

Robyn shivered. "Oh, Eric must be terrified—"

"Scott too," said Laura. "They're just innocent boys. They won't know how to deal with a violent, insane man."

"They'll do all right," said Justin. "Both boys have good heads on their shoulders. Maybe they'll even win Bryden over."

"Do you really believe that?" asked Laura.

"I have to."

Five minutes later, Sgt. Perez came over and said, "I suggest you folks go wait in the drugstore. You'll get frostbite out here."

"We want to be here in case the boys need us," Robyn insisted.

"Suit yourselves," said Perez. He nodded toward several officers with a bullhorn. "I'm going to make contact with Bryden again. One more time. After that—"

"We'll wait here and listen," said Justin.

Sgt. Perez scowled. "Yeah, like the TV newscasters are doing?"

Robyn looked over at the large white van parked beside the curb with the Channel 5 News logo emblazoned on its side. "Oh, I hope they don't make things worse."

"The publicity may make Bryden furious," Laura cried.

"Or he may do something drastic just to get attention," said Chris. "We can't let this become a public spectacle."

Justin nodded. "I'll talk to them, but I'm not sure what good it will do."

He was back a moment later and said, "For what it's worth, they assure me they'll proceed with caution and keep a low profile. We'll just have to—"

A loud voice bellowing through the bullhorn drowned out Justin's words with a stern pronouncement: "Richard Bryden, this is the police. Release the two boys. Come out and give yourself up."

Silence. The officer repeated his demand.

More silence. Then a distant, muffled voice from somewhere inside: "Let Victor Cahill tell me himself!"

Justin turned to Sgt. Perez. "Listen, my dad can't come here. He's ill." He faltered on the words, "He's on his—deathbed."

"Tell Bryden he can talk to us," said Chris. "We'll listen to whatever he has to say."

The four of them followed Perez over to the bullhorn. "Bryden, listen," shouted Perez. "Victor Cahill can't come here. He's sick. Dying. His sons are here. They'll talk to you. How about it?"

A long, heavy silence.

"Bryden's taking his sweet time replying," said Chris irritably.

"Sergeant, tell him I'll come in," said Justin, "if he'll let the boys go."

Chris shivered. "Me too. *Us* in exchange for our sons."

Sgt. Perez lifted the bullhorn and delivered the message. Silence. He repeated it.

Finally, Bryden's voice wafted from the building like an echo on the thin winter air. "I want Victor Cahill! No one else!"

Justin sighed with pent-up frustration. His breath came out in little white puffs as he said, "There's no way. Even if we could bring Dad over, the exertion would kill him. Not to mention the shock of all this."

Chris nodded. "What then? If the police storm the place, the boys could be hurt."

Sgt. Perez tried again. "Listen, Bryden, let the boys go. They haven't done anything to you. Your gripe is with their granddad."

A half hour passed. Perez tried three more times, but Bryden remained silent. Then, unexpectedly he shouted out, "Send in some food. These boys are hungry."

Robyn looked questioningly at Justin. "That sounds encouraging, doesn't it? He's thinking of the boys."

"Maybe, maybe not," said Justin. "Hard to tell what's up his sleeve."

"Listen, Bryden," Perez called back, "you'll all get a good hot meal as soon as you come out. Let's be a nice guy—okay? —before we all freeze out here!"

Robyn pulled her coat up tighter around her neck. Perez was right. They *were* freezing. She looked questioningly at Justin.

He brushed the frost from her hair. "Let's go to the drugstore. You girls need to warm up a little. Then maybe Chris and I can find a place that sells hamburgers at this time of morning."

"For the boys," Chris interjected. "Not us."

"I could use a strong, hot cup of coffee," said Laura.

Chris nodded. "I could use something stronger than that."

Justin told Perez, "We'll be across the street, Sergeant. Call us if anything happens."

"*Anything*," repeated Robyn.

Reluctantly they walked over to the drugstore and sat down at the lunch counter. Robyn gazed across at their weary reflections in the mirror as Justin ordered four coffees. While they waited, Robyn rubbed her hands together. They were numb. When her coffee arrived, she could hardly wrap her stiff fingers around the mug; but she swallowed the hot liquid gratefully, welcoming the warmth.

For a while she sat absorbed in her own thoughts—a whirlwind of memories of Eric, her only child. Eric's birth—the incredible pain and then the incredible joy, a squalling flesh-and-blood infant who nursed hungrily even as she lay with him cradled in her arms on the delivery table. Why was it?—whenever she feared harm for Eric, she always pictured him again as a baby. Her baby. No matter how old he grew or how independent he became, he would always be her baby.

But now, would he even have a chance to grow old? Silently, she prayed, *Please, God, please, please. Don't take him from me. He's Yours, but let him be mine a while longer too. I love him so much!*

"More coffee, Robyn?"

She looked at Justin. "What? Oh, no, I'm fine."

"What were you thinking about?"

"Eric. What else?"

"You looked so far away."

"I was remembering the day he was born."

"Me too," said Justin. "It seems so recent, like we've hardly had him at all." His voice broke slightly. "And I don't even know him."

Robyn wiped the moisture from her eyes. "He'll be all right. He has to be. Why would God let him get hurt?"

Justin shook his head ponderously. "That's the age-old question, isn't it? Why should anyone suffer? But we do. It happens every day. And we'll never know why one suffers and another is spared."

"I don't want a sermon—not now, Justin," Robyn said sharply. "We've got to believe. We have to have faith that Eric will be okay. Eric and Scott both."

Justin nodded. "I want that more than I've ever wanted anything in my life. But, Robyn, we've got to—"

Before he could finish, Chris reached over from his place at the counter and gripped Justin's shoulder. "Listen, Justin, I think we should call Mom. I don't want her hearing about this over the radio or TV. She's got to hear it from us."

"You're right, Chris. Do you want me to call her?"

Chris's brow furrowed. "Yeah. I think you're the one she'd want to hear it from."

"She was asleep when I left this morning," said Robyn. "I just left her a note saying there was a matter at the factory that needed our attention. I'm sure she's already worried, wondering what would call all of us away so suddenly."

"I'll call," said Justin, reaching into his pocket for some change. He was gone for several minutes. When he returned to the counter, his expression was even more troubled than before.

"What did she say?" asked Robyn.

"She was upset, naturally. And she's worried about Dad."

"Dad? What about Dad?" asked Chris.

"She says Dad's worse. The nurse had the television on in his room. He's having a lot of trouble breathing. She called the doctor. He should be there anytime."

Chris sighed deeply. "Well, that settles the question of involving Dad in all of this."

"Not really," Justin answered. "Do you know what Mom said? It's okay if we want to come get Dad. He'd want it that way. When I told her no, that we'd work it out, she offered to come and talk to Bryden. She was willing to sacrifice herself for her grandsons."

Laura began to weep.

"Chris, let's get back over there and see what's happening," said Justin. "The girls can wait here. We'll come back for you if there's any word."

Robyn was about to protest, but she whispered, "Go on over, but if there's any news—"

After the men had gone, Laura ordered more coffee and sipped it nervously. "I wish I had a cigarette," she said. "I gave them up when I was pregnant with Rudy, but I could sure use one now." She rubbed her fingertips over her eyes. In a monotone, she said, "I'm being punished, Robyn. I know it. I'm being punished."

Robyn looked at her in surprise. "Punished? Why?"

Laura shook her head slowly. "Because I'm a nagging wife and a shrew of a mother. I'm always yelling at Scott. You should hear me sometimes. And I ride Chris all the time. I hate our life. I've never been satisfied. I've always wanted him to be different, more confident and self-reliant. I've hated his family and I've hated myself for buttering them up. I'm such a hypocrite. I'm not a nice person, Robyn. Not deep down inside."

Robyn slipped her arm around Laura's shoulder. "I think you're a nice person, Laura. And I like you very much. I wish we lived closer so we could be better friends."

Laura managed a faint smile. "I wish that too, Robyn. Somehow I feel like we understand each other."

"We do. In ways that need no words."

Laura took another swallow of coffee and said, "I'd better go call home and see how Lauralee is doing with Rudy. She must be sick with worry about Scott too."

"Give her my love," said Robyn.

As Laura headed for the phone, Robyn realized that she was sitting alone at the counter. It was still too early for many customers. She shivered, feeling a bone-coldness that didn't come from the weather outside. She wished that she were somewhere private where she could cry out aloud to God and beg His mercy, where she could scream to the heavens that she needed her son, the precious child of her flesh and her heart. But here, at the Rexall Drug lunch counter where she had sipped sodas and munched hamburgers throughout her youth, she could not pray aloud or scream out to God for mercy. She could only sit and sip coffee and pretend that her world wasn't about to collapse.

Then she spotted him in the mirror—Alex, standing just behind her, saying, "Robyn, are you all right?"

She whirled around and looked up at him. "What are you doing here, Alex?"

He sat down beside her. "Justin told me you were over here."

"The boys—?"

"Nothing yet. I can't believe it, Robyn, that Bryden would go off the edge like this. But I don't think he would harm the boys—"

"How can you be sure, Alex?" The question was tinged with desperation.

He folded his large hands on the counter as if he were about to say grace. "I can't be sure, Robyn. But call it a gut instinct. Bryden's pulled some shenanigans, but he's never harmed a flea."

"Thank you, Alex," Robyn said softly.

"What for?"

"For making me feel better. Reassuring me. You don't know how I need it."

"I think I do." He reached over and took her hand and gently touched her wedding ring. "The other day at the office, Robyn, and again when we were alone at lunch on Sunday, I told you how you've made me feel something again—"

"Don't, Alex—please. Please, don't."

"I have to, Robyn." He turned on the luncheon stool and forced her to look directly at him. "I have to apologize to you. I had such a mixture of emotions and old memories. When I talked with you, I realized how much I missed Deanna. Oh, not at first. I thought it was you. Us. The old days."

"Alex, don't go on—"

He kept his hand firmly on hers. "Hear me out, Robyn. It's best for both of us." He seemed to be groping for the right words. "I sensed something in you, Robyn. An uncertainty. A loneliness. I misread it—"

She tried to pull her hand free, wanted to scream out at him, *My son is being held hostage, is perhaps wounded and dying, and we sit here talking of things that should never be!* But then she noted something in Alex's gaze. A plea for understanding. A gentleness.

"Believe it or not, Robyn, I was going to call you today. Risk everything. Seek you out. Yes, ruin my walk with God—to have you back again. And then—then all of this happened." He nodded toward the factory. "Even then, I wanted to be with you, to help and comfort you." He smiled sadly. "But when I took you and Laura to your husbands—when you saw Justin, you broke away from me. You ran into Justin's arms, where you belonged. I realized then that he was the one you wanted, the one you needed. Whatever was troubling you the other day, I know now that you and Justin belong together."

Robyn was crying now. "That's when I knew it too, when he held me there in his arms."

Tears rimmed Alex's eyes. "Will you forgive me, Robyn, for wanting you again, for thinking it was possible to go back?"

"If you'll forgive me, Alex . . ."

"I thank you, Robyn, for making me realize that I'll be able to love someone again someday. I've been so afraid of feeling anything since Deanna's death."

"I understand. You must have gone through such pain—"

"I'm getting better, thanks to you." He released her hand and ordered a black coffee; then he looked back at her. "I just wish I could do something now to help you."

"The only thing that will help me is seeing Eric come out of that building—alive."

"He will. I'm sure of it."

"Say a prayer for him, Alex."

He gave her a long, lingering look. "If things were different, Robyn . . . if we were young again . . ."

"But we're not, Alex. We're who we are, who we've always been . . . we can't change that . . ."

"Ships passing in the night," he quipped softly.

She smiled. "Something like that."

Suddenly there was the sound of hurried footsteps behind them. Robyn turned, her lips parting with an unspoken question. It was Justin, striding toward her, his gloved hand reaching out for her. "Come on, hon. The police are going to storm the factory!"

25

As JUSTIN ran with Robyn back across the street toward the central offices of Cahill Manufacturing, a television newswoman stepped in front of them and stuck a microphone in his face. "Rev. Cahill, can you tell us how you feel about the man holding your son hostage? As a minister, will you be able to forgive him if he harms your son?"

Justin shoved the microphone away and kept running.

"Rev. Cahill," she called after him, "are you optimistic that the police will be able to rescue your son?"

Justin drew Robyn protectively against him as they made their way through the growing throng of police, newspeople, and curious onlookers. "Oh, Justin," Robyn gasped, "they're turning this into a circus."

"Don't look at them, don't think about them," he told her. "Let's just concentrate on getting Scott and Eric free."

They made their way over to Sgt. Perez who stood beside the police car with the bullhorn. Justin spoke first. "Sgt. Perez, I want you to tell my wife what you told me." He looked around. "Just a minute. My brother and his wife are here too."

Perez eyed the two couples, and then said, "Bryden called out a warning a few minutes ago. He said we have until noon to produce Victor Cahill. If your father doesn't show, he's going to—uh—he said he'll shoot one of the boys."

"Oh, dear God, no!" Robyn said under her breath. She swooned against Justin, but he held her steady. *But who would hold him up?* he wondered fleetingly.

"Is Bryden serious?" asked Chris.

"We have no choice but to believe him."

Justin's cheek pulsated. "You said you would storm the place. Go for it."

"Right. With less than an hour before Bryden says he'll carry out his threat, we can't wait any longer."

"Can you take Bryden by surprise?" Justin asked.

Sgt. Perez nodded. "We sure hope so. We'll have one of our men talking to him, keeping him distracted, while two of the boys circle around and try entering by another route." He turned to Chris. "Mr. Cahill, here's where you can help us out. We sent for a plot plan of the building. Take a look at the blueprint and give us your opinion of the best route to your father's office."

"I'll do what I can," said Chris.

The officers conferred with Chris for several minutes; then Sgt. Perez drew two of his men aside and spoke privately with them. Finally he returned to Justin and said, "We're going to try to take Bryden off guard. Send up a prayer this works."

Justin nodded. As he watched the two officers dart stealthily around the building, he felt his own muscles grow taut as high-tension wires. There was a rock in his gut and an ache in his chest for his boy. *God—Father God—spare my son. Don't ask me to give him up. I'm not strong enough.*

Sgt. Perez stepped over to the loud speaker and shouted, "Hey, Bryden, can you hear me? Listen, we're gonna get some lunch for you and the boys. How about it? You hungry? I bet those boys could eat a horse. You said a while back you wanted us to get you some burgers."

"What's the catch?" Bryden shouted back.

"No catch, man," said Perez. "You said the boys were hungry. We figure after all these hours the three of you could use some nourishment. If you don't want hamburgers, how about those chicken nugget things the Colonel peddles?"

"No, we'll have the bur—"

A shot rang out. Then another.

"Oh, dear Lord, no!" cried Robyn.

The two officers came running from the building. One was wounded.

"You've done it now, cops!" Bryden shouted from Cahill's office. "You and your tricks! You made me kill one of the boys!"

Shock radiated through Justin's frame. He whispered, "Oh, God, don't let it be my son!"

Robyn sank against him and moaned, "No, no, no!"

The wounded officer confirmed their worst fears. "Sergeant, one of the boys took a hit. I don't know which one. I don't know how bad."

"What about you? Where were you hit?"

"A bullet grazed my shoulder, but I'm okay."

"What happened in there?" demanded Perez.

The officer gestured with his good arm. "Bryden spotted us before we could get him. We didn't dare shoot. The boys were too close. Bryden fired and hit my shoulder. He would have shot me dead if the boy hadn't lunged and deflected the weapon. He took the bullet instead."

Perez shook his head and turned toward the ambulance driver. "Over here on the double. We've got a wounded officer and a boy who was hit. It could be bad."

Justin gripped the sergeant's arm. "We've got to get those boys out of there. One may be dying . . . or dead!"

"We know, Reverend. We're doing the best we can."

"I'm going in," Justin announced. "Maybe Bryden will let me take the boys' place."

"No way, Reverend. That'd be suicide."

"Wait, Justin's right," said Chris. "If Bryden wants revenge against our father, who better to take hostage than Victor Cahill's sons? Both of us. Not his grandsons."

"You tried that before. It didn't work."

"Just let us talk to Bryden again," urged Justin. "It may be our only chance."

"All right, we'll give it our best shot," said Perez. "Come on."

Robyn clasped Justin's arm. "You can't risk your life like that, darling. I can't lose you both."

Justin drew her against him and nuzzled the top of her head. There were snow flurries in her hair. "I'll be careful, darling. Just remember how much I love you."

She held on to him, refusing to let go. "I love you too."

Gently, Justin held her at arm's length. She was crying, the tears glistening like ice crystals on her cheeks. He turned to his brother. "Listen, Chris, I have a plan. Remember when we were kids, how we used to . . . ?" He lowered his voice and talked privately with Chris for a minute. Then they approached the vehicle with the bullhorn and spoke with Sgt. Perez.

"No foolhardy heroics now," Perez warned. "I'll let you try to coax Bryden out here, but I won't let you two go inside."

"We'll do what we have to do," Justin said under his breath.

Moments later, the wintry morning silence was broken by the sound of Justin's voice booming over the loud speaker. "Mr. Bryden, can you hear me? This is Rev. Cahill, Victor Cahill's son. My brother and I have a proposition for you. Are you listening?"

"Yeah, I hear you," came the voice from inside the building.

"My brother and I want to trade places with our boys. It makes sense, Bryden. If you have a problem with our dad, we're the ones to deal with. We're the ones who can make things right for you."

"You can't make things right," Bryden shouted. "My little girl's dead!"

"And now one of our sons may be dead too, Bryden," Justin called back. "In respect for your daughter and our son, let's stop this violence and talk together like reasonable adults. We'll listen to whatever you have to say, and we'll do what we can to help you!"

For a minute there was no response. Then Bryden shouted, "Okay, you got a deal!" He paused for a long moment before adding darkly, "Only one boy's alive. I'll bring him out and trade him for you two. Only, no double-crosses, you hear?"

Justin felt a lump rise in his throat. *Only one boy's alive.* A sharp jolt struck him in his middle. He met Chris's gaze. It was a tragic irony. They were both waiting to learn whose son had died, whose had survived. As automatically as breathing, Justin sent up prayers that had no words . . . groanings that could not be uttered.

Suddenly, there was a noise inside the building, a door opening and shutting. Then, incredibly, there stood Richard Bryden in the doorway, holding Scott in front of him like a shield.

Scott! Scott alive—not Eric! Oh, God, no, how could You let it be Eric! Justin felt himself reel momentarily, heard Robyn scream behind him. Tears dotted his eyelashes and turned to ice crystals; his nose ran and became frost above his lip. Rage pierced his heart.

Chris was weeping too, with relief and joy. "Scott, you okay, boy?"

"Yeah, Dad, . . . but he got Eric! He's not moving, Dad. He's all bloody!"

Instinctively Justin fell into step beside Chris. *Keep moving,* he told himself. *Block out the pain. Don't think about Eric now. Dear God, just get us out of this!*

As he and Chris approached the office building, Justin spotted the weapon Bryden held against Scott's temple. With a fresh wave of panic, Justin realized they weren't out of the woods yet. At any moment, Bryden could pull the trigger and Scott would die too.

From the corner of his eye Justin glanced at Chris. Chris's eyes were fixed on Bryden, but he closed his left fist briefly, then flexed his fingers. Their signal. Almost imperceptibly, even as they continued walking toward Bryden, Justin began moving away from Chris. With each step, Chris moved to the right, Justin to the left.

As the distance between the brothers widened, Bryden shouted angrily, "Get back together, you two. Come on, what's going on? Whaddaya think you're pulling?"

Justin paced himself at a slow, measured gait, staying even with Chris, but constantly lengthening the space between them. His heart hammered in his chest, maintaining a strange rhythm with his stride. In a bizarre sense, it was like a carefully orchestrated game, like something he and Chris might have played in their youth. He and Chris were only a couple of yards now from the doorway, one on each side of Bryden.

Bryden looked confused. He had to turn his head to look from one brother to the other. His thick-jowled face was ruddy from the cold and reddening with rage. "Stop or I'll shoot!" he demanded.

"You'll get only one of us," warned Chris. "And the other one will get you."

"Okay, so you wanna play games?" Bryden challenged, cocking his revolver against Scott's head.

Chris shouted, "No, Bryden!"

Bryden glanced Chris's way. Instinctively, Justin leapt forward and slammed the weapon from Bryden's hand. Even as Bryden scrambled to retrieve his gun, police officers converged on him, immobilized him and took him into custody. Justin stood momentarily dazed by the confusion of the moment—police, newspeople, and bystanders swarming over the area, Chris and Laura gratefully wrapping their son in their arms, Robyn running to Justin and clutching him to her. Before Robyn could utter a word, Justin said with a start, "Eric. He's inside."

They broke into a run, bolting into the Cahill lobby and down the hall to his father's office. Two policemen and a paramedic were already inside, kneeling over the sprawled body of his son. Justin bent down beside them. "Is he—?"

"We found a heartbeat, Rev. Cahill, but it's thready. Only God knows if he'll make it!"

26

ROBYN CLUTCHED Justin's arm as he sped along the snowy streets following the screaming ambulance to Southfield General Hospital. The shrill siren song could have been her own mournful lament. Eric was in that ambulance. Her son. Her only child. He was barely alive . . . but at least he was alive. Or maybe by now he was dead. No, she couldn't think like that, refused to entertain the possibility.

But it was more than a possibility. Face it. Eric was dying. She had seen it in the faces of the attendants as they worked on him, as they lifted him into the ambulance and slammed the doors with such finality. She should have ridden with Eric in the ambulance; she could have; she had considered the possibility and then decided to ride with Justin.

He needed her. She could see it in the tautness of his expression, the desperate glint in his eyes. How rarely she had seen the look of need in his face. She knew, as a man of God . . . a man of faith, Justin could not bear to be anything less than invincible, or at least he needed to *appear* invincible.

But now all the masks and defenses were gone; raw neediness was evident in every line and angle of his features. It was the same shameless, blatant neediness that Robyn felt now too. Emotional or spiritual neediness did not terrify her the way it terrified Justin. She was too well acquainted with her own weaknesses to deny their existence.

It struck her suddenly that these shattering moments ahead would test her frailty to the limits. Would she survive them? Would God ask more of her than she could handle? God's Word said that He would not, that He would give her grace to endure. Why then did she feel as if she might fly apart? Why did she feel as if her emotions were hanging by a tenuous thread?

Oh, God, help us! Please help us! Please spare my son!

Robyn's silent pleas snapped as she turned her attention to the road ahead. Justin was entering the emergency parking area and pulling up now near the ambulance. She could hear the tires crunch in the rutted snow. As Justin turned off the ignition, Robyn jumped from the car, hoping against hope to catch a glimpse of Eric as they whisked him into the emergency room.

But she was too late. The attendants were already entering the emergency room and pushing the gurney that held Eric's still form down the hall, where they disappeared quickly behind closed doors. There was nothing now for Justin and Robyn to do but go to the information desk and sign the necessary papers. They performed the task with a dutiful numbness. Name and address. Insurance carrier. Social Security numbers. Information about Eric. *Eric, my baby. No, he's a little boy. No, a high schooler. Almost a man.* The blank spaces seemed endless. When they had finished, the receptionist smiled politely and told them to have a seat in the waiting room.

"But what about our son?" Robyn cried. "When can we see him?"

"The doctor will be out after he's examined him, Mrs. Cahill."

Robyn wanted to shout at the woman, *Is he dead? Is my son dead?* But she shunned the idea of introducing death into the conversation. Even speaking the word aloud would give it a grim reality Robyn wasn't prepared to cope with. She and Justin had no choice but to retreat to the waiting room . . . and *wait.*

Ten minutes passed. Fifteen. Robyn and Justin sat like zombies in the nearly empty waiting room. Patients came and went. A young woman with a crying baby. A man with a broken arm. An elderly woman in a wheelchair. Robyn watched them all with a remote curiosity. Justin missed them all, sitting forward on the vinyl sofa with his elbows on his knees, his head in his hands. He was so quiet she wondered if he were praying. Somehow she resented the idea, as if he had gone into his closet with God without inviting her. After all, this was the most devastating moment of their lives. They needed to share it together. How dare Justin shut her out and leave her comfortless while he alone found consolation in their God?

I'm crazy, thinking these thoughts, she told herself. She clasped Justin's arm. "Are you okay, honey?"

He looked over at her and blinked as if he were not quite sure where he was. She repeated her question and he said quickly, "Yes. You?"

"Terrified," she whispered.

"They've taken long enough," he said impatiently. "I'm going up there and demand to see someone." He stood up and straightened his shoulders. His clothes looked rumpled. Robyn couldn't recall ever seeing him look so disheveled, except when he wore his workaday clothes for gardening or puttering with the car.

Robyn trailed him back to the reception desk. She had a feeling the receptionist was about to resort to evasive tactics when a fortyish, sober-faced physician emerged from a nearby room. He strode directly over to Justin and Robyn and held out his hand. Even as he greeted them, he withheld a smile. "Reverend and Mrs. Cahill? I'm Dr. Ferris."

"How's our son?" asked Justin, his voice gravelly with emotion. "How's Eric?"

"Your son is alive," Dr. Ferris answered.

"Will he be all right?" cried Robyn.

"Let's go over here and sit down, and we'll talk."

They followed the doctor over to a private alcove and sat down.

The physician cleared his throat, and then spoke with a precise modulation. "Your son's condition is critical. He's being prepped now for emergency surgery."

"Surgery?" echoed Robyn as if the word were foreign to her.

Dr. Ferris nodded. His voice was calm, almost matter of fact. "We'll need your permission, Mrs. Cahill."

"For what?"

"The bullet is lodged near his heart. It's in an extremely dangerous position, but it must be removed."

"Will he be all right?" Robyn ventured again, her voice barely a whisper.

For the first time, Dr. Ferris's expression softened. "I don't know. If he survives the surgery, he has only a fifty/fifty chance of recovery."

"You're saying Eric might not live?" Justin uttered incredulously. "He might die in surgery? He can't—!"

"We'll do our best," Dr. Ferris replied. "I must go now. The surgery can't wait. Dr. Ben Randolph will be there. He's one of the best cardiac surgeons in the state."

Robyn and Justin returned to the empty waiting room. As Justin sat down, Robyn said, "I'd better go call Laura. I promised I'd telephone as soon as there was some word on Eric."

"Let me call," said Justin. "I want to find out how Dad's doing after his spell earlier today. And Mom's probably beside herself with all that's happened."

"Give them my love," said Robyn absently.

Justin nodded. He was back a few minutes later. "They're okay," he said. "Everyone's there at Mom and Dad's. Dad's weaker, but Mom's holding her own. Chris and Laura are spending some time with Scott, but Chris will be over here once he has everyone settled."

"That's kind of him," said Robyn.

"Yeah. Know what else he said? 'Tell Robyn our prayers are with Eric.' It's the first time he's acknowledged that he prays."

"That means so much to me, Justin."

"Me too." He settled back on the vinyl sofa and rubbed his temples.

"One of your migraines?" she asked.

He nodded.

"I'll ask the nurse for something."

"No, don't bother. I'll be all right." He sat forward and put his head in his hands.

He remained motionless for so long that Robyn asked, "Are you okay, Justin?"

He didn't answer. She shook him and repeated the question. Still, he was silent, his face hidden from her.

"Justin, talk to me," she begged, gripping his arm. "Don't shut me out. I can't bear it."

He turned his face away. Suddenly his shoulders and back began to heave as he broke into great, wracking sobs.

Robyn was stunned. She had never seen Justin weep, let alone dissolve into such convulsive grief. He was out of control. She tried to gather him into her arms, but she could not contain him, could not absorb his torment. Mournful sounds of pain and regret erupted from deep within him and echoed hauntingly in the empty room.

For what seemed an eternity, he wept like a baby in her arms.

She spoke soothingly over and over. "It's okay, darling. Everything will be okay."

Then, as quickly as the torrent had broken, it ceased, and Justin drew himself up and squared his shoulders and dried his eyes and shut her out again. She clasped his hand, urging him to bid her enter the secret place of his feelings. But already his jaw was set and his mask back in place.

"Why did you cry? Tell me," she pleaded. "What are you feeling, Justin?"

"It's nothing. I'm okay now, Robyn. It's just the tension—"

"It was more, and you know it, Justin. It was more than Eric, more than your father, more than me. Tell me, Justin. What happened to you just now?"

He remained silent, methodically rubbing his hands together and flexing his fingers.

Robyn said quietly, "I'm frightened, Justin. If our marriage is to survive, you must let me in. If we're ever going to cope with what's happening to Eric, you must let me share your feelings. And let me share mine."

He shook his head ponderously. "You don't want to know."

"Yes, I do. Whatever it is. Tell me. We'll deal with it."

After a long, deliberate moment, he said softly, "I failed."

Had she heard right? "Failed?"

"Failed Eric. Failed you. Failed God."

"Justin, why on earth would you say such a thing?"

"It's true." His voice was a low monotone. "I'm a hypocrite."

"What?"

"Today, when I knew one of the boys had been shot, I said, 'Don't let it be my son.' Robyn, I wanted it to be Scott. I wanted Scott to die, not Eric. Even knowing that Scott's not a Christian and Eric is, if God had given me a choice, I would have said, 'Let Scott die.'"

Robyn reached over and rubbed Justin's forehead. "Darling, that's only human. No parent would choose death for his own child. I felt it too. You can't expect to be rational at a time like that. God understands. He forgives."

Justin gazed intently at her. "That's just it, Robyn. God may forgive me, but I can't forgive myself."

Robyn uttered a sigh of dismay. "Oh, Justin . . ."

"I caught a glimpse of myself today, Robyn," he continued unevenly, "and I hated what I saw. I saw a man who wants to be perfect when only God can be perfect—a man whose eyes have been fixed on himself, on his own achievements and weaknesses, when his eyes should have been fixed firmly on Christ. I am not worthy to serve God or His people, Robyn. I'm not worthy to utter His name."

"Justin, are you saying you don't feel you belong in the ministry?"

"I'm saying I'm too flawed to serve Him effectively. I want Chris to come to know God, and yet today I would have chosen his son to die over Eric. Even now I feel that way. I'd trade Scott's life for Eric's. Don't you see, Robyn? I'm not the person I thought I knew. I had an image of myself all tied up in a neat little package, but I'm not that person at all. I don't know who I am, or what I am. All I know is, I'm ashamed, Robyn. I don't like the man I've discovered inside me."

"So you're ready to give up before you bring shame on the name of God?"

He coughed uneasily. "I don't know—"

Robyn clasped his arm urgently. "Listen, Justin. Listen to me. You are not the glory of God. I'm not either. Only Christ is the glory of God. Even if you met every standard of excellence you require of yourself or that you think your dad or others require, you still fall short of God's standard. We all do. That's the message of Christ, the message you try to give to the world. Don't hold up the messenger as the example, or you'll fail every time. Hold up the *message*, darling, that God can save the worst of sinners . . . even you and me, Justin."

Tenderly he drew her into his arms and buried his face in her hair. "Oh, Robyn, my little Robyn." He held her that way for what seemed forever, until she could feel the wetness of his tears against her scalp.

He held her until she heard Dr. Ferris in the doorway saying, "Your son made it through surgery. He's in the recovery room. We can only wait now. And hope."

27

JUSTIN AND Robyn arrived back at the Cahill homestead short-ly after dusk. Chris, who had joined them at the hospital, returned now to his parents' home too. Laura met them at the door with little Rudy in her arms. The toddler stretched his pudgy arms out to Chris and squealed, "Da-dee, Da-dee!" Laughing, Chris gathered him into his arms and squeezed him tight.

Laura turned questioningly to Justin. "How's Eric?"

"He made it through the surgery." Justin removed his overcoat with a weariness that shot through every muscle.

"The doctor hasn't held out much hope," said Robyn, slip-ping out of her coat. "But he was quite encouraged that Eric made it through surgery."

"Will he be okay?" Laura asked, her voice tentative.

"We don't know yet," said Justin. "The doctor says the next few days will tell the story." His voice broke. "It could still go either way."

Laura took Rudy back from Chris. "Did you see Eric?"

"Just for a few minutes." Robyn sat down on the sofa. "He was asleep, or unconscious, I'm not sure which. He had all these tubes in him, and he was hooked up to these strange machines. He looked awful. So still. So vulnerable."

"Where's Scott?" Chris asked, looking around.

"Upstairs in the spare bedroom. He was so upset. The doc-tor gave him something to help him sleep."

"Then you're all spending the night?" asked Robyn.

Laura nodded. "We figured we should be close by, for you guys . . . and for Mom and Dad Cahill."

"How is Dad?" asked Justin.

"Your mother's upstairs with him," said Laura. "He knew something was wrong. He heard bits and pieces on the TV. So your mother felt she had to tell him about Bryden taking the boys hostage."

"I'm not sure that was a good idea," said Justin.

"She told him while the doctor was here, in case he had an adverse reaction. But he seemed to handle it all right."

"Good. I'd better go on up and check on him."

Laura nodded. "I made a big pot of chili, whenever you're hungry. It might help to warm you up. I don't know about you all, but I haven't been able to stop shivering."

"That's nerves, Laura, not just the weather," said Robyn. "I feel the same way, trembling inside and weak-kneed."

"Well, listen, I'll dish us up some chili. But first I'd better call Lauralee. She just went over to Kaylie's. Those girls are beside themselves worrying about Eric. They would have been right there at the hospital with you this afternoon if I'd let them. I told them I'd call the minute you got home."

Justin headed upstairs to see his father. His mother was just leaving the room as he approached the door. "How's Dad?" he asked.

"Better than this morning," she said. She gripped his arm. "Son, how's Eric?"

"He's alive, Mom." Justin repeated what the doctor had said.

"We'll keep him in our prayers, Son," his mother said softly. There were tears in her eyes.

"Thanks, Mom." He leaned down and kissed the top of her head. "Thanks, too, for offering to come talk to Bryden at the factory today. That means a lot to me."

"I meant it, Son. And your father would have been there too."

"I know, Mom. I need to see Dad. I'll be downstairs in a few minutes."

"Take your time, Son. Your dad's eager to see you too."

Quietly Justin entered his father's room and walked over to the bedside.

"Justin? That you? How's my grandson?"

Justin sat down in the chair beside the bed and repeated the words he had just told his mother. Each time he said it, the grim reality struck him afresh, like a lancer's blow.

"The boy's made of strong stock," said his father, his voice raspy but full of conviction. "He'll pull through."

"I pray to God he does," said Justin. "I just don't think I—" His voice broke and his throat filled with a lump that ached all the way to his chest. He could feel the tears coming again. He hadn't wept in twenty years, and now twice in one day? With a wave of horror, he thought, *Oh, God, I can't—not now, not in front of my father!*

But the sobs came, rippling over him uncontrollably. He fumbled for his handkerchief and blew his nose and turned his face away in shame. "I'm sorry, Dad," he said when he found his voice again.

Unexpectedly he felt a hand on his arm. He looked around. Amazingly, his father was weeping too. Great tears rolled from the wrinkled, runneled face. Justin grasped the familiar, ancient hand in his own and pressed it against the wetness of his cheek.

"Dad, I don't know what to say," he tried again, his voice swollen with emotion. "I always thought I had an answer for everything, but right now I'm—empty. Worse than empty. I'm going to lose him, Dad. I may lose Eric. And you too. I didn't know it could hurt like this!"

"You're a strong man, Justin. You'll do what you have to do."

Justin shook his head. "I thought I was strong, but today—today every preconceived notion I had about myself was shattered."

"That's the shock talking," said his father, his breathing labored. His eyelids drooped, and then opened again. "You'll be your old self in the morning, Son."

"No, I don't think so, Dad. I—I hope not." He studied his father's graying pallor. "Am I tiring you, Dad? Maybe I'd better let you rest."

"No, stay here. I've got an eternity to rest."

The two men were silent for a minute. Justin listened to his father's uneven breathing. He realized he was still holding

217

his father's hand. He couldn't remember their ever holding hands in his entire life, certainly not since he was a very young child. Now, he felt strangely warmed by his father's touch, reassured. Was it possible? *Comforted.*

He said quietly, "Dad, I have something to ask you."

"What?" There was a note of suspicion in the gravelly voice.

"Dad, will you—" Justin groped for the words. "—forgive me?"

His father's feathery brows shot up in astonishment. "Forgive?"

Justin struggled to keep his voice even. "I've failed you, Dad. I—I've failed the whole family. I've been proud, resentful, unyielding . . . unloving."

His father eyed him skeptically and growled, "I expected a sermon, not a confession."

"I know. I've always felt more comfortable preaching than expressing my feelings. Maybe that's the trouble."

"Nothing wrong with keeping your feelings to yourself, Son. My dad was that way, I was that way. You get it fairly."

"But sometimes there are things that should be said and never are. Either we're too proud or too busy or too blind to see what's really important."

"What are you saying, Son?"

Justin cleared his throat. "I'm saying my son may die and I don't recall ever telling him I loved him." His voice broke. "I don't want that to happen with you, Dad. I don't think we've ever said the words to each other—"

His father looked wary. "We don't need words. Isn't it already understood?"

"I don't know, Dad. Is it?" Justin squeezed his father's hand. "I—I love you, Dad."

His father turned his gaze away. Justin winced. Had he gone too far, said too much, embarrassed his father? After a long moment, the old man said huskily, "I love you too, Son."

Justin feared he might weep again. "Why didn't you ever tell me, Dad?"

"Tell you? I showed you. Everything I ever did was for you."

"I know that's . . . how you feel. But I felt like you were trying to—to control my life. I felt that I could never please you, Dad."

His father coughed fitfully, his chest rising and falling with the effort. Finally he barked, "Please me? You were the pride of my life. I gave you everything."

"All I ever really wanted . . . was your love."

His father said solemnly, "I didn't think my love mattered a whit to you."

Justin stared at his father in surprise. "How can you say that?"

"I figured as far as you were concerned, I was just an unrepentant sinner bound for hell."

Justin lowered his head in dismay. "Is that how I came across?"

"Isn't that the truth? Isn't that what you think of me?"

Justin weighed his words carefully. "My feelings for you are far too complex to put into words, Dad. I have felt great devotion, respect, awe, even fear. When I was growing up, I thought I could never measure up to what you were. I could never earn your love. Then my life changed. I came to know God. And suddenly my life had a whole new meaning, and I had Someone else to please. God Himself. The profundity—the immensity of it nearly blew me away—the fact that God cared about me. Loved me. I wanted you to have a taste of Him too, Dad. Know His love. Experience it for yourself. You don't know how it hurt when you wanted nothing to do with Him."

His father coughed, and then shook his head solemnly. "I didn't have anything against God. Still don't. I've got a healthy respect for the Almighty. It just irked me that you started looking up to Him instead of me. You wanted to go into His business and not mine. I figured I gave my life for you—"

"So did He," said Justin simply.

"Yeah, I guess so. Anyway, I couldn't tolerate you thinking of me as some heathen—"

"Dad, I only wanted to share the joy I'd found in Christ—"

"It's not that I don't believe, Son. I'm no atheist, you know."

"But have you ever accepted the gift of His love?"

"Maybe not officially."

Justin bent close to his father. "Listen, Dad, God loves you. He died so you could have eternal life—"

"I don't go for a lot of hocus-pocus—"

"There's no hocus-pocus about it, Dad. It's very straightforward. By an act of your will you admit you need a Savior. You put your faith in Christ." Justin's voice rose with excitement. "Dad, it's like admitting that we can't fly by ourselves. We need an airplane. We can say it, but it doesn't mean anything until by faith we actually step onto that plane and have the experience of flying."

"Okay, okay, I get the picture—"

Justin slumped back in his chair. "I was doing it again, wasn't I? Preaching?"

"Why should I expect any different? It's what you are."

Justin felt strangely warmed by his father's remark. *It's what you are.* Had he finally accepted the fact?

Justin sat forward again. "I asked you a question earlier, Dad, but you never gave me an answer."

"What question?"

"I asked if you'd forgive me."

"You don't need to be forgiven," his father scoffed.

"Yes, Dad, I do," Justin persisted. "I've had hard feelings, against you, against the family. I was wrong, and I'm sorry. Will you forgive me?"

His father met his gaze, and then looked away self-consciously. "If you think you need it, you're—forgiven."

"Thank you, Dad." Justin sighed deeply. What he was about to say now could undo every gain he'd made in these past few minutes. "Dad, I've got to ask you something. I'll never be able to live with myself if I don't."

"What it it?" his father asked warily.

Justin's pulse raced. The words broke over his own deepfelt emotion. "Will you think about asking Christ into your life, Dad . . . giving Him a chance . . . giving yourself a chance to know Him personally?"

There was a long, unsettling silence. Something shifted in his father's expression, in the creases of his eyes and the folds of his jowls. His dry lips moved imperceptibly as if he were debating with himself before committing to a reply. At last he turned his somber gaze on Justin and said, "You've struck a chord deep down, boy. Something in your manner is different. You don't stir the antagonism in me. You stir something else, something I haven't felt since I was a boy wanting to reach out to my own father. I wish I could be what you want, but I can't. I'm no righteous Holy Joe. I can't pretend I am, for you or anyone else. I'm just me, Victor Cahill, a decent, God-fearing man. You're going to have to take me as I am."

Justin felt tears sting his eyes again. "That's just it, Dad. I do accept you as you are . . . at last. More important, so does God. He's always wanted to accept you . . . just as you are. No pretense, no sham. You don't have to make yourself good enough. You don't have to earn His love. It's yours just for the asking."

Are you listening, Justin? a small voice said within him. *Do you really hear what you're saying?* Yes, it was the lesson he himself needed to learn, over and over: *You don't have to earn God's love. It's yours for the asking.*

"I'll think about it," his father said.

"What?" Justin asked in surprise.

"I said, I'll think about what you said." He coughed, that deep, familiar, hacking sound. "I'm a proud, stubborn old man, Justin. God has a tall order if He wants to crack my hide, but I suppose it's possible. That's the best I can do for you tonight." He coughed again. "After all these years, I'm not about to be rushed into anything, even for God Almighty."

"But you will consider—," Justin said dubiously, sounding like a tongue-tied schoolboy.

"I said I would, didn't I, Justin? I'm a man of my word."

"Fine. That's all I ask." Justin stood up. "We'll talk again tomorrow, okay, Dad?"

His father nodded wearily. "Tomorrow then, Son."

28

LATER THAT evening, as the family prepared for bed, Robyn told Justin, "I know it's late, but I'd like to drive back over to the hospital and see Eric. I need to be with him, need to look at him and touch him and be sure he's still breathing."

Justin nodded. "I need to see him too."

They drove through a gently falling snow that had given the landscape a fresh coat of frosty glitter. The night air was crisp and dry and bitterly cold. Because it was so late, Justin had his pick of parking spots at Southfield General. He and Robyn ran from the car and went straight to the intensive care unit.

Eric was in the third cubicle, lying just as they had left him. Robyn looked up anxiously and whispered, "I wanted to come back over to reassure myself, but seeing him like this, so pale and lifeless, just brings the terrible reality of it back to me."

Justin had to admit he felt the same way—utterly powerless. He hated standing by helplessly while his son fought for his life. "There's only one thing we can do for him now, Robyn," he murmured, placing his hand on Eric's forehead. Earnestly he prayed, entreating God to have mercy on their son.

When he had finished praying, Justin leaned over the bed rail and talked to Eric as if he could hear him. "Son, you've had a part in something good for Grandpa. For the first time in my life I really believe my dad—your grandfather—is ready to accept Christ as his Savior. Do you know how long your mother and I have prayed for him, Eric? And now, mainly because of what happened to you, he's on the verge of making a commitment."

"So this terrible day has had one bright spot," said Robyn as she brushed Eric's hair from his forehead.

Before leaving Eric's hospital room, Robyn and Justin held hands across his bed. "Robyn," Justin said hoarsely, "I haven't told Eric I love him—not out loud, not since he's grown older. I'm afraid he won't know."

She gazed down at her son's face; then her eyes met Justin's. "Then tell him now, darling. Tell him while there's still time."

For the third time that day tears grazed Justin's cheeks. He leaned down, avoiding the tubes that served as Eric's lifeline. Then low in his ear he whispered, "Eric, my son, I love you. I have always loved you. And I'm so proud that you are my son."

When Robyn and Justin arrived home, the house was dark. "Everyone must already be asleep," Robyn whispered as they tiptoed up the stairs. Alone in their room, as they undressed for bed, Justin told her more about his conversation with his dad. "It's incredible. I've never seen him so open. Tomorrow I'll talk to him again. I can't tell you what it means to have this happen on the heels of such a tragic day. It's like the Lord has given me something to hold on to, a sign of hope."

He climbed into bed and stretched out on his back, his eyes on Robyn. He watched as she slipped a shimmering night-gown over her naked body. Suddenly he felt fire in his groin, an overwhelming sense of longing to take her in his arms. But he held back, horrified that he sought such comfort from Robyn when their son lay alone in a hospital bed fighting for his life. But there was something else that quelled his desire too—the deep, instinctive fear that his manhood was gone.

Robyn sat down on the bed and absently ran her hand over the eiderdown quilt. She smiled at him, but there were lines of sadness etched in her face. "Do you know what I considered a sign of hope, Justin?"

He reached over and turned off the light as she slipped between the sheets. In the darkness, he edged closer to her warmth. "What did you consider a sign of hope?"

"Your openness today at the hospital. Your tears."

"Three times in one day," he murmured. "Some sort of record."

"I never felt closer to you, Justin."

He slipped his arm around her and drew her close. "We've got to hang in there together, or we'll never get through this."

"I wasn't sure that's what you wanted," she said softly.

"What? You mean, being close? Why wouldn't I want it?"

Silence, then: "I wasn't sure you loved me anymore, Justin."

Her words sent new shock waves through his body. "What are you talking about, Robyn? Of course I love you."

"Then why haven't you . . . shown it?"

"I do, Robyn."

"You haven't . . . for a long time."

His pulse increased. He felt suddenly on the defensive. "Listen, Robyn, after all we've been through today, I don't think this is the proper time to discuss our sex life."

"It's because of what we've been through that we need to get things out in the open." Her voice sounded resolute but wounded. "If you don't find me attractive anymore, Justin, then tell me what I can do to change things."

He rolled over on his side, still holding her against him. "Darling, you're more beautiful now than the day we were married." He kissed her face and realized she was crying. He could taste the salt of her tears on his lips. The knowledge of her pain filled him with wrenching guilt. How could it have happened? In trying to protect himself, he had hurt the woman he loved.

She said urgently, "If you still want me, then why do you always turn away?"

"I don't," he said quickly. "Life is busy. I'm tired. I have things on my mind. But I never meant for you to take it personally."

She made a little sound in her throat, like a scoffing laugh. "Not take it personally? Justin, how else could I take it?"

He wracked his mind for another excuse, a way out, anything to derail this conversation before he said something he would regret. "We'd better get some sleep, hon. We're going to need all our strength for Eric tomorrow."

"Oh, Justin, you were so open today at the hospital. Why are you pulling away from me now?"

"I'm not, Robyn. I'm just dead tired. After what happened today to Eric, sex should be the last thing on our minds."

"It's not just sex. That's only part of it."

He kissed her on the forehead. "I promise, honey, one of these days when things get back on an even keel, we'll talk this all out, okay?"

There was a long, weighty silence. Justin wondered for a moment whether Robyn had fallen asleep. Then, just as he felt himself beginning to doze off, she said matter-of-factly, "I thought I might still be in love with Alex Lanigan."

Every nerve in Justin's body jumped to attention. He leaned up on one elbow and stared down at Robyn through the darkness. He couldn't see her face, only the shadowy outline of her head. "What are you talking about?"

"Alex Lanigan. I didn't know how I'd feel about him when I saw him again after all these years. I still had feelings for him, Justin."

Justin's voice came out labored and rocky. "Are you telling me you still love Alex?"

"No, not the way you mean. I care about him. I'm even still attracted to him. But I love only you."

He settled back down. "Then why are we having this conversation?"

Her voice was light and soft. "Because for a while I wasn't sure how I felt, and the confusion made me feel guilty and afraid."

"Afraid? You mean, of what you might do with Alex? Are you telling me he came on to you?"

"No, Justin. He still has feelings for me, I suppose, but I was never tempted to—well, you know, to have an affair with him—"

"I should hope not," Justin snapped. An irrational anger surged through him. He was suddenly angry with Robyn, angry with Alex, angry at himself. Why did Robyn have to bring up such a distasteful subject now when all he wanted to do was sleep? "I considered Alex my friend," he grunted. "And here all the time he was making a play for my wife."

"He was not!" Robyn protested. "Not really. He's lonely and hurting too, you know. And I was just trying to be as open with you about my feelings as you were with me today, but obviously I was wrong to mention Alex." She rolled over abruptly, away from him. "Good night, Justin. Like you said, we'll talk some other time."

He reached out and massaged her shoulder. "Listen, sweetheart, you threw this at me from left field. I never thought about you still having feelings for Alex, but I guess it stands to reason. He's a nice guy, you loved him once—"

"It has nothing to do with Alex," she retorted. "It has everything to do with you."

An edge of resentment crept into his voice. "Now what is that supposed to mean?"

She turned back toward him. "You make me feel lonely, Justin, and unwanted. I can lie here in bed beside you and feel like I'm all alone. Do you know what that does to me, to feel so cut off from you, to feel you recoil from my touch? I need . . . tenderness. I need you, Justin, the way it used to be."

He pulled her against him so that the planes and angles of her body fit his like a puzzle. They lay that way for several minutes, both of them silent, resting in each other's arms. He knew she was waiting for him to prove that what she feared wasn't true; she was still desirable to him.

He drew in a deep, shuddering breath and said, "I want to love you, Robyn, I long to . . . but I'm not sure I can."

"—Not sure you love me?" she echoed in dismay.

"No. Not sure of myself."

"I don't understand."

He gently rubbed her bare arm. "It's not easy to say, Robyn."

"Tell me, Justin. Please. I need to know."

He grappled for the right words. He could feel his heart hammering against his rib cage. He wondered if Robyn could feel it too. "It's just that sometimes lately when we started to make love, Robyn, you thought I lost interest. That wasn't the problem. The problem was I—I couldn't do it. I don't know why. All I know is that the more it happened, the more I dreaded risking failure again."

There was silence for a few moments as the meaning of Justin's words took hold. Then: "Oh, Justin, my poor darling." Robyn's voice was filled with amazement and relief. "Why didn't you just say so? Right from the beginning? I would have understood. We could have gotten help. We still can. We will!"

"You're right, honey. I just figured I could deal with it myself. I felt—I guess I felt ashamed."

"Oh, Justin, I thought it was because you didn't love me anymore!"

He kissed her lightly on the lips. "Nothing could be further from the truth, my darling. I realized it today more than ever, when I thought we might lose everything we've built together, . . . and even more so now that we're fighting for Eric's life."

"Justin, I need you so."

"You're trembling. What's wrong?"

"It's just—we've come so close to death today. It still hovers over us even now. I feel the horror of it, its icy fingers in my veins."

"You feel warm to me."

"But I'm cold inside. Nerves, I guess. I can't stop shaking."

"Relax, sweetheart. That's it. Let yourself unwind."

"I love you, Justin," she whispered. "Hold me. No promises, no expectations. Just be close to me."

Huskily he said, "I love you, Robyn. Terribly."

"Whatever happens, Justin—"

"Yes, whatever happens—" Slowly, hungrily he kissed her face, her eyelids, her lips.

"—Whatever happens," she murmured dreamily, ". . . we fall asleep . . . in each other's arms."

29

Justin dreamed.

In his dream he and Chris were young again and stood in the Southfield High football field facing Richard Bryden. Bryden was laughing and jeering, saying over and over, "You'll never see your son again!" Then, out of the blue, Eric was there, beside Bryden, shouting, "Do something, Dad! Do something!"

But Justin couldn't move; it was as if he were frozen to the spot. He turned to Chris and cried, "I'm powerless! I can't help my son!"

Chris only threw up his hands and said, "You know me. Dad doesn't think I've got what it takes. I can't help Eric either."

Justin looked around frantically and saw the young, smiling faces of his boyhood friends, but none of them seemed aware of his dilemma. They were running, darting across the field, playing a game of touch football.

Then, suddenly, Justin was no longer in the football field but in a long, narrow room with gray walls. He squinted through the shadows and spotted his father in a hospital bed. Urgently he called out, "Dad, you're the most powerful man I know. Save Eric!" But the old man shook his head and said, "I'm too sick to help Eric, . . . but I'll listen to what you have to say, Son. I'll try your faith. For the first time in your life, I'll be a real father to you."

Just as Justin reached out for his father, he heard Robyn's voice coming through the shadows. Sunlight washed away the darkness as she moved sinuously toward him. He heard her say, "Whatever happens, Justin, I love you." Then the sunlight broke, and Justin realized he was standing in his pulpit facing his congregation, and they were all chanting lyrically, "Whatever happens, Rev. Cahill, we want you!"

Justin woke with a start. The first pastel ribbons of dawn were spilling through the window, chasing away splinters of darkness. As the fragments of his dream dissipated, Justin's consciousness jolted him back to stark reality: Eric had been critically wounded yesterday; at this very moment, Justin didn't know whether the boy was dead or alive.

Still groggy with sleep, Justin made his way over to the phone and dialed the hospital. Not until the intensive care nurse assured him his son's current condition was "serious, but stable," did he let himself collapse back into bed and think of other things.

Like his father. And Robyn. Last night he had had the first positive conversation of his life with his father. Was it possible? The great Victor Cahill had agreed to consider the claims of Christ. It was Justin's first real breakthrough with the old man. As incredible as it seemed, the purpose of Justin's trip home to Southfield might still be accomplished. His father was open to the gospel.

And there was another bright spot. Robyn. Last night Justin had confessed to her the secret that had tormented him for so many months. And she had understood! Now, the possibility of his being impotent had lost a little of its nightmarish horror. His problem was something he and Robyn could deal with. It was not the end of the world.

He was not helpless. He was not powerless. He was not less of a man. *God has not given a spirit of fear, but of power, of love, of a sound mind . . .*

Justin reached over and touched Robyn's arm. She was sleeping soundly beside him, her auburn hair curling loosely around her face, her pale pink lips parted in slumber, her long lashes casting a fine shadow on her cheeks. Justin felt warmed, watching her. Somehow they would get through the days ahead; Eric would recover and they would take him home. They would be a family who knew how to face their problems and survive.

Just as Justin was about to doze off again, he heard someone stirring in another room. Probably his mother, he mused sleepily. She was nearly always up at dawn. His mind grew pleasantly fuzzy as he ebbed into sleep, but a muffled cry from another room snapped him back to wakefulness. He leaned up on one elbow.

Moments later he heard his mother's voice outside his door, sounding urgent, out of control. "Justin—Justin, are you awake?"

"Yes, Mom." He jumped out of bed, threw on his robe, and opened the door. "What's wrong, Mom?"

She looked small and fragile in her blue quilted robe. Her face was pale and her eyes filled with alarm; she was shivering. "Justin, your father—!"

Instinctively he knew. He dashed down the hall to his father's room. He heard his mother padding hurriedly after him, and Robyn behind her. He burst in the door and stared through the shadows at the bed. "Dad?" he said as he approached the sleeping form. But as he gazed down into his father's ashen face and vacant, staring eyes, the horrifying truth struck him. "Oh, my God," he uttered under his breath.

His mother went into his arms, weeping. "He's gone, Justin."

Justin held his mother close, pressing her head against his chest, but his gaze remained fixed on his father's gaunt, lifeless face. The eyes mesmerized him, sent shock waves through him. How could it be? How could his father be dead?

"What happened? Were you with him, Mom?"

"No, son. I—I just came in to check on him. Mrs. Pringle was due soon. I found him—" Her voice broke. "I found him like this. Oh, Justin, I wasn't even with him when he died!"

"He—he didn't suffer, Mom. He probably went in his sleep." Justin was mouthing the words automatically, saying the appropriate thing, but his mind screamed out against the terrible reality. *God, it can't be! It's too soon. I wasn't ready. He wasn't ready!*

Robyn was beside them now, wordlessly embracing Justin, and then wrapping her arms around her mother-in-law.

Justin leaned down and gently closed his father's unseeing eyes; then he placed his hand on the still forehead. The skin felt cold and smooth as a stone. "We must call Dad's doctor," he told his mother, his voice sounding tight and strangled. "And the coroner. And the funeral home."

His mother let out a muffled little sob.

"I'd better wake the family and tell them. Then I want you to sit down and rest while I make the necessary phone calls."

While Robyn stayed with his mother, Justin walked down the hall and woke Chris and Laura. They all gathered for a few moments of quietness around his father's bed and whispered their good-byes; then solemnly they filed downstairs. Laura fixed coffee while Robyn sat in the living room consoling Justin's mother.

Justin made his phone calls in a calm, perfunctory monotone. The doctor and coroner would be over within the hour; the funeral home would send a hearse as soon as the coroner called them to pick up the body. Dutifully Justin relayed the information to his mother.

"Son, I want to go back up and be with Dad," she said, standing unsteadily.

"Okay, Mom, I'll help you up."

Moments later, when Justin returned to the living room, fully dressed, Robyn said, "I called the hospital about Eric and they said he's holding his own.

Justin nodded. "I called an hour ago myself."

"When can we go over?" Robyn asked. "We've got to be there when he wakes up."

"Go get dressed," said Justin. "We'll wait for the doctor and coroner, and then run over before the hearse comes for Dad's body."

Robyn's expression looked as if it might shatter. "Oh, Justin, I can't believe all of this is happening."

He drew her into his arms. He wanted to say something, offer some comfort or reassurance, but his mind was blank; his feelings were numb. Finally he said, "I'll be back in a few minutes, Robyn."

"Back? Where are you going?"

"Out for a minute. I—I need to be by myself."

"Outside? Justin, it's freezing. You can't go out."

"I'll be right back. I just need some fresh air. You get ready to go over to the hospital. I promise. I'll be okay." He went to the hall closet and grabbed his overcoat, a scarf, and cap. He was out the door before Robyn could utter another protest.

He strode purposely down the icy sidewalk as if he actually had some destination in mind. In fact, he wanted desperately to escape all signs of humanity and civilization. He wanted to find a spot alone where he could scream out his anger and frustration. At least it was so early and so cold that few people were out walking or even in their cars. He increased his pace, his breathing growing heavier, his exhalations sending out little clouds of frosty air. He kept his hands buried in his overcoat pockets, but already he could feel them aching with the cold. His nose felt like an icy appendage and the sinuses in his cheeks ached. He fought back tears because he knew they would freeze on his eyelids and in his nostrils.

Aloud he said, "What are You doing to me, God? Are You trying to destroy me? If You are, You're doing a good job. I'm going down for the last count. It won't take much more to crush me into the ground with Your foot."

He slowed his pace. His breathing was so labored, he couldn't speak, and the crisp wintry air left his mouth stiff and dry. He swallowed several times to start the saliva working again. He coughed a dry, hacking cough and blew warmth into his hands. In spite of himself, he could feel the tears coming, the wracking sobs swelling in his chest, demanding release. He stared up into the clear, salmon-pink sky and shouted, "Why are You doing this to me? You've taken my church, my pride, my son, and now my father! Are You laughing at me? Have You turned Your back on me?"

The tears spilled out, crystallizing on his cheeks. "I was so close," he wept, "so close to winning my father. After all these years! How could You let him die now? He was ready to make a commitment. Oh, God, he was so close! How could You take him?"

The cold was turning Justin's limbs and fingers numb. Everything ached. He had to go back home. He had to face his family and offer comfort. He was a minister of God, for heaven's sake. He was supposed to know what to say and how to behave. He was trained; he was experienced. He was expected to be in control.

But everything in his life was flying apart; he was caught in a whirlwind, buffeted like dry leaves in a hurricane. He would perish. Or worse, he would not perish. He would be forced to live the long, bleak years of his life with the unspeakable anguish that was flooding over him now.

30

JUSTIN RETURNED to his mother's home with a feeling of dread. He didn't want his family looking to him for strength just because he was a minister. At the moment the title and position seemed irrelevant. He was merely a man, all too mortal and fallible to be an example for anyone. In fact, he wasn't coping well at all right now. Life had thrown him too many curves in the past twenty-four hours. His father was dead and his son's life hung by a thread. How did people expect him to react?

As Justin walked up the porch steps, he noticed the hearse pulling up to the curb. They were early. He wasn't prepared to have strangers come bursting in and removing his father's body from the house he had lived in for over forty years. They were intruders, thieves stealing the very soul of this rambling, old, memory-filled house.

Justin chided himself. *I can't let my mind trap me like this and weigh me down. There are too many responsibilities now, too many decisions to be made.* So in the hours that followed he put his emotions on hold as he mechanically tackled the tasks at hand. There were papers to sign, options to consider; there was information to relay. Did his father have a burial plot? When would the family be picking out a casket? When would the funeral be held?

There was the obituary to prepare for the newspaper, and there were insurance companies to contact. And Dad's lawyer. And the Social Security office. And his father's old friends. The duties seemed endless.

Chris efficiently handled many of the details, setting up an appointment with the funeral home and making one call after another to acquaintances, friends, and business associates.

As the day wore on, Justin's sense of frustration grew. He knew his mother needed his comfort, but he wanted to be back at the hospital with his son. Robyn was there, sitting by Eric's bedside—if the intensive care nurse allowed it—waiting for him to regain consciousness. That's where Justin belonged too, but how could he leave his mother to face her grief and the quandary of decisions alone?

Finally, shortly after noon, Justin drove over to the hospital and stood with Robyn at the bedside of their son. Justin's heart ached as he gazed at the boy. Eric looked so frail, so vulnerable, so young. "He looks the way I remember him at ten," Justin murmured, his voice edged with wistfulness. "He looks like a child again."

"I know," said Robyn. "I've thought that all day. I just want to gather him in my arms and kiss away his hurts."

"I wish it were that simple."

Robyn nodded. "Nothing is simple anymore."

"Don't I know it," said Justin with a perturbed sigh as the nurse gestured that their time was up. They walked out to the intensive care waiting room and sat down.

"How is everything at home?" asked Robyn. "Pretty bad, I suppose."

"Chaotic is the word," said Justin. "Everyone's stressed out. In shock. Chris is trying to handle things. Doing a good job, in fact. Laura is trying to comfort Mom. I keep thinking we'll all wake up and things will be like they were . . ."

"We thought we had problems when we arrived in Southfield," mused Robyn ironically. "Now those days seem absolutely idyllic."

Justin grimaced. "We didn't know how minor our problems were."

Robyn reached over and squeezed Justin's hand. "God is still with us, darling. He's still in control."

"I'm glad someone is," Justin quipped darkly, "because I'm not."

"Listen, darling, I'm so sorry about your dad. I know you felt you'd just made a breakthrough with him—"

Justin doubled his fist and punched his other palm. Actually, he wanted to slam his fist against the wall. He wanted to punch someone out. He couldn't recall ever wanting to express his anger physically the way he did now. He wanted to take his rage out on something, but there was nothing—no one!—he could attack. He could only gather the dark, billowy clouds of fury back inside himself and hope he could contain them.

Robyn noticed his expression because she said, "I'm worried about you, Justin."

"Why?"

"Your feelings. I can see what a hard time you're having. Maybe if you talked about it—"

"Talk? Oh, I could talk all right, but you wouldn't want to hear it. God wouldn't want to hear it." He kept working with his fist, massaging it as if he were preparing for battle.

"God does want to hear it, Justin. He wants our honesty."

"Honesty?" Justin's voice rose unevenly. "Honesty means I think it stinks that my son is lying in there fighting for his life. And it's lousy that my dad died just when I finally had a chance to win him to the Lord!"

Robyn moved closer and gently rubbed his arm. "Did you stop to think, Justin, that maybe your dad did come to Christ?"

He eyed her curiously. "What are you saying?"

"I'm saying that you had a wonderful talk with him last night and he was open and responsive to the gospel. He told you he would think about accepting Christ as his Savior. Your father was a man of his word. Who's to say he didn't make that commitment last night before he went to sleep? His heart was ready. He could very easily have made the decision."

"You really think so?" The idea was wonderfully compelling, and incredibly simple and obvious. Yes, it was possible that his father had yielded his life to God in those moments before sleep. It was possible. But had it actually happened? "There's no way of knowing," said Justin. "No way I can be sure."

"No," said Robyn. "You'll have to take it by faith, just as we take our own salvation by faith."

"It's not the same, Robyn. I need to know. I need to know whether I'll see my dad in heaven someday."

"Oh, Justin, I wish you could know. I wish it was all clear-cut and certain—"

"Do you realize, I'll have to go through the rest of my life not knowing? Why didn't I press harder, urge him to make a commitment last night?"

"You did everything you could, Justin. Your father was a proud, stubborn man, like you. Do you really think he would have made a decision if you'd pushed too hard?"

"No, no, of course not. There was such a special rapport between us last night, so fragile. If I'd pushed him or cajoled him, that special camaraderie would have been shattered."

"Then you have nothing to regret, Justin. It's in God's hands."

"Like the life of our son."

Robyn winced and tears started in her eyes. "Yes . . . exactly. Like the life of our son."

Justin held Robyn close for a minute; then he said, "Let's look in on Eric again. Forget this ridiculous five-minutes-every-hour routine. Come on. Then I'd better get home and see how Mom's doing."

When Justin arrived home, the first shadows of evening were falling across the drifting landscape, turning the snow a deep azure blue. Justin entered the house and smelled the first pungent fragrance of death. Roses and carnations. Floral bouquets were already arriving. Justin hated that smell. It reminded him of a hundred or more funeral services he had performed, always with that sweet, repulsive aroma in his nostrils. And now the funeral was for one of his own, and Justin himself was the bereaved.

With a distracted greeting, Chris loped into the hallway with papers in each hand and a harried look on his face. "Hi, Justin, how's Eric?"

"Still no change. The doctor says we have to sit tight. We should know something by tomorrow. How's Mom?"

"The doctor gave her a sedative. She's resting now."

"How are you doing, little brother?"

"Managing. Going through some of Dad's papers. We're going to have a lot to attend to in the days ahead."

"I'll help," said Justin. "Let me know what you need."

"There is something," said Chris.

"Yeah?"

"Mom—it was her idea. I told her I wasn't sure how you'd feel about it—especially with Eric—"

"What? Tell me."

"Yeah, okay. Mom wants you to perform the funeral service for Dad."

"Me?"

"You're a minister."

"Yes, but—"

"You know Mom and Dad have never gone to church. They don't know any preachers. And we don't want some stranger coming in here and spieling off something about Dad when he never even knew him."

Justin shook his head incredulously. "Listen, Chris, you don't know what you're asking. I mean, with Eric in the hospital near death, and Dad gone so suddenly—"

"It's okay, Justin, I understand, if you feel you can't do it."

"That's not it, Chris. It's just—"

"You will do it, won't you, Justin?" His mother's voice. He whirled around. She was standing in the hallway, one hand holding the wall for support. "Your father would want you to speak at his funeral, Justin. He wouldn't want anyone else."

Justin went over and took his mother in his arms. She felt so small, so terribly fragile. After a moment, he said, "Whatever you want, Mom. If you want me to perform the service, I'll do it."

But even as he held his mother close, he wondered somberly, *How can I offer solace to my unsaved family when my own heart is filled with such bitterness and disappointment?*

31

ON THE day of his father's funeral, Justin rose at dawn and roamed restlessly through the silent, memory-filled house of his birth and boyhood. He was short on sleep. He had been at Eric's bedside until almost one in the morning, holding his hand, rubbing his arm, willing his son to live. For hours he had said, "Eric, if you hear me, if you know it's Dad, squeeze my hand." Shortly after midnight he had tried it again, and Eric's limp hand moved, touched his own. He knew it wasn't his imagination. His son had heard him! It was the sign of hope they had been waiting for.

Now, there were matters Justin had to resolve within himself before his father's funeral. It was as if in a few hours he must tackle a crash course in self-understanding; he must work through the spiritual conflicts that had plagued him for half his life. It was a monstrous task, but it must be done, for at the moment he did not have the spiritual fortitude to face his family at his father's grave site and utter words of comfort and hope.

As Justin wandered through the shadowed rooms, he resurrected memories from the long-forgotten past. In fact, these old, familiar walls brimmed with reminiscences just waiting to be collected and relived. In the front room he recalled the large, antiquated TV set where he and Chris had watched cartoons and adventure shows by the hour. His parents often said they watched too much TV, but even in the fifties television was still an exciting new medium, one they couldn't resist.

Unexpectedly, Justin recalled watching "Peter Pan" when

he was about five. He had stared transfixed at the lithe, elfin Mary Martin flying around the nursery of the Jim Darling children, and laughed when she crowed so audaciously. For weeks afterward he had pretended to be Peter Pan, had even stood boldly on the porch railing in the chill late March evenings pretending he could fly. He would leap into the dew-wet grass, his arms flapping, and then would roll several feet in disappointment, wondering if it would help if he only had a smidgen of pixie dust, and wondering whether he, in fact, could ever lose his shadow like Peter had done. His flying antics ended abruptly and unceremoniously when one soaring leap from the front porch resulted in a badly sprained ankle. After that, he decided to leave flying to the birds—and to Peter.

Justin chuckled inwardly at the grim irony of it all. He knew now what the boy in him had never accepted, that no one can be Peter Pan, or Superman, or even the perfect Christian. Never-Never Land never was, nor could he ever soar above his own human frailties; they were with him every day, from the moment he awoke until the moment he drifted into slumber each night.

Where was the Holy Spirit when he needed Him? Where was the source of inner power and strength? He knew the textbook answers, but they weren't enough for him now when everything in his life seemed so out of focus.

Or perhaps he was being too analytical, too introspective. It was a habit of his, analyzing everything to death, seeking the hidden meaning of things when perhaps there was none. Or perhaps he was too critical of his own weaknesses, too unforgiving. He realized he had the peculiar habit of viewing his life from two perspectives—first person, through his own eyes; and third person, through the eyes of a detached and mildly skeptical bystander. The bystander watched always, impassively, or with a shrewd, wordless scrutiny, so that Justin had the unsettling task of acting out his life as well as watching himself act it out. It was especially disconcerting, even dismaying, when he fumbled the ball or bumbled his way through some embarrassing situation. Never could he quite let himself go because someone was always watching from the sidelines, judging his motivations and behavior: He himself! That perplexing, exasperating side of himself could never be fooled, could not be argued or bluffed away. He was simply there, always there, never missing a beat, never batting an eye.

It was that way now. Even as Justin had wept and raved at God these past two days since his father's death, a part of himself stood impassively by observing his behavior and musing, *That fool of a man. A Christian all these years and he hasn't learned a thing. He still behaves like a buffoon, a spoiled, ungrateful child.*

Justin agreed with everything his impassive self observed. He was behaving irrationally; he was throwing stones at God's window, trying to get His attention, and bad-mouthing his Creator because he'd been dealt a bum hand. But, regardless of what he understood rationally, there was an entire undercurrent of feelings and behaviors that could not be touched with the conscious mind. Justin wanted to do the will of God, but he also wanted to do as he pleased. He wanted to love God with all his heart, but his heart was filled with so much clutter. The love was there, of course, but it was lost in the debris of his own self-will.

Justin knew that he needed to find a place in this house where he could be alone and cry out to God from his heart, a place of such privacy that not even his cynical self could loom nearby, making him feel self-conscious. If Justin Cahill was to survive, he needed to turn himself inside out before God. But where? Where could he and God be utterly alone?

And then he thought of the attic. Not truly an attic, but a storage room above the second floor where Chris and Justin had played as boys, where they had kept secrets and planned daring escapades and dreamed incredible dreams. At times that room had been a pirate's ship, or a foreign land, or a distant planet. It was limited only by the boundaries of their imaginations.

Justin climbed the stairs quickly, already anticipating the cozy familiarity of that wonderful room. He opened the door, flipped on the light switch, and gazed around with keen disappointment at the bare walls and old trunks and storage crates. Where were the dreams and secrets and pirate ships? There was nothing here to fuel a boy's imagination. It was only a very small room with very close walls.

Justin went in anyway. At least it was clean and neat; the housekeeper had done her job even here where no one came anymore. There were no chairs, just the old tapestry-like carpet on the floor that had once graced the dining room downstairs. Justin shut the door behind him and stood in the center of the room.

What am I doing here? he wondered. *Trying to recapture something from the past? Trying to make sense of the present or find strength for the future?* "God, I'm trying to make sense of my relationship with You," he said aloud. "A few days ago I thought I'd worked everything out. I realized I'd been bitter against my dad, and I asked his forgiveness, and for the first time in our lives we were no longer locking horns. I felt close to him. We weren't two bucks clashing antlers in the wilderness anymore. We were simply father and son. Oh, God, I thought I'd learned all my lessons that night. I even talked things out with Robyn. I thought things were on the upswing ... until Dad died."

Justin sat down on the floor and crossed his legs Indian-style like he and Chris had done as boys when they'd confided their secrets. It was strange. In this room, he felt like a boy again. He felt small and vulnerable and needy. It wasn't a feeling he was accustomed to ... or comfortable with, usually. But this was different. At this moment he wasn't Rev. Justin Cahill, man of God. He was simply Justin, a man in need, who painfully felt the limitations and shortcomings of his humanity.

Was this what he had come to after so many years of trying to be Christlike? He had never been more keenly aware of how far short he fell from that lofty goal. But then again, what did it really mean to be like Christ?

"I talk so glibly about wanting to be like You, Lord," he mused aloud, "but do I have the slightest idea what that means? Even as a minister ..." His voice trailed off as he absently twisted a raveling in the rug. "Oh, Lord, it's absurd, isn't it? Everything in this culture pushes me toward establishing myself professionally, making a name for myself, being number one. Even if it means being a professional minister." He sighed heavily. "Father, is that what I've become? A shrewd, cold-hearted professional?" He turned the question over in his mind several times, and then bowed his head. "No, Christlikeness has nothing to do with that. Christ, You were lowly and despised; You had a servant's heart. You were willing to wash feet and be spit upon. Nothing in my seminary training has taught me how to be that kind of man."

He thought a moment. "Maybe it's not something that's taught. It's not even something that's humanly possible. It's what only Christ can be." He nodded to himself, savoring the insight. "It can only happen when Christ's Spirit does it through me, when I open myself to Him with nothing held back. I have to want to be like Him more than I want to be myself."

He gazed up at the ceiling, seeing beyond the walls, beyond the room itself. "Do I, Lord? Do I want to be more like You than like myself? More like You than like my father? Do I want to please You more than I wanted to please him?" He shook his head solemnly. "I don't know, Lord. I honestly don't know. How much of what I see in You is really myself? How much of what I know of You is only me? Where do I leave off and You begin? And how can I know the difference? How can I truly serve You when I glimpse You only through the kaleidoscope of my own flawed understanding?"

He was silent a moment, mulling over the endless questions, the doubts, and yes, the fears. Admit it. He was afraid. He was indeed filled with doubts. In fact, it seemed that the closer he tried to get to God, the more magnified his sins became. Larger than life. There were so few times that anything he did was out of a pure motive; weren't his motives always a mixture of good and evil—wanting to help someone but also wanting to boost his self-esteem, wanting his sermons to draw people to Christ while he also desired admiration for himself? Did his flawed motives negate the good he tried to accomplish? Did the bad he had done contaminate the good?

Was he allowing himself to live by law rather than grace? How well he knew the Word of God . . . but how well did he know the God of the Word? And how could it be that he, a man with his seminary training and years of experience, was struggling now with such basics of the faith? Perhaps it was the weariness in his mind or the stress of these past few days. Or perhaps it was dangerous to ever get far from the basics, no matter how scholarly one considered himself.

Justin sat and listened to the stillness. What did he hear? Did he hear the voice of God? Was God speaking to him in the silence or in the wintry wind that whistled through the eaves? Was God speaking to him in a still, small voice that his pride kept him from hearing?

Aloud, Justin recited the familiar childhood hymn. "Jesus loves me, this I know . . . for the Bible tells me so . . ."

Except you become as a child . . .

The thought jarred him.

It had been many years since Justin's faith had been child-like, many years since he had felt like a child at the feet of Jesus. But, surprisingly, he felt that way now. And why not? He had just been orphaned. He was a fatherless child. He had only his Heavenly Father to cling to now.

He became aware of a feeling inside that he had felt only rarely in his life—a deep, gnawing hunger for Christ's presence. He ached for the Spirit to cleanse and fill him. "Oh, God, touch me, change me, break me—do what You must, but let me feel Your presence!" He felt a sob rising in his chest. It convulsed inside him, but there were no tears, only a dry, heaving anguish. He was in the throes of struggling with God and he must see it through to the finish. He stretched out on the floor facedown and cried, "Lord God, I throw myself on Your mercy. Do what You must with me. Break my will. Forgive me. Kill me, if you choose. I am Yours. My wife and son are Yours. All that I have is Yours."

Do you love Me?

It was as if the question had been spoken aloud. He answered, "Yes, Lord. Haven't I lived for You? Witnessed for You? Left my family for You?"

The words assailed his mind again: *Do you love Me?*

"I've tried to," he said aloud, "but how do I know it was real?"

Do you love Me?

Tears came at last, freely, unchallenged, unguarded. "Oh, God, I don't know. Have I loved You? Or have I loved only myself? How long since I've really seen You . . . focused only on You . . . felt love for You flaming in my heart?"

He raised himself up on his elbows. "Oh, Jesus, I want to love You. I do love You, but it's grown so cold. It's been crowded out by so many things—duties, distractions, rituals of habit, busy work, my own goals and desires. And lately by my anger and resentment. I've blamed You for what happened to Eric. I've blamed You for Dad's death. Forgive me. Oh, God, forgive!"

In the stillness that followed, he added quietly, "And forgive me for trying to *be* You instead of simply loving You and letting You *be* Yourself through me." He lay his head on the floor and became aware of his heart beating in a steady, pounding rhythm. His emotions spent, his body exhausted, he allowed his muscles to relax and opened his mind and heart to God. "I love you, Jesus," he uttered softly. "I love you."

He felt the spaces of his heart swelling with Christ's Spirit, filling to overflowing. He felt one with God, one in purpose, one in sweet communion. He didn't want to move lest he disturb the Spirit of oneness within him. It was too good, too satisfying to let it slip away. All of life's turmoils, struggles, and perplexities were worth the bliss of having all his senses attuned to Christ.

32

AT THREE that afternoon, the Cahill family and close friends gathered for a private graveside service on a snow-cloaked hillside in Southfield's oldest cemetery. It was Victor Cahill's wishes, written in his own hand at the bottom of his will, that there be no pompous ceremony in a fancy church with strangers gawking at his defenseless remains. So Justin stood by his father's closed casket under an icy, bare-limbed oak, his Bible open in his gloved hand, and spoke from his heart. His resonant voice was caught by the chill wind as scattered flurries wafted from the overcast sky.

"All of us here today have one thing in common: We have been profoundly touched and influenced by one man, Victor Cahill. He was a powerful man, a complex man, a faithful husband, a man who labored hard all of his life so he could pass on his dreams to his children. He was the father I spent half my life trying to please, and I was never sure I came close until the night before he died.

"Actually, I had two fathers," Justin declared. "My earthly father and my Heavenly Father. And I learned very different things from each one. From my earthly father, I learned how to ride a bike and throw a ball, how to work hard and be a good provider, and how to treat people honestly and fairly. From my Heavenly Father, I learned how to be prepared for this life and the next life, and I learned the real meaning of sacrificial love. And I realize now, perhaps more than ever before, how much I love both my fathers."

Justin paused, steadying his emotions. His gaze traveled around the little circle of mourners—his mother huddled against his brother Chris, Laura holding a gurgling little Rudy, Robyn standing beside Alex Lanigan and their pastor, Joe Wyden, and Scott and Lauralee beside Kaylie Hollis. Beyond them, a handful of friends, neighbors, and Cahill employees. Only Eric was missing.

"As a Christian and as a minister," Justin continued solemnly, "I have chosen to live my life by faith. You ask, What is faith? The Bible says it is 'the substance of things hoped for, the evidence of things not seen.' Without faith it is impossible to please God. Long ago I placed my faith in Christ for my own salvation, and now I have faith that my father met Christ and was ushered into His glory when he died. By faith, too, I believe that my son Eric, who hovers between life and death, will be healed and returned to his family, who loves him dearly."

Justin's tone grew softer, more confidential as he said, "I hope you'll forgive me if I depart from the typical funeral format. I need to say some things to my family, and I think this is an appropriate time." He gazed from his mother to his brother. "I've realized since coming home that I am quite capable of communicating the judgment and justice of God to others, but I have never truly succeeded in communicating His love."

He cleared his throat, swallowing against the coldness. "I am not a man given easily to forgiveness of others for supposed misdeeds, or even of myself. I find it hard to let myself feel God's forgiveness. Because I have been such a hard taskmaster on others as well as myself, I have collected grievances over the years that have left me bitter and resentful. I realize now how wrong I was, and I want to ask your forgiveness.

"And if I have foolishly led you to believe that I am a spiritual giant walking in clouds above the earth, let me assure you I am a very fallible mortal man, too often afraid to let people know how really human I am. The true gospel—the gospel that God has laid on my heart to preach—is that Jesus came to save sinners, of whom I am chief. And if I have managed to catch an unexpected glimpse of God along the way, it has only been on the road of faith and obedience."

He looked now at his mother and said brokenly, "I have failed you. I'm sorry. I have failed to love you with Christ's unconditional love. And I have judged you—and Dad—for what I perceived as your lack of love for me." After a moment, he turned his gaze upon Chris and said, "Forgive me. I have tried to hold myself up as an example of what you should be, but I'm no example, except as a sinner saved by the grace of God. Again, I have been guilty of representing to you the judgment of God, but not His love. Let me assure you that I stand before you as a man who can never hope to measure up to God's standards, who can never match Christ's fathomless love."

Tears welled in Justin's eyes. His voice rose as he declared, "But I am a man who has tasted the love and forgiveness and glory of God, not because of what I am or what I have done, but because His grace extends to me, a sinner, and His grace extends to you, a sinner, and His grace covers us and makes us righteous in His sight.

"So, my dear family, I do not hold myself up to you as an example of goodness but as an example of how far God's grace extends, for He reaches down and covers my sinfulness with Himself when I can't begin to reach up to Him."

The wind whistled through the trees, and distant church bells chimed the hour. Justin stepped forward and placed his hands on his father's casket. He stood motionless for a long minute, his head bowed, his emotions brimming. "I loved this man," he said with feeling, his gaze still on the mahogany casket. "He was strong, and industrious, and honorable. He was a man a son could be proud of. And I was proud of him. But I was almost too late to tell him how I felt." He looked around, his gaze settling on each member of his family. "I don't want to be too late in telling you. I love you, Robyn . . . I love you, Mom . . . I love you, Chris . . ." Softly, as he spoke their names, they whispered their love back to him.

After the service, the mourners filed by Justin one by one, shaking his hand, giving him a hug, sharing words of encouragement. When Rev. Joe Wyden clasped his hand, Justin said, "You know our talk last Sunday? I'd like to try it again. There are some things I should have discussed with you, but my pride got in the way."

The pastor nodded. "Sure thing. Call and we'll set up a time. Is it about Eric . . . or your father?"

"Neither," said Justin. "It's my . . . career. The ministry. I've got some heavy decisions to make in the next few months, and I need some help. The benefit of your counsel. In other words, I'd welcome your advice."

Joe Wyden smiled. "I'll do my best, but I may be a little prejudiced. I've got a church that could use a good man like you."

Justin returned the smile. "Joe, you never change. You always know just what a guy needs to hear."

Kaylie Hollis shook Justin's hand too and asked, "Do you think it would be all right if I took a little Christmas tree over to Eric—you know, once he's feeling better and out of intensive care?"

"I think he'd like that," said Justin, genuinely touched.

She smiled gratefully. "Now we just gotta pray he makes it, like you said, right, Rev. Cahill?"

Justin nodded. "I've never hoped for anything more, Kaylie."

"Yeah. Me, too," she said softly, and slipped on by.

Alex Lanigan was next, shaking Justin's hand with a startling energy even as he put his arm around Robyn's shoulder. "I'll be praying for you two," he told them. "I know how it hurts to lose someone close. But you and your family—you've got everything going for you. You'll be okay."

"How about you, Alex?" asked Robyn. "Will you be okay?"

He looked down tenderly at her. "Don't worry, Robyn, I've learned that God has a way of working things out for the best—if we let Him."

Robyn lifted her chin and lightly kissed his cheek. "I know you'll find someone again, Alex—the right one to love, who'll love you for the wonderful person you are."

"I wish you the best, Alex," said Justin. "Thanks for coming today. Thanks for being a friend."

Chris came over, started to shake Justin's hand, and then

gave him a big bear hug instead. His voice was emotion-choked. "Thanks, big brother, for what you said today. I'll never forget it."

"I meant every word," said Justin.

His mother went into his arms too. "Son, I'm so proud of you. I just wish your father could have heard you."

"Maybe he did, Mom. Maybe he did." Justin kissed her cheek and held her close. "Are you ready to go home, Mom?"

She dabbed her eyes with her handkerchief. "Yes, Son. But I'll ride with Chris. I know you'll want to go on to the hospital and see Eric."

Justin nodded and turned to Robyn. "Give me a moment alone at the casket, okay? Then we'll be going." He walked across the frozen ground and placed his hand reverently on the polished casket. Aloud, he said, "Good-bye, Dad. I love you. I'm sorry those words were so hard for me to say to your face. I pray to God I'll see you again someday. I'm going to believe it. Faith is all I've got now—for you, for Eric, for myself. But then, maybe faith is all I need." He thought a moment and added meaningfully, "Faith . . . and love. Help me remember, Father, the greatest of these is . . . love."

Robyn slipped over beside him and hugged his arm. "You okay, Justin?"

His throat and chest were too filled to speak, so instead he pressed her against him and nuzzled her snow-flecked hair. Finally, he murmured, "Let's go see Eric, honey . . . and then let's go home."

In a small, anguished voice, she whispered, "Oh, Justin, with your dad gone, and Eric hurt, and everything in our lives still so unsettled, I'm not even sure where home is anymore."

"We'll find it, darling," he soothed. "In California, in Southfield—wherever God wants us. I know our life's up for grabs now, with no written guarantees. But whatever we've got to face, we'll face it together."

"With the Lord," she vowed.

He nodded. "No other way."

Arm in arm, braced against the gathering flurries, they walked away from the lonely casket beneath the gnarled tree.

Delicate strains of "Silent Night" drifted from the little country chapel down the road. In the distance they could see the first lights of evening, like welcoming beacons against winter's burnished sunset.

Date Due